Praise for *The Divine Conspiracy Continued*

"I know of no more important voice on spiritual tr~~~~ ~ our day than that of Dallas Willard. To be able to recei~~~~ ~~~ds from him along with Gary Black Jr. on the rea~~~~ ~~~~ in our midst is a priceless gift to every foll~~~~

—John Ortberg, a~~~~

"I consider *The Divine Con~~~~ ~~~~ant book in the field of Christian spiri~~~~ ~~~~ ~~fetime. So, I welcome the publication of *The ~~~~ ~~racy Continued*. Gary Black Jr., working on this project ~~~~ ~~llas Willard right up until Dallas's death, helps to expand and enrich the themes that moved us so deeply, articulating the same grand vision as the original text and adds many penetrating insights into our life in the kingdom of God. May *The Divine Conspiracy Continued* find an eager audience ready to grow in the life that is Life indeed."

—Richard J. Foster, author *Celebration of Discipline and Sanctuary of the Soul*

"The name Dallas Willard is one you hear a lot in our house. He's somewhere between a family member and a saint to us, as we've been so deeply shaped by his words and ideas. What's so deeply special about this book is that Gary Black Jr.'s respect and love for his friend and mentor shines through every page, but never stands in the way of Dallas's extraordinary wisdom. I'm so thankful for this beautiful book."

—Shauna Niequist, author of *Bread & Wine*

"*The Divine Conspiracy Continued* is a continuation of the divine conspiracy to implement kingdom principles in the professions and to influence the structure of our institutions for good and for God. In my search for evidence of kingdom practices in business, I have found them in the exemplary practices of many executives in the U.S. So I know this can be done just as Willard and Black describe. The question is, 'how to proceed?' I believe it must start in the church and much effort should be devoted to mentoring lay leaders

in the kingdom principles as described in this book. I will return to its teachings again and again. May the kingdom come!"
—Joseph Maciariello, The Peter F. Drucker and
Masatoshi Ito Graduate School of Management,
Claremont Graduate University

"*The Divine Conspiracy* is a Christian classic that deserves to be mentioned in the same breath with Augustine's *Confessions* and Brother Lawrence's *Practicing the Presence of God*. For years, I have longed for a sequel. Unfortunately, Dallas—a genuine treasure to the body of Christ—passed away. However, unknown to me, Gary Black Jr., who did his doctoral dissertation on Willard's thought and knows as much about Willard's ideas as anyone living, and who spent considerable time with Dallas before his departure, gathered Dallas's ideas, added his own, and has produced a truly coauthored book that satisfies the hunger of so many of us. *The Divine Conspiracy Continued* focuses on extending important ideas about the Kingdom of God into the areas of spiritual, moral, and cultural leadership, and into the spheres of education, economics, and politics. For those of us who desire to influence the culture in a distinctively Christian way, this is must-reading. I thank God for its release."
—J. P. Moreland, Distinguished Professor of Philosophy,
Biola University and author of *The Kingdom Triangle*

"*The Divine Conspiracy* shaped an entire generation. Now Willard and Black have turned their attention to leaders becoming Christlike disciples instead of institutionalized church members . . . reshaping our thinking at an even wider and deeper level."
—Scot McKnight, professor of New Testament,
Northern Seminary

"If I could have one spiritual guide alongside me in life's deeper waters, it would be Dallas Willard. Dallas, and his protégé Gary Black Jr., have given us all a guide in *The Divine Conspiracy Continued*. Picking up where Dallas last left us in *The Divine Conspiracy*, this sequel lays out a sweeping vision of what we as leaders can and must do both within our fields of influence but also in our own hearts. This is the book for every follower of Christ who seeks to be a light in and through every vocational and professional arena of contemporary life. Willard and Black tell us all how we can live truly significant lives in God's Kingdom—now. *The Divine Conspiracy Continued* is a must-read."

—Bob Buford, cable-TV pioneer, philanthropist, founder of Leadership Network, and author of *Halftime and Drucker & Me*

"Willard and Black offer leaders a hopeful vision that steers the wobbly structures of this world onto the road of love, justice, and truth."

—Richard Swenson, M.D., author of *Margin*

"You hold in your hand a deep and compelling continuation of *The Divine Conspiracy*. The outworking of an individual's life in the kingdom of God is the effect of one's calling for the greater good of the world and the glory of God. Willard and Black have given us a prophetic writing, so bold that if embraced and embodied might just produce a Christian community that actually is 'salt and light' to a world in desperate need of it! I recommend this book with great enthusiasm."

—Keith J. Matthews, chair and professor of Spiritual Formation & Contemporary Culture, Graduate School of Theology, Azusa Pacific University

"It is not very often that I encounter a new idea, but *The Divine Conspiracy Continued* has good, new, surprising, and challenging ideas at every turn. Willard and Black help move serious Christians from 'renovation of the heart' to renovation of their professions to renovation of their cultures. If lawyers, doctors, teachers, and ministers take this book to heart it will go a long way toward making our world, in John Calvin's lovely phrase, a 'theater for the glory of God.'"

—Robert F. Cochran Jr., Louis D. Brandeis Professor of Law and Director, Herbert and Elinor Nootbaar Institute on Law, Religion, and Ethics, Pepperdine University School of Law

"This is a fantastic book that provides a grand masterpiece for how we pursue and embrace personal transformation in order to be God's transforming agents in the world. These pages are filled with the great themes that call us to pursue and embrace the with-God life that is life indeed."

—Gayle Beebe, president, Westmont College

I read this book with a group of people from different vocations and professions. The conversations we had were absolutely riveting. The book created a space where we could wrestle with dangerous, paradigm-shifting questions. The process reminded me how the people in our churches long to know how to live out the reality of the kingdom of God and 'be genuinely good' in the complicated and conflictual situations of their vocational life. This book speaks marvelously to this longing. It is an invaluable resource that can help pastors enter more fully into their congregation's world and discover together the wisdom of Jesus and the way to real life."

—Mike Lueken, coauthor of *Renovation of the Church*

"*The Divine Conspiracy Continued* brilliantly combines the legacies of Dallas Willard the disciple-maker and Dr. Willard the scholar. He helped us grasp the nature of truth and justice, and illuminated the deeper causes of the transformations unfolding in both Western culture and in the human heart. In this book, Willard has joined forces with theologian Gary Black Jr. to help us know better how leaders can mobilize as disciples of Christ to renew truth and justice within the modern world. Don't miss this book."

—Greg Forster, program director, Kern Family
Foundation, and author of *Joy for the World*

"Dallas once said 'True social activists are those who live as apprentices of Jesus in their ordinary relationships.' While many try to change society by laws, Willard and Black illustrate that changing society requires leaders, in every area of life, to live a Christlike life."

—Ihab Beblawi, M.D.

The Divine Conspiracy Continued

Fulfilling God's Kingdom on Earth

Dallas Willard and Gary Black Jr.

HarperOne
An Imprint of HarperCollinsPublishers

HarperOne

THE DIVINE CONSPIRACY CONTINUED: *Fulfilling God's Kingdom on Earth.* Copyright © 2014 by Dallas Willard and Gary Black Jr. All rights reserved. Printed in the United States of America. No part of this book may be used or reproduced in any manner whatsoever without written permission except in the case of brief quotations embodied in critical articles and reviews. For information address HarperCollins Publishers, 195 Broadway, New York, NY 10007.

HarperCollins books may be purchased for educational, business, or sales promotional use. For information please e-mail the Special Markets Department at SPsales@harpercollins.com.

HarperCollins website: http://www.harpercollins.com

HarperCollins®, ®, and HarperOne™ are trademarks of HarperCollins Publishers.

FIRST HARPERCOLLINS PAPERBACK EDITION PUBLISHED IN 2015

Library of Congress Cataloging-in-Publication Data
Willard, Dallas.
  The divine conspiracy continued : fulfilling God's kingdom on earth / Dallas Willard and Gary Black Jr. — first edition.
    pages cm
  ISBN 978–0–06–229612–2
  1. Jesus Christ—Kingdom. 2. Kingdom of God. 3. Christian life. I. Title.
BT94.W545   2014
231.7'2—dc23   2014004992

15 16 17 18 19   RRD(H)   10 9 8 7 6 5 4 3 2 1

Contents

Remembering Dallas

DALLAS WILLARD SUCCUMBED to the effects of pancreatic cancer prior to the publication of this work. His death has proven to be one of the most significant losses I have experienced, a fact I accept with equal measures of foreboding and gratefulness. I was wholly unprepared for losing Dallas as a mentor, guide, and friend. I was also unaware of how his loss would cause me to discover how deeply our relationship and his teachings affected me.

Although Dallas was candid with me about his illness and I was aware of the difficult challenges of pancreatic cancer, we remained optimistic about his ability to finish this project until only shortly before his death. Therefore, from the beginning of our work together we were both under the impression, and there were reasonable signs of hope, that his condition would improve enough that he would be able to at least finish the manuscript together. Perhaps I didn't allow myself to seriously consider the alternatives. Nevertheless, even up to the final few days of his life, we were progressing toward that goal. However, as events transpired, I found myself needing to do what I hoped would not be necessary, which is to describe some of the overarching vision that motivated Dallas to create this work and how I came to be involved as a coauthor.

I will begin near the end. On May 5, 2013, I received a phone call from Jane Willard, Dallas's wife, at about nine thirty in the morning. She told me how Dallas's health was deteriorating and asked if I would be able to stay a few days to help him get around the house. He needed assistance moving from place to place safely. She and I had talked a few weeks earlier about the possibility of my staying in the guesthouse and working on the book projects we had in process. I had previously mentioned that I was with my grandmother as she succumbed to pancreatic cancer, and I offered to help in any way I could. Jane asked if there was any wisdom or experience that I could relay about the issues they might face toward the end of Dallas's life. I told her all I knew. Like my grandmother, Dallas was experiencing the highs and lows, times of strength and clarity followed by moments of significant weakness. When Jane called that Sunday morning, she was characteristically deferential in her request, making me promise nothing would inconvenience my family. I told her we were all happy to help.

As I packed an overnight bag, my wife gathered our two teenage daughters to pray with me before I left. It was difficult for me to tell my children about Dallas's prognosis, and I struggled with my emotions as I discussed what might lie ahead. My elder daughter asked me, "Dad, what is it about Dallas that has had such a strong impact on you?" As I looked into my daughter's eyes, my mind raced back some twenty-five years to my first encounter with Dallas. For a person who often can't recall exactly what he had for breakfast the day before, for some reason I have been able to maintain a vivid memory of that first introduction. Even now, whenever the weight of that distant memory hits my heart, tears are not far behind. For me and countless others, God saw fit to use Dallas and his teachings to spark a foundational shift in our lives, our understanding of the gospel of Jesus Christ, and our awareness of the grand purposes God has for humanity in and through his kingdom. Though unknown to me at the time, my daughter's question can serve us well as a means to both explain my participation in this work and start our journey into the objectives and hopes we have for this book.

I was first introduced to Dallas's work in 1991. I had been out of college for two years and had two years of marriage under my belt. My wife and I were living in the San Francisco Bay Area, and I was attempting to establish a business career in the "real world." As my new bride and I were settling into our cramped little apartment and the challenges of adulthood, we also began to attend a local Covenant Church. There I met a fresh-faced associate pastor named Keith Matthews, who soon invited me to an early morning breakfast. After pleasantries and personal histories were exchanged, he suggested we consider a regular one-on-one breakfast session during which we would discuss a chosen book. Keith was then, as he is now, encouraging, energetic, and intentional about discipleship to Jesus, and I was beginning to miss all the deep, late-night conversations about God and the meaning and purposes of life that I so enjoyed during my university days. So I agreed.

The next week Keith handed me Dallas's first book, *In Search of Guidance: Developing a Conversational Relationship with God* (available today as *Hearing God*). I remember immediately balking at the title.

"Developing a *conversational* relationship with God?" I asked incredulously.

Keith only smiled. He told me Willard was a philosophy professor at the University of Southern California and also a Southern Baptist minister. Keith was toying with me now. He knew of my deep Southern Baptist roots, and we had previously discussed some of my growing discomfort with the eccentricities of modern evangelicalism. Having studied postmodernism briefly in college, I was familiar with some of the emerging ideas in epistemology that conflicted with the traditional modern conceptions of knowledge used to underpin many Christian doctrines. I assumed Keith had to be mistaken.

"You don't mean *the* USC, as in the Trojans' USC?" I asked.

He assured me I had understood him accurately.

My head was spinning. An ordained Southern Baptist minister

who taught philosophy at one of the most prestigious secular universities in the country? I was more than a little intrigued at the iconoclastic possibilities. That little résumé, along with the title of the book, caused a surge of hope and excitement to stir within my heart. Could someone possibly have found a way to break out of the Christian bubble I felt closing in around me? I agreed to read the book.

As it turned out, *In Search of Guidance*, which was followed by *The Spirit of the Disciplines*, began to reveal a spiritual life that was significantly foreign to my previous Christian experience. Little did I know at the time, but those two seminal works allowed me to take the first steps on a journey that I had been yearning to take, even though I was not fully aware of my longing. I am not alone. Increasing numbers of Christians are looking for a reality that is as big as the beliefs we profess. I knew, I just knew, there had to be more to my faith than mental assent to a set of doctrines and practices. I knew that reality was not limited to all that I saw around me. I hoped against hope that there was more to this life and to life in the kingdom of God than hanging on by my fingernails until I died and entered eternity. I knew there had to be a greater purpose for both my life and all of creation than was currently being realized. I was a closet, hopeless, C. S. Lewis–esque romantic who deeply longed to find a Narnia. And just when I was about to let go of that lingering sense of what the world could be, to begin rationalizing away my dreams and longings as nothing more than misplaced exuberance and youthful naiveté, God used Dallas's insights and wisdom to stoke those fading embers of hope in my heart and mind.

Still, this transformation wasn't easy or quick. Keith was a willing and able guide, and together we waded purposefully and sometimes painfully through the pages of Willard's work—often staying stuck on one idea for weeks on end. Keith was patient and committed, despite my stubborn resistance to the revolutionary ideas I was encountering. What was most compelling to me, then as now, was the level of courageous critique I discovered in Willard's writing combined with an encouragement to seek a deep level of personal authenticity. This blend of critical analysis and a vision for change was missing in most other Christian authors of the time and more accurately reflected the style, rigor, and insight of Dietrich Bonhoeffer's works. Still, my traditional evangelical roots kept me mildly skeptical of Willard's description and use of the spiritual disciplines. It all sounded a little too "Catholic" or works-centered for my "Protestant" grace-first tradition.

A short time after finishing *The Spirit of the Disciplines,* Keith invited Dallas to come to our church to speak at a weekend retreat and then preach the following Sunday morning. I eagerly anticipated meeting Dallas. To say the retreat was influential would be the height of understatement. I would learn later that Dallas was lecturing from notes that would eventually become *The Divine Conspiracy.* I was captivated by his lectures. Dallas solved the grace-versus-works dilemma in the first half hour. His words seemed to tax every inch of my being. My mind hurt from the challenge of wrestling his elusive ideas to the ground. My heart ached from both the level and degree of inspiration. My body was fatigued because I was not used to this level of exercise of the spiritual muscles of contemplation, meditation, focus, and study.

Yet the most compelling and memorable aspect of that weekend was the effect that the authority and power of his teachings on the nature of the kingdom of God had on my vision and understanding of the purposes God had for my life. Dallas was the first teacher or minister I had met who inspired me to pursue the idea that I could know Jesus—really know him, and be convinced of that fact—in an experiential and relational way.

When Dallas spoke, I sensed that I had encountered a man who knew Jesus just as completely as the original disciples—John, Peter, or even James, Jesus's brother. There was an undeniable authenticity in his teaching that emanated from a unique combination of the way he spoke and what he described; he almost seemed to reminisce about Jesus as if he had just moments before been on the Sea of Galilee with the other disciples, rowing along in Peter's fishing boat, telling stories, hearing new teachings, and witnessing miracles. The nature of the testimony Dallas gave of his experience of the kingdom of God was so fresh, it was as if I could still smell the aroma of fish on his clothes and hands. Of course it wasn't fish; it was, instead, the savory essence of authentic relationship. It was then, for the first time in my life, that I believed Jesus was actually knowable in much the same way I knew any other person. Not as a myth, an elusive mirage, or a historical relic, but as a living, talking, engaging, personal reality. Dallas helped me to discover something more grand, far beyond just religion or profession of belief. Dallas introduced me to the possibility and benefits of knowing and loving Jesus as he actually is, in the minute-by-minute experience of my existence.

Dallas's objective for that retreat, and the many other retreats and conferences that I attended over the years, was to open the doors of the kingdom of God and invite everyone in. I remember remarking to my wife after that first evening of lectures that Dallas reminded me of Willie Wonka in Roald Dahl's *Charlie and the Chocolate Factory*. Not that Dallas was silly or fanciful. In fact, he appeared quite the opposite. But the Wonka analogy came from the similar way that Willard stood at the threshold of the kingdom of God and, with glee and the kind of excitement that comes only from encouraging the hopeful anticipation of children, invited us into the most wonderfully delicious experiences that life could ever offer. And I, like Charlie, was awestruck—not by Willard, but by the tales he told of his experience inside God's amazing castle of wonders. Willard invited us in, all of us, telling us and showing us we have nothing to fear and everything to gain.

In the many years since, I've listened to numerous stories similar to mine. People from all walks of life, often deeply steeped in a particular faith tradition, tell of sensing that Dallas was revealing the gospel for the first time as "good news" and not simply the opposite of "bad news." Congregants, students, doctoral candidates, pastors, philosophers, and psychologists alike were routinely stunned to see how Dallas was able to use well-known and familiar scriptures and weave an altogether different theological conclusion from them. I routinely watched Dallas, like no one I had encountered before or since, wipe clean people's vision of who God was, what his Son did and why, and what the Holy Spirit wishes to do in and through his church and then replace it with an all-consuming, hope-filled, grace-empowered, joy-seeking, love-giving gospel of God's boundless goodness and power. All the while he never manipulated emotions, overcame people's will, or used fear as a motivator.

I can't remember the number of occasions I've been asked when I was "saved." Since meeting Dallas I have several ways I can answer that question. One answer is that Jesus saves me from myself nearly every day. Another is to tell of the day when, as an eight-year-old boy, I realized and confessed my need for a savior. In that manner I can consider myself "saved" very early in life. But that is certainly not the only time God has saved me. I have been saved so many more times in my life than that original decision would suggest. One of those miraculous saving events occurred during that retreat. God corrected my view of him. He opened a window into the eternal reality of life, life as I had hoped it could be or thought at times it should be. Dallas confirmed that those deep instincts were even more grand than I could expect or imagine. And the God who created and called me into that life stood with open, loving arms and the offer, "Whosoever will may come."

In the decade that followed I gradually lost sight of that early vision of God and his kingdom. Like the weeds that grew up and choked off the seed, my desires for my professional career began to take precedence in my heart and pull me away from the easy yoke of Christ. Mercifully, it was during this period that, while in the waiting room at my doctor's office, I came across a *Christianity Today* article discussing *The Divine Conspiracy*. I raced to the bookstore, bought it, and read it cover to cover that weekend. And the hope and grace that had become a fleeting memory started to gradually flood into my heart once again. All those distant longings for wonder and excitement began to percolate toward the surface. I read it over and over during the next several months. In many ways *The Divine Conspiracy* introduced me to a Jesus that was so much more than my religious stereotyping had allowed. Dallas knew a Jesus far grander than I had assumed him to be and as a result my love and respect for Christ grew exponentially. The weeding had started.

But habits are hard to break, and transformation can be slow, especially for a stiff-necked person like me. It wasn't until nearly another decade had passed that I fully relinquished myself to God's call on my life. I retired from my career in the financial services industry and entered seminary. It was also around that time I was able to reconnect with both Keith and Dallas. What amazing grace those two reunions represent in my life.

My seminary experience helped me to place Dallas's theology in context and recognize his insights were more than just another commentary on Christian doctrine, a program of discipleship, or plan for spiritual formation. I realized Dallas was articulating and advocating an understanding of the gospel that was often significantly at odds with the theology taught in the institutions and traditions of mainstream evangelical religion in America. As a result only a few pastors, and even fewer theologians, were critically engaging Dallas's work. Once again with Keith's guidance and Dallas's encouragement, I began to recognize the need and opportunity to introduce Dallas's theology and understanding of pastoral leadership more deeply into theological education. After completing my seminary degree, I entered a Ph.D. program in the United Kingdom, where I completed my dissertation on "Willardian" theology, hoping to offer some insight into and remedy for this situation.[1]

During those years Dallas offered tremendous assistance. He spent countless hours with me, patiently enduring my endless inquiries, sharing materials, e-mails, phone calls, encouragement, wisdom, and prayer. He faithfully read through each chapter of my dissertation and my revisions, as I endeavored to accurately portray his theology and its effects. I completed my degree in April 2012, and accepted a position in the Graduate School of Theology at Azusa Pacific University.

A wonderful benefit of moving to southern California was the opportunity to be closer to Dallas. We took advantage of that proximity during the last year of his life. One of my most treasured moments was presenting Dallas and Jane with a bound edition of my dissertation and news of a publishing contract to adapt the dissertation for a wider audience. We shared a wonderful afternoon together reminiscing about all God had done for us in the twenty years since we first met. Those were good times.

It was in June 2011, when, in passing, I first suggested to Dallas that he should consider writing a follow-up to *The Divine Conspiracy*. As I was combing through his writings, interviews, and lectures for my dissertation, it seemed to me there was a collection of insights, explanations, and applications he had developed related to the kingdom of God that had not been given ample treatment in his other published works. I thought readers could benefit from the way he had expounded on several issues and realities of contemporary life in the years since *The Divine Conspiracy* was published. We kicked around some ideas and potential chapter topics over the next several months. Eventually he agreed about the potential benefit of such a book. It was only when his medical condition was not improving as rapidly as he hoped that he suggested the idea of coauthoring the book. By January 2013, we had formatted the basic structure of what eventually became the final product.

In March 2013, his health continued to weaken. By then we had formal outlines of each chapter, discussed particular examples, and made a myriad of choices about what to include and what to omit. Before his death, we had several chapters complete and a clear understanding of what was left to finish. We tried diligently to finish the manuscript before he passed. We were very close. As it turns out we were only six weeks short. It was just a few days after we had arrived at our completed outline for the final chapter that I received that fateful call from Jane and kissed my family good-bye to join Dallas as he began his final journey into eternity. What I would have given for just six more weeks. We tried.

As I drove to the Willard home, I had a feeling this was the beginning of the end of his life. In some ways that drive allowed me to prepare. I didn't know what exactly the next days or weeks held, but I did have a sense that difficulty and sorrow were ahead. Yet I also sensed that there would be a significant blessing as a result.

I spent the next four days with Jane and the family watching over Dallas's final hours. It was a very sacred time, one I will treasure for the rest of my life. We talked about many things and were able to conclude some of our conversations we had engaged in off and on for months, if not years. Some of these discussions were very intimate and private, and will remain so. Yet, as Dallas was coming to grips with his own physical death, and our talks tended to naturally turn toward the subject of our life and hope after death, heaven, and eternity, we also began to discuss how our character developed here on earth continues into eternity and all the implications that fact might carry for our life both now and then. As our conversations developed, Dallas and I began to realize others might benefit from the fruit of these interactions. Therefore, before his death he encouraged me to continue thinking and writing on these topics. I promised him I would. It was his final request of me. I am hopeful that work should become available in the near future.

In terms of worldly fame, Dallas was not what most would consider a "famous" man. Although he maintained a very faithful following, there are still many devoted Christians who have never heard of Dallas or his ideas—a surprising fact I routinely encountered as I was researching his theology. Undoubtedly he had earned respect and acclaim in certain arenas such as academic philosophy and the field of spiritual formation. But his notoriety did not reach as far as those who love Dallas and are familiar with his works often presume. Much of his work and a good majority of his ideas remain relatively unknown to a wide spectrum of Christian readers. Therefore, it is likely this work will find itself in the hands of those previously unaware of Dallas and his unique, life-giving perspectives on the gospel.

The book before you is an attempt to extend a set of proposals and perspectives on the kingdom of God and the gospel of Jesus first published in *The Divine Conspiracy* (1998). *The Divine Conspiracy* was originally conceived as a set of teachings Dallas started developing during his time at the University of Wisconsin while completing his doctoral work. In summary, *The Divine Conspiracy* is an articulation of the intent and effect of the gospel of the kingdom of God, which Jesus revealed most pointedly in the Sermon on the Mount. In laying out Jesus's plan for attaining life to the full, Dallas not only deconstructed some significant alterations to Jesus's original message contained in both liberal and conservative forms of contemporary Christianity; he also simultaneously reconstructed a positive and hopeful vision of the kind of existence human beings were created to experience under the loving and grace-filled reign of God.

The widespread acceptance and appreciation of *The Divine Conspiracy* hit a significant chord with many readers seeking a more robust and authentic vision of Christian faith. It became Dallas's most recognized and celebrated work, achieving *Christianity Today*'s award for Book of the Year. Scot McKnight, a New Testament scholar and professor who has tracked the movements of contemporary evangelical Christianity for decades now, suggests that when historians look back at the key influencers of the twenty-first century, Dallas will arguably be among the few names mentioned as offering significant influence on the Christian faith.[2] Long before becoming the director of the Dallas Willard Institute at Westmont College, Gary Moon argued Dallas's thoughts and insights should be considered as revolutionary and catalytic as those of Martin Luther. John Ortberg, a leading preacher, psychologist, and writer, has stated that, in his considered opinion, no one has been able to articulate the power and depth of the gospel better than Dallas.

In large measure, the success of *The Divine Conspiracy* stems from Dallas's unique, life-giving, and commonsense description of the intents and purposes of God for human life, both individually and collectively. Questions such as, "Why are we here? What are God's purposes for human life? What is the purpose of the church?" are the kinds of philosophical and theological questions that Dallas brought the full force of his mind to bear upon. He knew God had called him to preach the gospel, the good news, or, as he sometimes called it, "the benevolent knowledge of the way things really are" to answer these crucial, essential human questions. *The Divine Conspiracy* and his later work *Knowing Christ Today* focus on helping human beings grasp the nature and reality of God and his kingdom ways.

Although *The Divine Conspiracy* was a revolutionary work of inestimable value in its own right, one need not have read *The Divine Conspiracy* in order to understand the perspectives presented in this sequel. Those familiar with Dallas's previous publications and ministry will recognize this work as a consistent application and continuation of his vision, ideas, and concepts. What is new here are the situations and circumstances of contemporary society we chose to engage and overlay that original vision upon.

Our desire for this work was to cast and articulate a broader vision for the way the gospel must move first *in* and then *through* the church. The church is the means God uses to bring his kingdom to fruition. Such a transformation from the kingdoms of our world into the kingdom of Christ can best occur when discipled leaders of all types and in all contexts are poised to influence and direct the institutions and systems of government, education, economics, commerce, law, medicine, and religion. When this occurs, Dallas believed, the "kingdom of goodness and blessing" would begin to permeate every arena of life, every family, every street corner, every neighborhood, every city, and every citizen throughout the world. This was Dallas's understanding of purposes behind the Great Commission.

Dallas believed God's kingdom is firmly established and grown when followers of Jesus incarnate the virtues, faith, wisdom, power, and godly character enough to infect the world with an insatiable virus of goodwill. This is the primary thesis of this book.

The chapters that follow coalesce around three areas of interest that Dallas spent nearly forty years developing and honing. The first area conjoins his thoughts on moral knowledge and leadership. These are topics Dallas has already engaged in his more academic writings, but here we broadened his more philosophical and theoretical approach to include the way the nature of moral knowledge demonstrated in the gospel must move into the arenas of Christian leadership, discipleship, and spiritual transformation if there is to be a positive effect for the kingdom in both our communities and the broader culture at large. Dallas was devoted to helping Christians—from every walk of life, in every workplace, and in every social organization, business, or institution—to realize their full potential as leaders and ambassadors of light for the kingdom of God. Therefore, he attempted to cast an encouraging vision that bridges the gap separating Christian leaders ministering in the local church from Christian leaders in the broader secular workforce who minister in the institutions of government, education, business, service industries, commerce, and other professions. Closing the sacred-secular divide was the primary way he believed the local church could become the essential beachhead of the kingdom of God within contemporary society. Only then could the kingdoms of our world begin to experience the benefits and blessings of the kingdom of our God and of his Christ.

The second area centers on how the revealed knowledge of God, applied through moral leaders with integrity and courage, would positively impact the individual vocations that are central to the establishment and maintenance of flourishing societies. This includes, but is not exclusive to, the key institutions of government, business, commerce, education, and ministry. The final area dovetails with the first two. Dallas was devoted to the work of the church and its leaders. He never stopped seeking new and better ways of equipping and training disciples of Jesus to inhabit each of these key positions of societal governance and bear their responsibility for administering the manifestations of light, life, and hope to the world as a gift of a good and loving God. In one of our final conversations, Dallas made it clear that his great hope was to help Christians better understand what it is that Jesus is doing today. He said:

> Gary, we must help the church understand that Jesus is leading a subversion of all human governance. And that [subversion] will happen by the transformation of individuals, through the power of the gospel. And the community that emerges as a result is the divine conspiracy. They will not be overcome by evil but will overcome evil with good. That's the whole deal. And of course Christian leaders in every area of society are at the very heart of that mission.

Much of the material covered here grew from lectures and notes Dallas compiled for the very popular course he taught at USC on professional leadership and ethics. Many of our initial conversations also surrounded an article he had written and spoken about at Trinity International University in 2008.[3] A third resource we often discussed and expounded on was a two-day lecture series given at a Kern Family Foundation conference in January 2013. Dallas's thinking, writing, and research compiled from the class and those two proceedings were our springboard to dive deeper into what he believed were the essential core issues for Christian leaders and professionals to reconsider. His overarching desire was to provide persons of influence in every arena of society with a vision for what our collective lives might accomplish if given over to the ethics, power, wisdom, and grace found under the shepherding care of God's kingdom. What you now hold is the culmination of those ideas.

Dallas was devoted to the idea that our societies need well-placed, well-informed, thoughtful, gifted, effective, and supremely devoted persons of moral integrity to lead us through the opportunities and trials of contemporary life. He worked long and hard at helping the future leaders of our world, represented by his USC undergrad students, to develop the vision and means through which their leadership could actively pursue and attain common flourishing, prosperity, and general welfare. Likewise, the primary motive and intent of this work is to catalyze conversation, imagination, cooperation, and reconsideration of the ways and means we as Christian leaders participate in the "coming" of God's kingdom to the realms touched by our own spheres of influence.

Dallas's greatest hopes, and mine, would be for men and women from every walk of life and every profession and vocation that serves our societies—teachers, attorneys, physicians, pastors, accountants, tradespeople, and businesspeople alike—to read and discuss this book together. The book and the discussion questions are designed to instigate and facilitate these conversations, in coffeehouses, living rooms, elder board meetings, conferences, and retreats—wherever leaders gather to discuss their vision and hopes for God's mission to our world. The church, though not only the church, should be a perfect place for such a transformative discussion.

Yet this is not explicitly a "how-to" book. We would not presume to tell professionals how to apply these ideas to fields and endeavors outside our areas of expertise. Instead, as outside observers we engage a few professional disciplines as case studies in order to better highlight situations where Christlike leadership is essential and offer a few suggestions, viewpoints, and insights that we hope will prove profitable in assisting Christian leaders as they reconsider or reengage the crucial issues that affect our lives.

Christian leaders must engage in deep reflection and then robust dialog before we can begin to transform our world. God has invited us to help him revolutionize the world so that his good will is accomplished throughout all of creation, just as it is in heaven. For this reason disciples of Jesus need to be knowledgeable of good so they can be effective in achieving it. In the end, we are attempting to assist leaders who are already seeking to faithfully discern the good way, the right path, and the beneficial news of the kingdom in the workaday world right where they are. We believe these ideas will not only assist discussion, but that they will also encourage a growing sense of unity, a broadening vision, and the development of mutual respect, encouragement, and support that must remain the trademark characteristics of those who live and lead as followers of Jesus in our world.

I praise God for what he accomplished in and through Dallas's life and ministry. I am thankful for the gift of that first meeting. Finishing this project alone has forced me to face the stark reality of Dallas's absence. His smile, his loving laughter, his personal guidance, and his active engagement in our lives are gone. His soul will never die, but his body is no longer living. What remains for us to engage is his extensive body of work, his wisdom, his words, his ideas, his faith, and our use of these invaluable gifts. This book is part of the attempt to carry on that heritage. For his family and countless others, perhaps millions, just like me, we can choose to dwell on what is only in our memories, or we can expand and expound upon his impact for the greater glory of God and the advancement of his kingdom. At Dallas's funeral a prayer was offered that we would all be allowed to dream once again of a new vision that continues and builds upon the legacy of our friend, mentor, and guide. My prayer is that this work is one step in that very direction.

Gary Black Jr.
July 2013

CHAPTER I

God's Call to Leaders

Of this gospel I was made a minister according to the gift of God's grace which was given me by the working of his power. To me, though I am the very least of all the saints, this grace was given, to preach to the Gentiles the unsearchable riches of Christ, and to make all men see what is the plan of the mystery hidden for ages in God who created all things; that through the church the manifold wisdom of God might now be made known to the principalities and powers in the heavenly places. This was according to the eternal purpose which he has realized in Christ Jesus our Lord, in whom we have boldness and confidence of access through our faith in him. So I ask you not to lose heart over what I am suffering for you, which is your glory.

For this reason I bow my knees before the Father, from whom every family in heaven and on earth is named, that according to the riches of his glory he may grant you to be strengthened with might through his Spirit in the inner man, and that Christ may dwell in your hearts through faith; that you, being rooted and grounded in love, may have power to comprehend with all the saints what is the breadth and length and height and depth, and to know the love of Christ which surpasses knowledge, that you may be filled with all the fullness of God. Now to him who by the power at work within us is able to do far more abundantly

than all that we ask or think, to him be glory in the church and
in Christ Jesus to all generations, for ever and ever. Amen.

EPHESIANS 3:7–21

L ET US START by clarifying the major point of this work as straightforwardly as possible. God's "divine conspiracy" is to overcome the human kingdoms of this world with love, justice, and truth. This includes the whole world and all of human society—at the individual, corporate, and governmental levels. "The kingdom of the world has become the kingdom of our Lord and of his Messiah, and he will reign forever and ever" (Rev. 11:15). This is what Handel proclaims again and again in his famous "Hallelujah Chorus." This is reality. We could even say an eternal reality. The kingdom of God has indeed come; it has a past, it is with us now, and it has an unending future. The scriptures describe this future as the "day of the Lord," when God will have his turn at bat. The primary question this book pursues is this: How can we best participate in this reality?

In these pages we will suggest to followers of Jesus who are leaders, spokespersons, and professionals that they must responsibly and explicitly address the public issues, proposals, and processes of society within their spheres of influence through teaching, proclaiming, modeling, and manifesting the reality of the benevolent rule of God, which includes working together as the body of Christ by God's empowering grace. This influence encompasses every sphere of human action, not just those we think of as religious in nature. Such ambassadorial representation need not be overt or delivered in "Christianese" in order to be effective. No flag-waving and banner carrying are required. Such is the nature of a conspiracy, even a divine one. This is a tactic Jesus employed on many occasions with great aplomb.

Spokespersons for Christ are under the overarching imperative to love God and to love their neighbors as themselves. Their responsibility for what honors God and what is good for the public as well as for their closer "neighbors" dictates that they deal with economic, political, professional, and social issues that seriously impact life and well-being. It is not a religious conspiracy we are to pursue, but God's conspiracy, founded, led, and empowered by Jesus the Christ.

It is the task of Christ-following spokespersons, leaders, and professionals to keep before their own minds as well as those of the public they engage—through whatever vocation they maintain—an understanding of what is good and what is not and what conditions are required for human beings to experience well-being. No one person need have exclusive responsibility in this regard, nor does there need to be some sort of continual media event to make a significant fuss about every issue or decision. At times some leaders and spokespersons may be required to take on a special, higher-profile responsibility because of their position in society or because of the sources of knowledge and power that come with a certain activity or expertise. Even in such cases, we are seeking things that benefit the common good and the flourishing of all peoples. We are not advocating for a special-interest group or that people use public positions or notoriety as a platform to promote a certain ideology or theology. We are not necessarily endeavoring to stack political power on one issue against that of another or to privilege one candidacy over another. Instead, we seek to present the wisdom of divine love in order to be a light shining in the darkness that cannot be missed, whatever the issue.

THE KINGDOM HERE AND NOW

A significant part of our Western Christian heritage over the past few hundred years and much of the explicit practical teaching that we hear from our pulpits, which becomes routinely modeled in our Christian communities, argue that the kingdom of God is something that is not readily available or accessible in the here and now. Thankfully, this view has shown signs of changing, in fits and starts, and to very good effect. But overall there remains a sense, sometimes overt, sometimes more covert, that one fine day, far in the future, all the earthly kingdoms of our current world will eventually come under the reign, or rule, of Jesus Christ. But until then we are left to hold on by our fingernails, if we can, to our piety and faith, doing our utmost to ride out the many storms of life that threaten our sense of well-being. This has remained a very familiar strain of thought and practice for many of our Christian preachers, teachers, and spokespersons today, as it has been over the past several centuries. Such ideas and images are difficult to reform and thus tend to leave Christians with only the fading hope that in the "great by and by" Jesus will return to finish his largely failed previous attempt to jump-start his reign as king over both heaven and earth.

What is less well known, let alone appreciated, is that such a perspective is not how the early church traditionally understood the rule or reign of Jesus. Nor is it what Jesus taught. Jesus's kingdom has not been deferred until his return or until after he is able to "clean house" at the final judgment. He will return, and there will be a settling of accounts, we can be sure of this. But until then, he is not biding his time, having been limited to changing a few minds here and there, saving individual souls at various religious services, and making a few mystical appearances now and again, until some unknown period in the future when he can get his original intentions back on track. In contrast to such a passive theology, the teachings of the church through much of its history demonstrate a consistent testimony, even if ignored at times, that Jesus's rule began when he said it began, at the proclamation of his "Great Commission," which, as you recall, occurred just before his ascension—after his death and resurrection, but just before he went to be with his Father in heaven, where he now is actively positioned in the seat of authority "at the right hand of the Father." As noted biblical scholars N. T. Wright and Scot McKnight, among many others, have clearly argued, Jesus was crowned king, is now ruling, and currently maintains all authority or dominion "in heaven and on earth." Theologian Amos Yong has also helped us better understand how the Spirit of God, as the "chief empowerer," is now "poured out upon all flesh" (Joel 2:28; Acts 2:17) and directs, leads, encourages, supports, and advocates for the reign of Jesus in and through the wills, minds, bodies, and even human institutions that serve his overarching purposes of holistic redemption.

What is important to understand here is that there is no "then" or "when" to the kingdom of God. This reign is a current, progressing, maturing reality, which means Jesus rules today. Jesus is the one who sits on the throne of the cosmos, and all authority, over all things, has been given to him (Matt. 25:31; 28:18). God is the God of all humanity (Jer. 32:27). God rules today through his Son, Jesus, the king, and he rules over everyone and everything—not just Christians or religious organizations. He is the King of Kings, the ruler of rulers (Rev. 1:5), and the dominion of his Spirit extends to every corner and crevice of the universe at this very moment—a fact even the demons appear to understand perfectly well (Mark 1:24; 5:7; James 2:19). The kingdom has come, and there is more to come. Thanks be to God.

Let's take a moment and contemplate the implications of what all this means. A loving and omnipotent God is now ruling. Therefore, he has a holistic vision for human life that necessarily includes all the political, economic, and social realms—not just religious realms—along with the innumerable personal kingdoms that compose all human activity.

As previously stated, this is not a new vision, but one present throughout the Hebrew scriptures, revealed through the prophets, partially demonstrated in the people of Israel, made abundantly clear in the teachings of Jesus, carried forward in the first century by the apostles, and propelled through the ages until landing on the doorstep of the contemporary church. Through Christ all things, everything, everyone, is in the process of coming under the sovereign benevolence (Latin: *bene*, "good"; *volens*, "willing") of God's *agape* ethic and ethos (1 Cor. 15:28). Through Christ all things are being, and will be, made new (Rev. 21:5; 2 Cor. 5:17). Eventually, every knee will bow and every tongue will acknowledge this current reality (Phil. 2:10–11). Both believers and nonbelievers alike will be confessing an appropriate degree of both wonder and ignorance regarding the magnitude of Christ's lordship and glorious representation of God, his Father.

BECOMING KINGDOM BUILDERS

It may be difficult to conceive of the effects that recognizing the full scope of Christ's lordship today could have on both the world collectively and each person individually. In the rough and tumble realities of our contemporary world, the glorious rule and reign of God can, and often does, become far too distant and foggy for us to even imagine, much less manifest within our personal and social situations and circumstances. Yet that is exactly what Jesus wants us and has empowered us to do. We can see, hear, experience, and realize, with confident assurance, that God is most definitely with us in our work as we seek to do his good will. And if God is for us, with us, guiding and empowering our efforts, we can be appropriately confident that good will result. But losing our vision for this reality has largely cost us the hope that it could ever occur. Therefore, in this increasingly foggy mire of futile doubt about the grandeur and glory of God's intentions for us and his creation, it is increasingly important that we endeavor to describe, as clearly as we can, what such a reality can mean for everyday life.

We face a significant problem today in our lack of awareness, interest, and critical thinking and teaching within our Christian congregations and institutions of higher learning regarding how

God, through his Spirit, is to guide us personally, communally, socially, politically, and economically into direct conformity with the blessing that is within his kingdom. We simply have not thought very long or hard about how the kingdom of God could, would, or does manifest itself within ideas and images that drive the current contexts of our church, work, school, play, family, business, health, and economic activities.

This is our primary task here: to reinvigorate the conversation about the ways and means of the kingdom of God, which will cascade over the walls of our Christian institutions to inform both Christians and non-Christians alike as to the beneficial effects and wonder-working power of God's love and goodness in every area of human existence. Yes, the kingdom of God is to be formed "within you," but it should never be understood as limited to or confined by the human heart. The kingdom of God is as big as the range of God's omnipotent will. Nothing can stop it. Nothing will. Not even the very gates of hell itself.

What we must begin to reconsider, given our immediate circumstances, is how to best focus our efforts and think deeply about this present and coming reality that Christ has made readily available to us. God's reign or rule is literally within arm's reach, at hand, near, close, right before us, in the midst of us, right where we live (e.g., Matt. 3:2; Mark 1:15; Luke 17:21). And this is exactly what people from all walks of life—our political leaders, educators, business professionals, and stay-at-home parents—are called to apply right where they live and work. We must reach out and grab this "kingdom of heaven" (Matthew's term for the "kingdom of God") by the throat, with gusto and vigor, and be willing to violate the established norms in order to accomplish with God his divine conspiracy to overcome evil with good (Matt. 11:12).

We so often find these kinds of violations of norms in the most unlikely of places. A few years ago the entire world was shocked by the love and forgiveness offered by a small group of disciples living in Nickel Mines, Pennsylvania, to a lone, troubled man who shot ten young children, killing five, before turning the gun on himself. There was no media circus, no political debate about constitutional rights versus public safety. These citizens of the kingdom didn't follow that well-worn path. Instead, trusting and modeling their confidence in their Savior's ways, they chose to forgive. While still mourning and comforting each other, they offered their love, grace, and even financial support to the killer's widow and parents. As a result the world looked on in awe as a shining ray of pure goodness illuminated a very dark hour. Such goodness cannot be hidden. People have to stop and look, in wonder. Forgiving those who persecute us and loving our enemies are ideas that still deeply violate our established norms.

Another simple example of such violation of norms and extension of grace is now routinely demonstrated in the innovative arena of microfinance. These are financial services for poor and low-income clients, including loans to unsalaried borrowers who have little or no collateral. The brainchild of Nobel Peace Prize–winner Muhammad Yunus, microfinance development has been utilized for over three decades by dozens of organizations, such as Opportunity International and World Vision. It has become so popular that both religious and secular organizations now offer small loans (the average loan is less than $400) to the world's poorest populations. When lenders focus on both "nurturing the profitability of borrowers' businesses—and, in turn, their clients' overarching economic and social well-being," the practice is so effective, it has now become the darling of poverty-fighting relief agencies all across the globe. In an age when institutional lenders seem to expect borrowers to demonstrate their lack of financial need before a loan is even considered, the concept of lending money to those with little to no resources but with an abundance of character has shown the potential for increasing not only income but also health care, housing, nutrition, and education. Client-centered microfinance is yet another idea that rattles the economic norms of our societies.[1]

We need to learn some very important lessons from our brothers and sisters in Nickel Mines and those creative innovators in microfinance. The people of God are to be ambassadors of good in our world, demonstrating, personally and through its systems and institutions, the ways of God for the benefit of all people. Just as John, writing Revelation, saw a vision of reality that needed to be revealed and understood by the struggling early churches scattered around the ancient world, we also must endeavor to recapture God's vision of our current world under the rule of King Jesus.

Part of our difficulty comes from a view that the world is on a countdown timer, which we sense is coming close to ringing. For so many believers, such an impending sense of doom creates a slow-burning fear that drains energy, optimism, and expectations of God's blessings in our lives and the lives of others. We can be assured God is worried about neither the present nor the future, and thus we need not worry about, or be distracted by, any doomsday scenarios that tend to cycle through our religious institutions. Yet just saying we shouldn't worry is very different from actually not worrying. Much of our preaching and teaching today that centers on fear of an imminent apocalypse and the unstoppable moral decay of our societies actually leads people to surmise that in fact Jesus is not in control at all. John's message was just the opposite. The risen Christ is very much in control, despite what we read and see on the evening news. All is well in his church.

TRUE BLESSINGS

A second difficulty is found in the rise of what has been termed the "prosperity gospel," which has created a sense that God is ready, willing, and able to provide for every consumerist desire or creature comfort vaguely connected to the American dream. Some have even argued that such God-ordained prosperity has become some sort of right or privilege we are entitled to, and believers are therefore righteously justified in demanding God's favor. Again, this appears to be a historically recurring twisting of the teachings of scripture. The Sadducees maintained a similar theology, to ill effect.[2] Today the same tendency is seen in the fact that our fascination with and confidence in materialism are working their way back into our interpretations of scripture.

Still, as is often the case, such "twisting" comes from a core truth of the gospel. The castle built on the rock is an undeniable blessing; it is strong, well developed, and withstands the storm. All kinds of people living in a state of confident assurance of God's love and care are blessed—not because of their condition, but despite any condition. The conditions we face are temporary. The blessings remain eternal. The people of Nickel Mines were richly blessed despite their situation by their willingness to let go of the bitter feelings of hatred and revenge. Those living in the most marginalized and impoverished cultures in our world who are learning to sustain their families with an incredibly small investment in a new business are also blessed through the intentional service and sharing of those with the gifts of education, planning, wisdom, leadership, and discipline. As he did with the boy's small lunch of fish and bread, Jesus is able to multiply our seemingly insignificant efforts in phenomenal ways. Such is the nature of the kingdom of God.

These applications of both the spiritual and material gifts of grace, service, and stewardship are just a few living testimonies that demonstrate that nothing can separate anyone from the love of God (Rom. 8:39) and that Jesus is with us, ruling in all things, even through our worst fears and largest problems, through the end of this age (Matt. 28:20). This king suffers violators, and the violators are forging dramatic new paths into the world. With this king, nothing is impossible (Luke 1:37).

The chapters that follow sketch out some new paths to consider as we follow God's calling to reflect his kingdom light in our world. We will explore a variety of social structures God wants us to change. We do not presume to offer a complete plan. Such a grand unfolding of God's intentions will require engagement with and contribution from the entire body of Christ. Here we simply seek to add to and further what is already occurring. This requires very explicit thinking in order to cast a vision or paint a portrait as grand as we can imagine in order to merely highlight some of the qualities and features of abundant living that mark the essence and beauty of the kingdom of God.

CHAPTER 2

Following the Good Shepherd

There was never a nation great until it came to the knowledge that it had nowhere in the world to go for help.

CHARLES DUDLEY WARNER

PERHAPS THE BEST place to begin our consideration of the central tenets, ethos, and ethics of the kingdom of God for contemporary life lies in the words David recorded in Psalm 23:

> The LORD is my shepherd, I shall not want.
> He makes me lie down in green pastures;
> he leads me beside still waters; he restores my soul.
> He leads me in right paths for his name's sake.
> Even though I walk through the darkest valley,
> I fear no evil; for you are with me;
> your rod and your staff—they comfort me.
> You prepare a table before me in the presence of my enemies;
> you anoint my head with oil; my cup overflows.
> Surely goodness and mercy shall follow me all the days of my life,
> and I shall dwell in the house of the LORD my whole life long.

Many people can recite Psalm 23. It is routinely treated as great literature and likened to words of Homer, Shakespeare, or

Cervantes. But there is much more to be gained here. Psalm 23 is not merely beautiful poetry. What many people miss is that this psalm spells out clearly what life with God is like.

THE LORD IS MY SHEPHERD

The kind of life David describes in Psalm 23 is one bathed in *shalom,* or "peace," which proceeds from understanding that Yahweh, the LORD, is a shepherd and hence a provider, protector, teacher, and loving host. The shepherd is one of the oldest and most enduring of Hebrew metaphors (Gen. 49:25; Pss. 77:21; 80:2; 95:7). What David understood and experienced was the reality of knowing a loving, attentive, present, powerful, and purposeful guide for his life. Our greatest assurance and soul-filling hope is that the LORD, Yahweh, is our shepherd. It is because of this simple, yet endlessly profound reality that we can begin to understand our place in the world and the joy that is ours forever.

The shepherd's vocation is largely lost on us today. There is an intimacy in shepherding. Shepherds know their sheep because they are with them all day, every day, for weeks on end, in solitary places. They learn the actions, habits, and preferences of their flock through constant oversight. They protect, feed, direct, and correct the sheep continually, developing a bond, perhaps even a love of their flock. Jesus says, "The good shepherd lays down his life for the sheep" (John 10:11), something that David knew was part of his responsibilities as well. As a result, the sheep respond and are benefited. Without a shepherd they are lost, in danger, and unable to endure the realities of the wild. To think of the LORD as a shepherd is to come to understand the intensely personal, comforting, attentive, and providing nature of God's love and care for his flock of humanity.

A first step on this journey of the Psalm 23 way of living is to confess that much of our resistance in placing our confidence (faith) in a Good Shepherd stems from the fear that God cannot or will not provide for us in times of great need or despair. Frequently this is a product of the belief that God simply is not good or that at least there are events on his "résumé" that put his character in question. This is often the tragic result of a significant trauma caused by bad theology; it simply should not stand. In fact, Psalm 23 speaks directly in opposition to such dismal theology. It is plainly foolhardy and oxymoronic to believe God is anything but perfectly good. The kingdoms of our world, including many religious kingdoms, run on doctrinal fear the way the kingdom of God runs on grace. Perfect love casts out fear, as will the love of a good shepherd. This image, of the Good Shepherd as Jesus describes him, is a far cry from the sort of vengeful, red-eyed, wrath-soaked Zeuslike deity popular with some. There is simply no reason to believe anything bad about God.

I SHALL NOT WANT

The sheep of the flock are at peace, never lacking or left wanting any good thing. Why? Because they know their shepherd can be trusted to provide all that they need. Fear is gone, needs satisfied, peace abounds.

In a consumer-driven society where newer and greater desires are both created and fed by increasingly clever advertisers and suppliers, it would do our own souls well, and by implication benefit our societies immensely, to meditate deeply on what our personal and social lives might be like if we were to experience the total absence of superficial want. Can we envision being free of want? Can we conceive of a place where the question, "How much is enough?" is thought as absurd as the answer, "A little bit more"?

What the Good Shepherd provides is of inestimable value and eternal quality, of the type whose value moths and rust can't diminish (Matt. 16:9). The Good Shepherd provides an understanding of what is essential and what is tertiary, what real needs are compared to artificial desires. What kinds of economies would we have today if we focused on essential needs first? How much debt would we incur if we realized our sufficiency and abundance in Christ? These are but a few of the key questions Psalm 23 brings to the fore.

> He makes me lie down in green pastures;
> he leads me beside still waters; he restores my soul.

Living under the care of the Shepherd provides a state of rest, or *shalom*, which involves plenteousness and brings restoration at the deep wellspring of our lives. Such rich and abiding rest replenishes our entire being or soul. It is the nature of the Good Shepherd to be good and to lead his sheep onto good paths, where what is good can be seen, experienced, demonstrated, and duplicated. These are the right paths and true ways of righteousness.

I FEAR NO EVIL

> Even though I walk through the darkest valley,
> I fear no evil; for you are with me;
> your rod and your staff—they comfort me.

Such goodness, provision, protection, soul care, restoration, righteousness, and flourishing that life with the Shepherd provides allows us to face shadowy dangers and uncertainties that threaten life. We can live without fear. Living without fear is, in fact, the same existential reality as living a life without want.

Can we envision being freed to the point where not a single thing on earth, above the earth, or below the earth could cause dread to creep into our hearts? Can we begin to imagine what living a life free from the plagues of worry, anxiety, and dread would demonstrate to a world whose societal engines are stoked day and night by media franchises devoted to peddling fear and anxiety?

Why does fear play such an oversized role in our lives and our culture? What exactly are we afraid of? Well, the list is long. We are afraid we will not be happy, that we will not flourish unless we take the proper offensive and defensive positions necessary to protect ourselves and provide for every possible existential need, both real and perceived. Our search for safety and contentment is endless and inexhaustible precisely because of the intrinsic futility of relying on human abilities to provide resolution to our problems. Thus, if telling the truth on a mortgage application or quarterly report, forgiving a family member or neighbor an offense, or giving time or money to an organization from our stockpile of resources is perceived to put us or our pursuit of our individual version of the American dream in jeopardy, our moral compass is adjusted to justify our own sense of self-fulfillment, pleasure, or even security. The result is one more brick of our lives laid on a foundation of shifting sand.

It only becomes a matter of when, not if, such a life and such a civilization will implode. The mental and emotional energy required for rushing about in the vain attempt to control the uncontrollable in order to preserve what tiny sense of security we can is an exhausting and deadening errand. The effort reveals a total lack of understanding of our Shepherd, his nature, the structure of the universe God created, and the ethos of his kingdom. Without such a vision generation after generation continues the desperate search for that elusive guarantee of holistic flourishing. And our social and political ineffectiveness continues to fuel the rage and shame of unrealized desire, which continues to fill our hospitals, prisons, and morgues with stories of cataclysmic sorrow and tragic despair. One sociologist has suggested that adults today represent the most numb, obese, addicted, medicated, and indebted generation in American history.[1]

The human problem has no human solution, because it is humans that are the source of the problem. We need a Shepherd.

GOODNESS AND MERCY SHALL FOLLOW ME

You prepare a table before me in the presence of my enemies;
you anoint my head with oil; my cup overflows.
Surely goodness and mercy shall follow me all the days of my life,
and I shall dwell in the house of the LORD my whole life long.

Such a Shepherd comes to the weary and burdened to whisper hope in their ears: "My dear little children: Really, truly, love one another. That's the big idea. When you do this, it will answer all your deepest questions and solve all your biggest problems. I've designed it that way" (1 John 3:18–20, paraphrased). Our point of breakdown is an opportunity to break through toward a new life. We must begin to imagine a new way of being. Green pastures, calm waters, restoration, safety, security, and provision—this is the life we all long for and seek, and it is exactly what Jesus came to provide. The Good Shepherd corrects all the gaps in our vision for life and fills the voids of our understanding of God's provision right now, where the rubber hits the road of our daily lives.

Ironically, the prophet Habakkuk makes the same claim, but from a different vantage point. He writes of God's sufficiency exactly at a time when he and the nation of Israel had been overrun by their enemies. These cataclysmic events at the end of the seventh century BCE left many Israelites' lives shattered. Not unlike the kinds of scenes we have witnessed during the many Middle Eastern conflicts through the centuries, Habakkuk saw the trauma caused by rapid political change, social turmoil, deadly military engagements, and endless rebellion.[2] In this cacophony of conflict Habakkuk reminds the people whence their hope springs:

Though the fig tree does not blossom,
and no fruit is on the vines;
though the produce of the olive fails,
and the fields yield no food;

though the flock is cut off from the fold,
and there is no herd in the stalls,
yet I will rejoice in the LORD;
I will exult in the God of my salvation.
God, the LORD, is my strength;
he makes my feet like the feet of a deer,
and makes me tread upon the heights. (3:17–19)

In light of such a state of sufficiency, even amid conditions of total desolation, an experience of joy, rejoicing, and strength remained. Neither fear of death, nor disease, nor danger, nor hunger, nor pain, nor person, nor creature, nor circumstance, nor loss can interrupt or overwhelm the life lived in the empowering love of the Shepherd's care (Rom. 8:35–39).

GETTING TO KNOW THE GOD JESUS KNEW

Psalm 23 and Habakkuk 3 lie before us as the result of reflection on the manner of being that fully establishes the ultimate goal of the divine conspiracy throughout all creation. Psalm 23, the God-breathed, with-God life, has already been initiated and is now being brought to pass in and through the lives and communities of his devoted students. As disciples of Jesus, following in his footsteps, listening to the Spirit's ever present counsel, we are to facilitate and lead a humble, peaceful, wise, and loving festival of goodwill, the result of which will overwhelm every competing agenda, every fearful scheme, and every desperate plan founded on the shifting sands of human fear or pride. It is a revolution of loving-kindness.

History reveals that acts of rebellion and resistance to God and his ways, whether overt or covert, conscious or unconscious, individual or communal, are most often committed by those with ears deaf to the music and eyes blind to the beauty of the plentitude provided by the Good Shepherd, who is the LORD of all things, Yahweh, the great "I am," who prepares a table of goodness that nourishes body and soul, family, tribe, city, and nation to the point of overflowing. It is from this position of lavish blessedness that God is set to deal with all creation.

Psalm 23 provides a step toward a primary change that must occur prior to any renovation of our thoughts and actions. We must come face-to-face with the king of the realm we seek to expand. The God that Jesus knew was perhaps very different from the God often described in our contemporary world. The God Jesus knew perfectly and testified to is a self-sustaining, all-encompassing being who is also immaterial, intelligent and free, personal and triune, perfectly good, wise and powerful, who created the universe and continues to sustain it as well as govern and direct it by his providence. The moral attributes of God as loving, beneficent, and generous flow out of the plentitude of his being. There is nothing to fear. We are in fact more than conquerors when we obediently follow in God's good purposes and plan (Rom. 8:37).

SEEING KING JESUS'S ONGOING WORK

It is also important for us to recognize and celebrate the fact that Jesus has made wonderful and glorious progress in accomplishing his divine conspiracy and building his church throughout our world. There are more improvements to be made, but we can and should marvel at the amazing achievements Jesus accomplished in bringing life and light into our lives, families, cities, and nations. Pages and pages could be filled recounting the miraculous, supernatural realities that have taken place right before our eyes that remind us and testify to how steadily God is moving in and through our world to turn hearts and minds toward his unending and boundless majesty. Truly "the whole earth is full of his glory" (Isa. 6:3).

Just some of the deeply satisfying improvements can be witnessed in the progress the church has made, in general, in dealing with many of the paralyzing debates and conflicts we have engaged in over the past two centuries. Of particular note are the advances made with regard to racial reconciliation and gender equality, the reduction in denominational acrimony, increases in cross-confessional and cross-cultural respect, awareness, dialog, cooperation, and relief efforts, to name just a few. Controversies still rage in certain corners, but much advancement has been achieved, and we should relish these developments.

Even still, much crucial discernment is needed regarding the kind and type of work Jesus would have his gathered disciples be about. When disciples of Jesus become more clearly able to see that we are also participants, and not only passive recipients, of God's empowering grace, what are we to do? What would God have us do? What is the big picture God is painting and how do we fit in? What is God's overarching mission for his church in our world? These are big questions, and they carry even bigger opportunities as we realize their answers are of great significance not only for followers of Christ, but for every human being. This is due to the fact that each of these questions stems from one core question: What is the primary objective and purpose for human existence?

Humanity has achieved much good. We've split the atom, learned to fly, traveled in space, probed the corners of our planet, cured countless diseases, invented amazing technological wizardry that boggles the mind, and steadily progressed in our understanding of our universe and the basic components of our physical world. Although we acknowledge there is more to do in a multitude of areas, humanity has made astounding progress. God has been with us, despite ourselves at times; he has shown us favor and helped us to thrive in many ways, in many arenas, and through many means. A great number of these advancements are not strictly "Christian," as we have come to understand that term. Electricity, for example, is not considered a "Christian" discovery. Nor should we expect it to be. Yet the world is a far better place because of it. God loves all people equally and can and does use all kinds of people, as he sees fit, for the good he desires to bestow on all of us. This is one of the most wondrous characteristics of God's mercy and grace. Certainly every good and perfect gift is from God, and he has graced humanity with many gifts and continues to do so. At the same time much progress remains in manifesting his kingdom "come" in and to our world today. Darkness still opposes the light. Only the most ardent of atheists would disagree with such a statement.

Even so, since our civilizations began, humanity has struggled, and continues to struggle, with discerning what thriving consists of, how best to do it, and how it will be measured. Our history reveals all the many experiments we have conducted to best organize our families, communities, cities, and nations. Each has been built on a variety of combinations of philosophical, ideological, religious, political, moral, legal, commercial, economic, and relational foundations. This will not change. Neither will the key questions driving these endeavors through the millennia: Why are we here? What do we want? How shall we live? Who is my neighbor and what is my responsibility toward my neighbor?

We can become weary and frustrated that the solutions our society provides to these questions continue to elude us. To paraphrase U2's Bono, humanity still hasn't found what it's looking for. Yet each succeeding generation has the responsibility of coming up with its own answers.

The many and varied secular gospels that seek to answer these questions fill our institutions of higher learning, our political discourse, and our airwaves simply because these issues concern the core needs of every human being. Consequently, the search for acceptable means of flourishing becomes a constant consideration for those who lead and direct our social institutions. Therefore Christians, in all the areas and disciplines that comprise our society, who are intimately acquainted with the Good Shepherd and his ways must be prepared to offer more than a memorized set of beliefs in reply. There must be a robust competency and willingness to examine and then demonstrate, model, and thus prove how and why Jesus's answers to these questions are both good and best.

It is at the intersection of human need and human knowledge that the Christian worldview, if it is what it claims to be, must offer hope, guidance, correction, and truth. Thus, we will now springboard from the ideas and implications first introduced in *The Divine Conspiracy* into the larger systemic issues we must begin to face in our world today.

CHAPTER 3

Leaders Who Follow the Shepherd

*So also, when the delight of eternity draws us
upward and the pleasure of temporal goods holds us down,
the identical soul is not wholehearted in its desire for one or
the other. It is torn apart in a painful condition as long as
it prefers the eternal because of its Truth but does not
discard the temporal because of familiarity.*

AUGUSTINE OF HIPPO

L ATE IN THE twentieth century the distinguished American sociologist Talcott Parsons observed that societal leaders had "become the most important single component in the structure of modern societies."[1] This is perhaps even truer today. Ready examples of the incalculable necessity for moral leadership can routinely be found over the airwaves and on the Internet. Consider the 2010 explosion and sinking of the offshore oil rig *Deepwater Horizon* and the spill that followed. This was a horrific catastrophe for both human lives and the environment. We may never know exactly who knew what and when. But as the investigations and lawsuits ensue, it is worth considering what kind of impact even one single, courageous, devoted individual could have made to avoid this disaster. What will likely never be discussed, much less probed, are the many factors that would have needed to be in place for a courageous, moral leader to have prevented such a calamity.

Laws protecting whistle-blowers do exist in the United States. Their effectiveness may be questionable, but they do exist. Still, having a law to protect whistle-blowers is not the same as mandating the character required to "blow the whistle" in the first place. One would need the integrity to avoid rationalizing away or skirting responsibility, the values required to prioritize safety over profits, the self-esteem to face the scrutiny and even disdain of supervisors and coworkers, and the courage to risk losing a job or career.

If one or more of these characteristics are absent, the temptation to cater to one's own fears and needs rises above what is morally true and best for all concerned. If moral leadership and courage win out, lives and livelihoods are saved, untold disasters are averted, and huge amounts of resources are preserved. In short, the world is a better place when leaders lead well. Such is the mentality that followers of Jesus must consider every morning as they enter the workplace to assume their responsibilities.

This is exactly what appears to have happened in the life of a low-level Google sales employee in the United Kingdom. *The Guardian* reported that Barney Jones came forward to give evidence against Google's claims that it did not close sales deals in the United Kingdom and therefore was not liable to taxation in the country. Upon hearing this, with no financial incentives and facing the prospects of diminished employment opportunities for himself, Jones presented to the public accounts committee his evidence that sales deals reported in Dublin were indeed closed in London. Why go to the trouble? Jones stated that he stood up, because he believes his Christian commitment requires accountability for pursuing and achieving the good. Therefore, he couldn't willingly "allow something within [his] power to just slip through."[2] There was no parade, no medal, and no reward, just an ordinary citizen doing his job with extraordinary courage.

The growing complexities of contemporary life make it increasingly difficult for us as both individuals and societies to know all that is occurring around us, so that we can discern both our needs and what is best. This was evident in the *Deepwater Horizon* disaster; there was no way for the fishermen, hoteliers, beachfront homeowners, or restaurateurs to protect themselves from the events that caused the massive oil spill. But the complexity of modern life also played a key role in the nationwide mortgage crisis and accompanying economic recession. Few people understood or were privileged to have the information about the nature and effect of the underlying investments that would threaten to demolish the world economy. In both instances, what was required, more than we realized, were leaders, professionals, and experts with the integrity and courage of Barney Jones to discern and pursue with all diligence what has for centuries been understood as the "general welfare." How, where, and by whom is the kind of personal character forged that is sacrificially devoted to the public good?

GOD'S DIVINE CONSPIRACY

Even though this book is coauthored, we see this present work as progressing naturally from and building upon Dallas's previous volumes. *The Divine Conspiracy* came as the third book in the series. The first installment, *In Search of Guidance* (later retitled *Hearing God*), describes how life in God's kingdom promises an intimate, conversational relationship with God. The king of this kingdom of goodness wants to be in conversation with us about our lives. The book explains how we can experience this reality.

The second, *The Spirit of the Disciplines*, seeks to explain another aspect of this intimate relationship with God. As we develop a conversational relationship with God through the Holy Spirit, we become apprenticed to Jesus—novices learning from the guidance of a master craftsman. And what this craftsman is teaching us is how to have a character like his and so embody God's goodness. The book explains many of the practices and tools that facilitate spiritual transformation.

The Divine Conspiracy then shows how this intimate relationship of being apprenticed to Jesus has a direction and goal, using the Sermon of the Mount as a means of articulating a vision of the good news as the good life available in the kingdom of God— that is, available now. Next, how God works through the nitty-gritty details of our lives, work, relationships, bodies, thoughts, feelings, and desires to teach us how to live our life as Jesus would live it if he were in our specific context is covered in *Renovation of the Heart*. *The Great Omission,* a collection of essays, discusses the great opportunity that lies before our churches today as they attempt the task of creating disciples, of bringing people into the life-giving reality of Jesus and his kingdom ways—and the great tragedy that occurs when this opportunity is not fulfilled.

These previous works provided a vision for personal transformation, the how and why for what we are to be working on in the Christian life. This work hopes to expand our vision so that we begin to glimpse God's kingdom goals over and above the work he is doing in our own lives and better see his overarching objectives for the world. In God's kingdom we are not solely concerned with our personal transformation (which by itself would be spiritual narcissism), but also with how we are part of a larger work of transformation: the reconciliation of all things. We are concerned with how God wants to accomplish this work both in and through us.

In the New Covenant Jesus has purchased, we are introduced to the true reality of all things. Through the Spirit of Christ we can draw from this reality so that we may know, in all of the areas that touch our lives—in our work, ministry, family, society, culture, government, institutions, art, play, research, religion— the goodness and provision of an all-sufficing, want-erasing, fear-eradicating, peace-loving Shepherd. Such a precious gift is not for sale, nor is it a chip with which to bargain in our society.

No doubt many will vehemently disagree with the notion that God is calling all leaders to extend the kingdom of God to whatever areas they are involved with. Some will insist that the church, or Christians in general, lack the expertise, competency, and responsibility for such a task. Many who hold this position argue from history's numerous examples of the ill effects that resulted when individuals, groups, or societies claimed Christian sovereignty over all areas. Horrific examples of cult practices, fundamentalist separatism, religious elitism, and doctrinal exclusivism are available for all to see. The so-called New Atheists have made a small fortune elaborating the ghastly tragedies that tarnish the history of the Christian religion. On the other side are those who argue that political power games that readily employ arm-twisting influence, backroom deals, and billion-dollar political action committees are the weapons and tactics that must be used by Christians on the battlefields of modern cultural warfare.

With regard to both these viewpoints, we simply note that making the claim that some activity or ideology is Christlike or is being engaged from a Christian perspective may not in fact be the case; it may be altogether unchristian and non-Christlike. What is advertised is often very different from what is delivered. Certainly issues of interpretation are involved, but interpretation is not the end of the matter. Many activities and motives ascribed to Jesus or the Christian worldview are verifiable misrepresentations of Christlikeness, despite claims to the contrary. Part of the means of discerning this difference is given by Jesus himself. When asked by John the Baptist if in fact he was who he said he was, Jesus gave a specific answer in reply: "Go and tell John what you hear and see: the blind receive their sight, the lame walk, the lepers are cleansed, the deaf hear, the dead are raised, and the poor have good news brought to them" (Matt. 11:5). Here again, contrary to popular "prosperity" gospel, Jesus is suggesting that

the kind and type of life he offers is better in essence and quality, both spiritually and physically, than the alternatives. This is
a question we, like John the Baptist, do well to consider during
periods of great difficulty.

But the base question underneath John's inquiry remains crucial for us today: Is the vision of life Jesus offers a better one, or
should we pursue another? If, during the first century, one were
to ask a Roman soldier, a Jewish religious leader, and perhaps a
dishonest money changer if becoming a Christian would better
their lives, such persons might honestly reply, "Absolutely not!"
Likewise, today there is vehement opposition to Jesus's understanding and revelation of what is good for us and how to discern
it in our individual and social circumstances. Still, no other ethical philosophy has yet been found or created that either matches
or exceeds the moral knowledge representative of Christ's life and
teaching. Jesus's teachings remain the solitary beacon of hope
for eliminating the elusive, cyclical crises of human existence
and thus represents the crucial first step that will lead humanity
toward achieving the life without fear and want that fulfills our
desperate search for human flourishing.

CITIES OF OUR GOD

Lest anyone consider this work advocacy for a new form of the
"social gospel," a fuller articulation of the "prosperity gospel," or
even an argument on which to base a new, better, or reformed
platform for virtue ethics that seeks the "general welfare" or
"holistic prosperity," let us put these claims to rest. We are simply recalling, reminding people of, and pursuing what both the
Hebrew scriptures and New Testament seek, articulate, and
instruct in the very old and elusive reality called *shalom*. It is
the enduring and encompassing experience and expectation of
restful, secure, holistic well-being, which every individual and
culture has struggled to find or create and maintain through-

out human history. *Shalom* is what Yahweh promised Abraham would be his, a blessing of God that would flow through him to all the other nations (Gen. 12:2; 15:15).

Likewise it is crucial that God's sufficiency and plentitude be manifested and experienced in the lives of those called by his name. Christians must eat their own cooking, follow their own teaching, and understand their own ideas. Judgment must begin with the house of God (1 Pet. 4:17). This encompasses the final hope of this work: to bless, equip, inspire, and encourage those leaders dedicated to working with Jesus in furthering the cause of the kingdom of God within the key institutions and structures of our society. It is crucial that a gospel powerful enough to save is also powerful enough to deliver us from evil. The local church must be moved from simply *advocating understanding of* or *professing belief in* the availability of life in the kingdom to *demonstrating* and *manifesting* a broader expression of what the gospel can accomplish when brought directly to bear on the weighty matters of our social realities. These matters are crucial and eternal, for they deal with the eternal souls of those individuals within our families, our neighbors, our society, and finally the world at large.

A very small percentage of those in the church stand behind a pulpit or sport certain kinds of identifiable clothing. The actual leadership roster of the church includes disciples ministering in every arena of life, in business, law, medicine, education, the arts, sciences, government, and religion. The objective of Jesus's church-growth strategy was not to build a single, behemoth social institution with a limited set of ordained authorities. Instead, his Spirit was to be poured out on all flesh to effect a widening, deepening base of influence within every nation, worldview, and social institution.

Today, we as disciples of Christ have the same opportunity and responsibility to abide in, and then manifest, *shalom* as a blessing for others as well as for ourselves. This is a significant aspect of what being a "light" to the world entails (Matt. 5:14). In every-thing we do and say, in word and deed, in worship and work, in politics and play, truly in all things—not just religious things—we are blessed to be a blessing to others around us, leading them toward *shalom*. And until this occurs, our world surely groans as it waits for just such a reality to be revealed (Rom. 8:18–23). It is these leaders, representing and maintaining the wonderfully rich and robust example of integrity of character in fulfilling honor-able duties, who exemplify and testify to the truth and goodness of God in a way that promotes, establishes, and maintains *shalom* for the benefit of all. If there is to be a next stage to the so-called spiritual formation movement, this must be it.

In 2 Chronicles, God says:

> If my people who are called by my name humble themselves, pray, seek my face, and turn from their wicked ways, then will I hear from heaven, and will forgive their sin and heal their land. (7:14)

The Chronicler reveals a significant result when God's people seek righteousness—the land is healed. The entire land. From sea to shining sea, one could say. Not just believers, not just God's faithful, but everyone in the land reaps the benefits of God's faithfulness to his people.

The scope of this blessing is what separates this work from the earlier books in this series. They necessarily focused on the individual realities of life with God, depicted primarily in Jesus's Sermon on the Mount. This work focuses on the responsibilities and opportunities inherent in the communal life that will come to the fore once the Sermon on the Mount has been applied. This new life is intrinsically tied to our relationship to our neighbors, our communities, and by extension our global community. It is the public "other," the *ethnos* or nations, those in all ethnic groups and from all walks of life, who can and must taste and see the eternal quality and quantity of life that is available in the manner and means God provides. The tasting and seeing of God's goodness in tangible, discernible ways is intended to lovingly woo people into willing obedience. Jesus wishes to bless all, everyone, at all times and in every condition. Such is the nature of the Good Shepherd.

Reaping the benefits and dividends from the applied ethos of the kingdom of God requires neither profession of faith nor understanding of how or why such blessings exist. God loves the world regardless of whether he is known or appreciated. Yet Christian leaders throughout society can never move forward into the areas of responsibility for manifesting the good life Jesus provides until there is a settled resolve regarding who we as disciples are called to be and must become. This is the arena of personal character formation from which all other activities of the good life are intended to proceed, first individually, then into and through our communities.

DISCOVERING MEANING AND VISION

Our world faces an overwhelming and unswerving epidemic of existential impotence, which can only be caused by an equally sweeping malignancy. The problem—our problem—lies in the shadows of the human heart. Unless and until the human heart absorbs and employs the sovereign goodness of God, the flourishing our societies seek will remain elusive, and the very means used to attain prosperity will end up only hastening our demise. As the writer of Proverbs predicts, we will return, again and again, to our regurgitated schemes (Prov. 26:11; 2 Pet. 2:22). Someone, somewhere, somehow, must break the cycle of moral relativism that creates substitute plans for human salvation and instead attempt to apply the answers in the vision God has provided. That this is widely assumed to have already taken place is a primary indicator of the depth of the problem Christian leaders must develop the courage to face.

This work endeavors to sketch a framework from which those who are ready and willing to take up the cause of the general welfare and flourishing of the public at large can proceed. To accomplish this, we have organized this work around the areas of society to which Christian leaders must turn their attention and influence in order to manifest the kind of flourishing God desires for all people. These areas can be defined as the institutions of government, education, business or commerce, the professions, and ethics. When these areas and their leaders come under the influence and direction of God, we can and will experience the kind of healing and flourishing human beings have searched for, longed to experience, and died trying to build. When leaders, spokespersons, and professionals (often synonymous terms, yet sometimes delineated for specific purposes to be defined and discussed later) become organized within the critical institutions of our society to most positively influence contemporary life for the common good, blessing, goodness, and grace will flow over the land as the waters fill the seas (Hab. 2:14).

What we hope to present here is the all-important sense of vision and perspective that will focus all our many efforts to seek and attain a life worth living for ourselves and our loved ones. What follows in these pages is not an attempt to outline a new gospel, but to reveal the radical implications for all of society of the original good news Jesus brought to earth. We want to provide a perspective to leaders and citizens of the way the gospel Jesus proclaimed can affect and transform our societies and lead them to *shalom*. This is not a Faustian effort. It's a revolution that happens one heart, one leader, one family, one neighborhood, one organization at a time.

An ancient parable tells of a traveler journeying through a medieval village one morning on his way to visit a relative in a distant town. As he enters the village through the far gate, he quickly encounters a stone carver struggling to load a very large, recently honed boulder onto his cart. The traveler asks the laborer, "What are you doing?" Frustrated under the weight of his task, the stone carver grunts to the stranger, "I am working for my bread." As the traveler continues through the village, he comes upon another laborer shaping a large stone with chisel and hammer. He asks the second stone carver, "What are you doing?" The laborer answers, "I am an apprentice perfecting my trade of carving stone." Finally, on the far edge of the village the traveler comes to another laborer sanding and smoothing his recently fashioned stone. He asks the third stone carver, "What are you doing?" Sweat dripping from his face, the laborer replies with pride, "I'm building a cathedral." We are building more than cathedrals. We are building the very kingdom of God.

The Divine Conspiracy dealt directly with *why* we might want to repent of our past understanding of life and living. But we can't stop with *why*. We have to get into *what* Jesus is doing and will do about his project of overcoming evil with good while simultaneously transforming the kingdoms of our contemporary world, individually and collectively, into the kingdom of our God and of his Christ, who will reign forever and ever. The *what* of the kingdom life comes into greater focus and ceases being such an overwhelming burden when we discover that it is found within the easy and light yoke directed by the hand of an expert guide and friend. We can know how to live, move, and have our being in the *shalom* of the Good Shepherd. Jesus introduces us to that reality and proves that we can know where our hope and power to thrive lie—both individually and communally. He frees us to actually find what we are looking for, right now, where we are, if we want to.

It is time we focus on *what* we must do to build the foundations for life and living that Jesus articulates and then helps to manifest among us. For those ready to engage the topic of our collective life with God that will eventually consume our lives for the rest of eternity, let's take a step into forever, now.

GOD'S KINGDOM AND THE
CALL OF THE GOOD SHEPHERD

Discussion Questions for Chapters 1–3

At the end of some chapters are discussion questions designed to encourage both individual reflection and group dialog. The authors' hope is that reflecting on these questions will allow readers to better unpack and integrate the insights and ideas within each section of the book.

In these introductory chapters, Willard and Black seek to make the case that all followers of Jesus Christ have the responsibility in their sphere of influence to teach, proclaim, model, and intentionally live out the reality of God's "divine conspiracy." Since we live at the "mercy of our ideas," the following questions will help you to examine your thoughts about the kingdom of God, the kingdoms of this world, and our vocations in light of God's calling upon our lives.

1. What life experiences led you into your present vocation? As a leader who influences others, you often reflect those who have influenced you. Who were the role models who worked to form you in your current role? How did they influence your vision, mission, values, conduct, character, and communication?

2. When was the first time you heard a teaching about the "kingdom of God"? Did that teaching include the idea that God's kingdom is presently available and accessible, or was it assumed that the kingdom of God is only a future reality? Share with one another how these dissimilar teachings on the kingdom of God affect our thinking, behaviors, and vocational responsibilities. Discuss what you believe is God's overarching mission or goal for our world.

3. Willard and Black suggest that there are significant problems (i.e., inaccurate views of the end times and of the purposes of the gospel) in many of our churches and Christian institutions of higher learning that have hindered us from experiencing God's rule through his Son, Jesus, the king. Do you agree or disagree with the authors' viewpoints? What *is* the "good news" according to Jesus Christ? What other problems may be created, although unintended, in our Christian doctrines and beliefs that have hindered both individuals and organizations from more fully living in the reality of God's kingdom? Give support for your views.

4. The authors suggest that one of the best places for us to begin developing a better understanding of the kingdom of God in our contemporary contexts is found in the concept of *shalom*, or peace, defined in Psalm 23. Do you believe a Psalm 23 kind of life is preferable or even possible? If so, how is it possible?

5. Fear is the absence of *shalom*. Proverbs 29:25 states: "The fear of others lays a snare, but one who trusts in the LORD is secure." How does fear separate us from the peace of God? How does our fear separate us from others? How does fear make us compare ourselves with others or seek dominance over them? In what ways does fear distort what is true? Give examples.

6. *Exercise:* Seek to memorize Psalm 23. Read it daily for the next thirty days slowly, focusing on both the images and ideas it conveys.

CHAPTER 4

Servant Leadership

A dispute also arose among them, as to which of them was to be regarded as the greatest. And Jesus said to them, "The kings of the Gentiles exercise lordship over them, and those in authority over them are called benefactors. But not so with you. Rather, let the greatest among you become as the youngest, and the leader as one who serves. For who is the greater, one who reclines at table or one who serves? Is it not the one who reclines at table? But I am among you as the one who serves."

LUKE 22:24-27

I F THE KINGDOMS of our contemporary world are to be transformed into a kingdom that manifests the grace, truth, justice, and mercy of Christ the king, there must be leaders who are willing and able to demonstrate Christlike qualities and courage and then use them to influence the power structures of contemporary society. Today, the roles and responsibilities of our leaders cannot be underestimated. In a world overtaken by an instantaneous, global media culture, leaders do not need to be of international renown for the consequences of their words and actions to have immediate, international effects. Thus, in many ways a leader's ability to influence, guide, and direct has never been more powerful.

However, the degree of impotent, misguided, and ineffectual leadership also appears to be on the rise. Evidence of it is seen not only in our elected officials and the political quagmires and deadlock they produce, but also in leaders responsible for our educational systems, our financial and medical institutions, our legal proceedings, and our religious organizations. Therefore it is imperative that we reimagine the overarching call or vocation of a leader in order to create the most beneficial environments possible for *shalom* and well-being to flourish.

Primarily, leaders are those who are followed or emulated because they possess the ability, experience, or knowledge necessary for achieving an objective that is pursued, valued, or required by others. Thus a leader is in the position of serving others by providing the direction and guidance necessary for a particular outcome or result. Leaders influence or persuade followers to work toward certain ends. But how do leaders accomplish these tasks, what ends do they seek, and why?

History helps us track the different ways God has attempted to develop and use leaders to guide the world toward his loving ways. The vision of life in the kingdom of God that has come to us in the example of Jesus the Christ is a very beautiful, dynamic story—one in which God is moving in and through human history. At the beginning of this story is God, the maker and creator of all things. We also discover in this story God's personal agency working to make righteousness and joy cover the earth like water fills the seas; his moral features are seen and experienced in his Logos, the cosmic Christ, Jesus the Nazarene, the reconciler of humanity to God.[1] The aim of God's story is the establishment of an all-inclusive community of loving persons, of which God is more than a participant; he is the prime sustainer, the prime minister if you will, and most glorious inhabitant.[2]

Human history demonstrates that the crux of this story has remained a catalyst for worldwide revolution; indeed, that is its aim. In every civilization, religious and cultural leaders have attempted, each in unique ways, to offer a parallel story that directs people toward answering the questions of why and how life should proceed. Even a cursory reflection on world religions demonstrates this point. Each society or cultural group has leaders who recommend precise sacrifices, ceremonies, propitiations, and other practices that play a significant role in directing their constituents toward a means of satisfying an enduring hunger for meaning, existential purpose, and universal well-being. Ultimately, the leaders and practices of these countless religious and political movements have left untold billions unsatisfied, to a greater or lesser degree, with regard to their ultimate pursuit. This is not an attempt to be overly critical of socioreligious movements or their leadership. It is simply a perspective gained from reflecting on the wide-ranging effects various worldviews have had on the course of human history.

The religious path is not the only means leaders have used in the quest for meaning, purpose, and well-being. Ancient philosophers also wrestled with four very basic questions they surmised formed the basis of all human problems. If these questions were resolved, classic philosophers believed flourishing could be attained and maintained. These four questions match four basic human problems and deal, respectively, with reality, well-being, virtue, and the development of personal character.[3] In the common parlance these questions can be posed in very straightforward terms:

What is real?

What is the good life?

Who is a good person?

How does one become an authentically good person?

The four questions are often framed in different ways, but each retains a singular core. This explains why the answers to the first three questions provide a predictable lead-in to the final question. Together the answers to these questions form a fairly sturdy framework on which many worldviews are built. From the creators of the Upanishads, to the ancient Israelites, to Karl Marx, political and religious leaders and thinkers throughout history have offered varying answers to these central questions. Societies have taken them, interpreted them, reinterpreted them, and sought further answers, a process that in turn has shaped and directed the evolution of those societies.

Still today our world is alternately blessed or hindered by the theories, strategies, philosophies, religions, and worldviews that have resulted from grappling with these four elusive inquiries. Each attempt left a wake, sometimes wide, sometimes narrow, of different effects and consequences. Thankfully, a great blessing of history is the guidance and wisdom available to inform current and future responses to these questions.

Part of what this history reveals is that one of humanity's great evils lurks in the recurring temptation for leaders to demonstrate their power and control over others. When this tendency rises to a fever pitch, we tend to build, out of sheer might, human will, and wisdom (such as it is), structures that highlight and glorify human achievement. The Hebrew scriptures describe some of these building projects. There are towers, temples, cities, and even nations, some of which Yahweh was involved in and some he was not. We can acknowledge there are traces of good in the desire to build. Leaders are intended to act in concert with God and his grace in doing good. Yet there is a significant absence of both imagination and effectiveness in human leadership, just as there are limits to what can be accomplished on natural ability alone. Still, humanity's recurring problem is that it does not possess the answers to its own problems. The failure to recognize and understand this simple truth is the genesis of the all-encompassing search by social, political, and religious structures and institutions to forge paradise on earth.

When cultural leaders seek to accomplish the goal of creating a utopian society apart from God, they simultaneously choose to leave grace, love, and truth out of their campaign. Such virtues are quickly discovered to be both inefficient and inconvenient when constructing human societies. Whatever variety of human rule or governance is imposed, inherited, or chosen, it seems to devolve into some form of rebellion followed by chaos. Social structures and their relational dynamics found in projects as grand as the Ming dynasty, Egyptian engineering, Roman military might, and Athenian democracy or as ordinary as a kindergarten classroom clearly demonstrate how social engineering projects devised by human beings routinely leave God and his creative, redemptive story out of the picture. At times we have come closer than others. Yet still we end up far from the idyllic pastures and still waters we long for. Certainly some leaders, societies, and eras of social development have reflected the shepherding goodness of God more than others, and when we learn of them, we instinctively feel hope rise in our hearts. This is evidence of the yearning God desires and intends to fulfill for our lives both now and forevermore. However, our past demonstrates the degree to which the whole world, now as desperately as ever, needs a shepherd, a Good Shepherd, to lead us into peace and security. Godly servant leadership sets out to manifest the *shalom* we seek.

ISRAELITE LEADERS STRUGGLING WITH GOD

The biblical depiction of the state and people of Israel is a dramatic illustration of the shepherding leadership God sought to provide to the world. To demonstrate his glory, God saw fit to elect a once impoverished and enslaved flock to manifest what a people could become when their hearts were transformed toward the Shepherd's ways. In God's plan, the sons and daughters of Abraham (the Jewish *ethnos*, or "nation") were commissioned to be his people, to be the community to which God would reveal himself and through which he would lead every people group on earth toward existential meaning, freedom from fear, and flourishing (Matt. 28:19).[4]

Sadly, the stiff-necked Israelites struggled, contended, resisted, and fought with God in God's attempt to accomplish this objective.[5] Their first and ultimate failure stemmed from their refusal to be consistently led by God alone. Instead, they wanted mediators, followed by human kings, and then rituals (Exod. 20:18–26; 1 Sam. 8:5–22). The prophetic response to these adaptations can be seen in Isaiah 1:11–17 and Jeremiah 6:20. God's desire is not for sacrifices, priests, or kings. Instead, God's pleasure was to be found in dwelling with humanity and abiding together as he led them into the experiential knowledge of his covenantal love. The inability to consistently be faithful to the covenantal relationship eventually led to Israel's destruction.

Yet the great success of Israel, despite its difficulties, was the creation of a social basis that would provide the springboard for the gospel of Jesus in the first century. This is what biblical authors describe as "the fullness of time" (Gal. 4:4), the moment in history when an adequate reception of God's revelation was possible and an advancement of the kingdom of God could proceed.[6] It is when the Messiah is announced and presented to the world that the stark differences between the kingdom of God and human kingdoms begin to rise from the ashes of the shattered nation of Israel.[7] During the last stages of Second Temple Judaism, God mercifully reintroduced the earth to the sweeping principle, the ideal, of an *agape* form of peace on earth. Such a proposition shook the foundations of human philosophy, psychology, religion, government, and law in ways and to degrees that have never been matched or reversed. First revealed to the ritually unclean shepherds, who were social outcasts living under the open stars, God's heavenly messengers proclaimed the arrival of a new reality that had fallen upon the entire cosmos (Luke 2:10–14).

From the beginning of his life, Jesus faced significant obstacles to God's pursuit of peace and goodwill. Today, many of these barriers remain and over the ages have only grown in breadth and depth. Primarily these hurdles center on the universal presence and experience of pride and fear, both of which are complicated and accentuated by individuals' relation to their particular group, culture, and context. It is important to realize that, even for the first hearers of the gospel, the pronouncement created great fear. The shining of the "glory of the Lord" terrorized the "Christmas" shepherds tending their flocks by night, just as it threatened King Herod's domination. This terror was, and is, well founded. Simeon the prophet predicted that the child Jesus was "destined for the falling and rising of many in Israel, and to be a sign that will be opposed so that the inner thoughts of many will be revealed" (Luke 2:34–35). Hearts being exposed, true motives revealed, kingdoms falling, rising, and resisting change—these predictions are indicators of world revolution. Fear and terror are often the preamble to changes in leadership, even benevolent change.

Just as Simeon predicted, the new wine of Jesus's new leadership paradigm caused the old wineskin of Judaism to burst, and fear has been a part of the journey of the gospel through human agencies ever since (Luke 5:37). Conversely, the kingdom of God, led by his Christ, does not abide in the pride and fear that have so often characterized and fueled the structures and institutions of human societies. There is endless irony in God's plan to lead the world back toward flourishing in his kingdom through the birth and death of a perfect human being, who was executed by God's own chosen people, in concert with the power of the greatest civilization then known, using the highest form of moral law to condemn him to the worst form of human execution, all of which occurred in Jerusalem, the "city of peace." Such hypocrisy exposes how fear wreaks havoc and eventually destroys even the best of human intentions and abilities. Fear must be done away with, especially in those endeavoring to lead as good shepherds.

The resurrection of Jesus marks the end of self-righteous, law-fixated religiosity advocated by much of the first-century Jewish leadership.[8] In its place, the church became the new spiritual community, birthed from within Judaism as a continuing fulfillment of God's promise to Abraham. Acts of the Apostles records the activities of two main leaders of this new movement, Peter and Paul. Both were Jews who were instrumental in the unfolding of God's new universal community tasked with the identical overarching objective previously reserved exclusively for Israel. No longer would the kingdom of God be accessed exclusively through the Jewish faith. This wondrous new way of being and living was now available to all people. Whosoever will may come.

Unfortunately this lesson of open access to a new creation is still to be learned (Gal. 6:14–15). We now know that the early Christian community did not fully escape its cultural and intellectual captivity to Judaism. But in time the captor changed from Judaism to Roman and then Christian sociopolitical systems. The Jews eventually became as despised as their gentile neighbors, and the early leadership of the church struggled with cross-cultural and cross-religious integration.

WHERE IS AMERICAN
CHRISTENDOM LEADING US?

Although much progress and some regress have been made over the past two millennia, this summary roughly brings us to the central question for leaders in our day: What role are Christianity and its leaders to play in our contemporary society?

The Divine Conspiracy discussed the hurdles American or Western forms of Christianity struggle to overcome. Together these adaptations fall under the umbrella of a single, daunting obstacle—the calcification of the message of Jesus into a form of nominal or civil religion. This has been a recurring phenomenon in the Western world from our earliest beginnings. In the contemporary context of the United States the resistance to the growing tide of nominalism sparked attempts by Christian leaders Jonathan Edwards, George Whitefield, and John Wesley, among others, to bring back to life (revive) the religion they saw dying around them. This resulted in what we now call the Great Awakenings. In the centuries before and since, Western civilization has labored to unshackle itself from a lukewarm brand of Christian religion that values profession of belief or outward acts of piety over transformed hearts, lives, and communities.

It is here, in the gaps and shadows of these key issues, where the gospel of Jesus must be understood, interjected into the discussion, and eventually manifested in the lives of our servant leaders, professionals, spokespersons, and pastors today. This is precisely why this work follows on the heels of *The Divine Conspiracy*, which addresses the problems of how and why our Christian culture may have allowed the inertia of previous generations to marginalize or obfuscate the central message and objective of Jesus. This is the key proposal that lay behind the ideas of the gospels of the left (concern primarily for the elimination of social and structural evils) and the right (concern primarily for the forgiveness of the individual's sins).[9]

Since the publishing of *The Divine Conspiracy*, another gospel has arisen that is similar in effect, but different in cause. This third gospel can be termed the *gospel of the church or "churchmanship."*[10] Here the local church—or more specifically those with church membership, affiliation, or commitment to religious structures and priorities—is understood as the means through which the good life, or salvation, is attained. Although there are many wonderful and beneficial aspects to local church membership and commitment in their own right, Jesus's gospel and the testimony of the entire New Testament oppose blind devotion to any religious tradition as a substitute for unbridled confidence in God as the way of achieving the truth for life and living (John 14:6).

The church is a marvelous and beautiful living reality that Jesus can be trusted to build and bring to perfection. Yet the gospel is not the same as the church, nor is the church identical to the kingdom of God. As has been previously stated, the local church is for discipleship, and disciples are for the world.[11] Thus, here we want to focus on precisely why leaders, spokespersons, and professionals who are disciples of Jesus Christ can and must enter the world, fully empowered by the Holy Spirit, to take on the responsibilities and duties of representing and pursuing the public good by holding fiduciary relationships with all they encounter. Such representatives will intentionally act as worthy ambassadors in a kingdom characterized by a just, benevolent, empowering, and endlessly loving king, with whom their allegiance ultimately lies. Therefore, such persons will be able to consistently testify and demonstrate, to all concerned, precisely how and why the best way, the clearest truth, and the fullest life are achieved by applying a Christlike model to both private and public issues.

The critical point to grasp in this discussion of servant leadership, as seen in the historical role of Israel and the ambassadorial role of Christlike disciples manifesting God's kingdom ethos, is the duty of *modeling* that our leaders are to accept and perpetuate in and through all of our societal structures. Leaders serve us best when they model the knowledge and beneficial effects that proceed from the life they first experience and then uniformly profess as worthy and honorable through word and deed to others. Israel and later the first disciples of Christ were intended to act as examples, lights, and beacons of the good news and the way of life with God. When this is done well, when individuals work together in dedicated, loving, and sacrificial service to God and his kingdom, their efforts will shine in such a way that all will see their benefits; it will be impossible to hide the effects. When leaders exemplify the reality of God's ways, everyone in society is well served. This is the sacred calling of servant leadership in the scriptures.

THE DIVISION OF LABOR AND THE
DEVELOPMENT OF LEADERSHIP

The history of God's use, direction, and purpose for leaders throughout the scriptures has brought us to a point where we can now consider, more precisely, the leadership function and why leaders are so integral and have such potential for either good or ill. Neither the Judeo-Christian perspective nor the theistic viewpoint, in either contemporary or historical terms, is alone in the pursuit of leading others to the good, peaceful, and just life. One example is found in Plato's *Republic*. There he records a genuine search for a reasonable cause for pursuing justice rather than injustice. What may now seem strange to the postmodern ear is Plato's presumption that injustice is the soul's greatest evil and justice the soul's greatest good.[12]

For Plato the greater good is defined as justice. This is not a theoretical statement. He holds that justice should be shown and understood simply by the consequences of its presence. In order to illuminate the reality of the goodness inherent in justice, Plato creates an illustration of the kind of social justice required of the city in order to better see the smaller reality of justice playing out in the lives of individuals.

At the beginning of this argument, Plato highlights Socrates's crucial statement regarding the division of labor that is necessary for life in a city. A city begins because individual life is not self-sufficient. The rural farmer or herdsman must become a jack-of-all-trades and fulfill every need individually, which is time-consuming and requires multiple skills. Conversely, in urban life a natural division of labor and services developed that provided a means by which individuals could act together to share and trade their talents for the common welfare. Socrates suggests that a flourishing life is not possible if one is forced to focus entirely on individual needs. Instead, specialization of effort allows for greater effectiveness and efficiency, since, as individuals are "freed from other work to do the one thing [they are] naturally fit for at the right time, more work gets done easier and better."[13]

Once cities are formed, city-states follow. We can say that the "public" is composed of the communal group of individuals who are affected by the consequences of certain actions and events to the degree that it becomes necessary and good for the potential results of those actions and events to be tended, watched over, and cared for. Since it is often the case that those who are directly impacted by these actions and events are not those in close proximity to their origin, it becomes necessary for certain individuals to be designated or elected as representatives. These persons are specifically tasked to ensure, to the best of their ability, that the "public's" interests are preserved and protected. Here the position of a "leading official" is a natural outcome of the division of labor, and one is specifically tasked to oversee the functions that concern the general prosperity and well-being of those they represent.

Philosophers who probed the nature of the four basic human problems mentioned earlier, who contemplated their various twists and turns, also knew that the impact of these questions is not limited to individual lives. Nearly every potential answer also carries significant implications for societies as well. Our social arrangements—how individuals relate to one another in their spheres of life—need to be taken into account when discerning human well-being and acquiring the knowledge to act appropriately. This is especially true in what is termed an "open" society, which includes our modern versions of a liberal democracy. In "open" societies, people are allowed to choose and cherish choice in these matters. In "closed" societies the ability to discern the common good and to gain access to knowledge itself are often severely limited. Therefore, in an "open" system the important questions become: *Who* chooses and *how* are choices made?

The origin of public leadership, in all its various forms, is simply a historical development resulting from the recognition of the need to divide our labors in the pursuit of good and beneficial ways of attaining flourishing communities. Officials in government, law, medicine, business, education, clergy, and so on are leaders, spokespersons, and guides whose job is to preserve and protect the public's best interest in their specific arena of community life. These leaders serve within a wide range of occupational fields that necessitate expertise, specific knowledge, and skill, also known as recondite knowledge.[14]

Our contemporary societies, cultures, and economies are as complicated and broad-scoped as our individual lives, because, in fact, we live in and either thrive or suffer through living social systems. As a result, a particularly vital issue that arises for modern democratic societies becomes who has knowledge, who has the expertise, who has the character, who can teach succeeding generations, who can protect, who can guide, and who can lead our public organizations in ways that position our society to achieve success? Where do we find these kinds of people?

WHO WILL LEAD US?

Some of the following questions are related: Do Christian leaders, professionals, and spokespersons have a responsibility (or even a right) to address social, economic, and political issues that concern the larger societal whole? Or is that none of their "business"? Are our institutions of higher learning, including Christian education in general, specifically undertaking to prepare those who administer in various ways—not just in those serving in pulpits, but those in classrooms, cubicles, boardrooms, courtrooms, at the front counter or the bedside, or on the congressional floor—that benefit the public welfare? Are our universities consistently or inconsistently producing men and women who are capable of speaking, writing, and leading with incisive depth, character, and wisdom in our society at large? Whom do we follow? Whom do we trust to lead and guide us, and why?

But these questions involve yet deeper and more difficult issues. In general, do spokespersons or leaders for Christ possess and bring unique and indispensable *knowledge* to the human world at large? Or are they merely advocates of certain traditional *opinions or beliefs*—dare we say dogmas and doctrines—in an attempt to motivate people to adopt a certain religious perspective? In particular, do Christian leaders bring *moral* knowledge and truth to bear on human life, and are such moral positions and attitudes (whether they amount to knowledge or not) even relevant to social, political, and economic understanding and the adoption of social practices?

Fortunately, the gospel, or the "good message" of Jesus the Nazarene, was specifically tailored to discuss and illuminate these very subjects. He not only focused on pursuing good; he also engaged the essential philosophical questions of his day, which centered on these quandaries.

In summary, we will argue here that the ethics and ethos found in the living reality of the kingdom of God are precisely what most, but not all, human beings want in the depths of their souls. Of course many may not be fully aware of their true desires. Individuals can in fact know something without being aware of their knowledge. They can know they desire to be loved and full of joy and not know that these very realities are indistinguishable from the character of God. They can want love and simultaneously not realize that God is love. Thus, the solution to Bono's lament is to discover what we are looking for in the everlasting and beautiful reality of God and his kingdom. God's original plan for Israel was to provide an example of what humanity was looking for. This is what Jesus's teachings pointed to and manifested as well. This is what the entirety of the scriptures encourages and bears witness to. This is what the church in its more focused and intentional eras has pursued and produced, and thus it remains the primary challenge we engage here. Christlike leaders must continually recast the vision of what God's kingdom is and can do in our lives and societies today, now, right where we are. We can leave the issue of perfection for later.

Many Christians today claim they have found, and are finding, what they are looking for. It should then be a natural consequence that those in close proximity to these individuals would be receiving the benefits and blessings of love, truth, and beauty that flow from the abundant life these Christians experience and share. Such a life is what Jesus described as an artesian well that spills over and nourishes anyone close enough to feel its spray (John 7:38). Such blessed people would gather, share, grow, invest, build, create, support, and enrich one another's lives in every aspect. As a result there would be flourishing, common goodness, and peace for all concerned.

Through time and eternity this has always been the mission of God for humanity. This remains the overarching goal of any people called by his name. What we must promote are discussions of what such a reality must look like for leaders and shepherds pursuing it in every aspect of contemporary life. We must consider in fairly concrete terms what the kingdom of God looks like in our families, communities, neighborhoods, corporations, and institutions, which together form the kingdoms of our world. Discussions on these matters are now taking place with greater regularity and to good effect. The Missional Church movement and its various branches are but one shining example of a renewed interest in focusing on concrete manifestations of God's kingdom among us. Yet part of the discussion must also include a rigorous analysis of the moral character of our leaders.

An interesting article in *Christianity Today* asked if there was an inordinate amount of arrogance and impatience evidenced in the lives of pastors planting new churches.[15] This is exactly the type of difficult and probing question we must ask not only of pastors seeking to build new congregations, but of all our leaders in every area of society. Any leader—banker, politician, engineer, pastor, teacher, tradesperson, or merchant (butcher, baker, or candlestick maker)—stands in the often precarious position of balancing power and privilege. There is no denying or escaping this reality. Therefore we require leaders who understand what is good and right, but who also have the means, both the courage of character and the actual facilities of positional authority, to achieve the common flourishing we all so desperately seek. It is to the subject of moral leadership that we next turn our attention.

SERVANT LEADERSHIP

Discussion Questions for Chapter 4

Robert Greenleaf was the first to coin the term "servant leadership" for our contemporary culture. Both parts of the term are significant for our theology and practice. *Servant* carries equal weight with *leadership* and fits the seminal description presented by Greenleaf: "The servant leader is one who is a servant first. . . . It begins with the natural feeling that one wants to serve, to serve first. Then conscious choice brings one to aspire to lead."[16] Such a perspective is in line with the statement from Jesus: "But it is not so among you; but whoever wishes to become great among you must be your servant, and whoever wishes to be first among you must be slave of all. For the Son of Man came not to be served but to serve, and to give his life a ransom for many" (Mark 10:43–45).

1. What are some of the challenges you face in leading others while at the same time seeking ways to best serve them? The authors ask several questions on pages 51 and 52. Which of these questions are most intriguing to you and why?

2. In what ways have you experienced the abuse of positional power in your vocation and/or organization? What were the specific behaviors and how did they affect you and those around you?

3. Servant leadership always begins with self-leadership, learning to govern and regulate one's thoughts, words, and deeds. The authors believe it crucial for leaders to assume the role of and responsibility for modeling life in the kingdom of God. What are the primary areas of your life that need attention with regard to self-regulation?

4. Willard and Black believe that all followers of Jesus have both the opportunity and the responsibility to appropriately address the social, economic, and political issues in our society. Do you agree or disagree? Which particular issues in society do you believe need more attention or have been a personal burden for you? What active steps have you taken to address these concerns?

5. The authors suggest that Jesus Christ has influenced the thinking, behavior, and development of people around the world more than any other human being. Do you agree with that viewpoint? Why do you think most leaders overlook Jesus as a role model for change?

6. *Exercise:* Leading others to a good, peaceful, and just life is a mark of a servant leader. Think about those around you who are less powerful, advantaged, or capable than you. What two or three tangible acts of service could you engage in to better their lives emotionally, physically, or spiritually?

CHAPTER 5

Moral Leadership

The first responsibility of a leader is to define reality. The last is to say thank you. In between, the leader is a servant.

MAX DEPREE

Nearly all men can stand adversity, but if you want to test a man's character, give him power.

ABRAHAM LINCOLN

IN ORDER TO transform our social systems, society's leaders must take the initiative and assume responsibility for ensuring their own personal honesty as well as the integrity of their particular field of expertise. In an age when more and more of our social and political lives require a level of knowledge and skill that few of us possess and even fewer can attain, trusting leaders and experts has become an increasingly perilous necessity.

Because our vulnerability grows as our dependency on others to make good decisions increases, it is important to make sure that our leaders are more committed to pursuing common flourishing than personal power and privilege. Therefore a vigorous investigation of the qualities and characteristics of moral leadership must accompany our debates about the status and qualifications of our leaders.

Here we discuss some of the key attributes of moral leadership, the unique and necessarily exalted position of a leader in contemporary society, and the conjoining of responsibility with accountability. We will then consider some of the unique opportunities of Christlike leaders in a democratic form of government, the prominent role of heroes, and the importance heroism plays in reshaping our imagination for exemplary moral character.

THE FAITHFUL LEADER

There is much value in the idea of equality, especially when considering the value and worth intrinsic to every human being. Yet few of us are actually equal when it comes to our responsibilities, and this fact is exposed most prominently in relation to the leaders, spokespersons, and professionals overseeing those institutions and organizations dedicated to business, law, medicine, government, religion, education, and so on. The allure of celebrity that surrounds many of our leaders, both Christian and secular, increases this perceived inequality and has often led to great harm for individuals and institutions alike. The decline in competency and reputation of leading professionals as a whole has even threatened the egalitarian ideals that form our American democratic way of life. Therefore, a renewed philosophy of society, one robust enough for our contemporary life, requires an equally renewed understanding of how the leadership substructures in our society operate, so that leaders can best protect the common interest their positions were created to serve.

And when we talk about leadership here, we are going beyond the limits of just a few fields. Included are any and all persons and groups engaged in a "fiduciary," or faith-filled, relationship. In fact, it does not take long to discover the innumerable arenas of contemporary life today where a fiduciary relationship occurs and is expected, yet is rarely overtly recognized. A fiduciary relationship only requires the consent of one. A fiduciary arrangement can begin when one individual makes the concerted decision and commitment to do what is in the best interests of the other, regardless of the consequences and circumstances.

To better define moral leadership and fiduciary responsibility, we must also admit that not every occupation is a profession, not every role is a leadership role, and not every job is a vocation. To say that every job is a vocation or that every person is a leader is to misunderstand the special and irreplaceable function of leaders and professionals in our society. What may be most difficult for many in thinking about differentiating professions from nonprofessions is the assumption that a professional is in general "better" than the nonprofessional, or a leader is "better" than a follower. This is absolutely not the case.

In this regard, a corporate attorney and a volunteer after-school soccer coach are both engaged in fiduciary (faith-filled) duties. One agreement is made officially between corporate officers and the court. The other is made every afternoon when a parent drops off a child for practice. Are both professionals? No. Are both leaders? Yes. Are the actions of both valuable? Certainly. Do both require a level of moral character to match the range of their responsibilities? Absolutely.

If you doubt this, consider the international outrage that resulted during the trial and conviction of Penn State football coach Jerry Sandusky. The field of coaching is not historically defined as a traditional profession (although many today would consider it one). Yet coaches carry immeasurable leadership responsibilities as role models and teachers who guide our children and young people in their development, which of course has a significant and lasting impact on the public welfare. Thus what is understood as public flourishing is composed of innumerable interconnected fields, and it is therefore crucial to engage and discuss the necessity of, qualities for, and responsibilities that make up the societal leadership that Christian men and women must bring to bear upon our world.

However, if we fail to acknowledge the uniqueness of the roles of leaders and professionals compared to those of nonprofessionals, then our communities will never be able to deal, in a more direct way, with the ethical and moral requirements that must be upheld by our professionals and leaders. Yes, there are privileges to leadership, and those with privileges must be held accountable. A great problem has arisen from instances in which some leaders have become divorced from ethical and moral behavior, and other leaders lack answerability for their mishandling of public "goods." In part this is due to the continued blurring of the lines between the qualities that constitute leaders and their accompanying duties and ethical responsibilities.

PERSONAL CHARACTER

Any conversation about moral leadership must also include the topic of personal character. On this subject there is an interesting line of questioning to consider: Do we believe it is more likely that a good person will perform leadership functions better than a bad person? Do we experience people who are good at their vocational duties as equally good people? Is there *any* connection between moral character and the performance of one's job, vocation, or calling? Do good people make better parents, spouses, citizens, or neighbors?

The answer that is assumed in the majority of our codes and standards of ethics specifically for professionals is a resounding, "*Yes!*" Yes, personal character does matter in the performance of the duties and responsibilities of leadership. Yes, a good person will also be a good doctor, coach, or lawyer. Yes, a good person will also be a good parent, spouse, citizen, or neighbor.

As may be already quite evident, the leadership tasks of servant leaders, because of the power inherent in directing the actions of others, contain a specifically ethical dimension that is fundamental to their nature and function. Leaders can serve the public good well, *only if* those individuals routinely act in ways that supremely promote the specific public good for which their particular leadership position exists. Further, leaders make a positive impact, *only if* they are prepared to sacrifice their own personal gain, monetary or otherwise, for that good. Last, leaders serve the common good *only if* they are appropriately vigilant in ensuring that members of their own peer group overwhelmingly conform to this moral ideal even when self-sacrifice is required. If these conditions exist, excellence as a leader or professional is never a matter of mere technical expertise or facility, nor is the attainment of a certain preferred status primarily a matter of personal success. One can be very proficient, highly regarded, and well rewarded, yet remain a failure as a leader. Thus, leadership positions in our society must provide the means for both moral fulfillment and productive flourishing. Not just one, but both of these objectives must be uniformly valued and pursued. We must develop leaders who are just as moral as they are effective. One cannot supersede the other.

Today, setting standards and guidelines for moral and ethical conduct that is accompanied by moral self-realization is something we must reconsider. When leaders or people with great responsibility in our societies fail, either morally or ethically, how should we respond? Unfortunately, there are ample examples of moral failures in our leaders, more cases than we would perhaps like to admit. The round-the-clock news cycle keeps us ever informed of the moral lapses of our public figures. Yet how do we as a society deal with these issues? There is now an industry of specialists in "crisis management" who swoop into these circumstances to do "damage control" or manage the "fallout." Routinely, pundits suggest taking a standard tack in these situations. In short, clients are counseled to confess, ask for forgiveness in some nationally televised or published interview, then move on.

Authentic confession is the acknowledgment of and agreement with the truth of a situation. It is aligning oneself with the real state of affairs. To confess in a responsible manner is often the correct response to all misjudgments and offenses. *How* this is done requires genuine reflection and wisdom. *Why* this is done, especially when it involves public figures, is a more complicated matter. Often it seems a public confession is merely an attempt to take the "air" out of the media uproar and allow the guilty party to "look forward" to the resumption of his or her position and authority. The question that rarely seems to be asked in these situations is: How, and under what conditions, can such a person be trusted again? This question proceeds from an idea that the authority that empowers leaders to act in our society rests on the previous demonstration of moral judgment and good behavior. How else are leaders to direct activities toward the common good if they do not demonstrate moral knowledge and behavior themselves? Celebrity alone will not suffice.

A brief example of this conundrum might help illustrate the importance of this point. Some may not remember, or care to recall, the significant debate surrounding the question of whether President Clinton's ability to lead the nation was irreparably injured after it was discovered he had engaged in and then lied about an inappropriate sexual relationship. All the many and varied opinions and positions regarding the scandal, the investigation, and the aftermath are not the concern here. What is important is the shift that seems to have occurred in the public consciousness: a partition was erected between a person's leadership ability in "public" office and his or her "personal" character as a human being.

It was proposed that Clinton was able to "compartmentalize" his life, separating the troubles of his private life from the responsibilities of his public office. In some measure, it appears the majority of the American citizenry and its elected officials in the Senate agreed with this proposal. As a result, in the majority of Americans' social consciousness, personal character has now been either marginalized or largely separated from leadership responsibilities. As long as you can "get the job done" in public, it matters little what kind of person you are in private.

This is a relatively new and troubling development. The idea is troubling primarily because it stems from an assumption that is blatantly false. A fact we learned from the Clinton case—and the Nixon case before that, and from countless similar but perhaps less dramatic instances—was that who our leaders "are" existentially, morally, psychologically, and religiously in private directly affects the way they handle their public responsibilities. To argue otherwise is to choose to ignore the facts. Clinton's and Nixon's personal character and private behavior did affect their ability to govern in public. It is simply a fantasy to believe that one can fully separate and distinguish the moral demands of their leadership responsibilities from the integrity of their personal character. Human beings simply are not made to function as disintegrated persons. Moral leadership and personal integrity are conjoined, and for good reason. To disconnect them is to court disaster, both personally and publicly.

BUSINESS ETHICS?

Another way to get at this issue of moral obligation within our societal leadership roles is to consider a book by John Maxwell entitled *There Is No Such Thing as "Business" Ethics.*[1] What does Maxwell mean by this title? He unpacks the concept in several ways. First, Maxwell states that the only principle that really matters for ethical conduct in business is one that is not peculiar to business (or any other profession or occupation)—the "Golden Rule," commonly understood as doing unto others as you would have them do unto you.[2] Second, Maxwell believes that anything short of this ethical standard, and especially anything peculiar or specific to a given profession, will not and cannot provide the moral character necessary to bring people to in fact "do the right thing" within their vocational practices. The point Maxwell drives home again and again is that one has to become the kind of individual who can treat others in a loving, altruistic manner in order for the Golden Rule to appear in the first place. It cannot be legislated in policy. It has to be incarnated in people.

Since this kind of ethical character is not routinely required or developed in our leaders and professionals, industries have instead created what we call "professional ethics." These are policies that have been developed in our contemporary context to deal with specific circumstances and situations, but rarely if ever do they deal with actually "being" an ethical person. Instead, "professional ethics," or "business ethics," only educates people about ways to stay out of trouble with the law, fellow professionals, and customers or clients. Ethics have come to be defined only as legal behaviors or practices, not qualities of character in moral agents who are tasked to pursue and achieve general flourishing and common welfare.

This was demonstrated during the "tech bubble," in which several Wall Street securities firms were fined huge sums by the SEC for misleading clients with investment advice. Yet five years earlier, the SEC commissioned a study on compensation and demanded across the board "ethics training" for investment brokers.[3] One wonders if regulators truly believed such "ethics training" would prevent breaches of fiduciary responsibilities and unethical treatment of clients. Is it knowledge alone that will stem the tide of unethical abuse?

In fact, neither the SEC nor any other governing agency has the power to achieve what ethics training must actually produce in practice. What all our ethics training courses, both secular and religious, fail to do is forge moral agents. The result of any course of study in ethics must be both the *knowledge* required to make ethical decisions and the *character* to take appropriate action. Simply staying out of trouble is not an adequate guide to becoming a moral person who naturally does the right thing. People with only ethical compliance in mind almost always look for ways of eluding "the rules," the consequences of which are witnessed in glaring cases of unethical dealings.[4] Furthermore, a discussion of ethics in business at this level restricts "ethics" to only what one does. It does not deal with the issue of what business "life" is about or what kind of person a merchant, salesperson, or manager actually is.

ACCOUNTABILITY

Personal character formation and ethical standards of behavior in our leaders will only change when and if such traits and actions are actually accounted for. Movies and television series are routinely full of dramatic examples of elected officials, professionals, and leaders who use their unique and privileged positions to twist and contort facts to their own self-interested ends while escaping any negative consequences or accountability.[5] In fact, one wonders if power and authority today are understood as synonymous with the ability to escape the bounds of accountability.

In perhaps a case of life imitating art, the Congress and President Obama reversed their position on insider trading laws (STOCK Act) enforced against certain appointed and elected officials.[6] As a result it is now legal for politicians to make investment decisions in light of information they attained as a direct result of their government duties, something that is illegal and unethical for any other citizen.

Similarly, it is also important to note that to date very few have been charged with crimes in the economic crisis brought on by the mortgage meltdown of 2008, which threatened to bankrupt the national economy. This is perhaps due to the fact that many practices that led to the crisis were deemed "legal" while remaining highly unethical. The catastrophe directly exposed both the power and responsibility of contemporary business professionals and elected officials to ethically manage our economic structures. The resulting economic woes also demonstrated how the extraordinary expansion of opportunity and prosperity—which has in the past made the United States the economic wonder of the modern world—can simultaneously foster a deadly sense of aristocratic entitlement and elitism within the professions overseeing massive economic engines. That many of the professionals involved remained largely unscathed and unrepentant for the tragedy they created is proof of the very power leaders wield and the essential position they hold. The "bailout" (an interesting term with judicial connotations) was never seriously debated. It was assumed. Why? The professional experts who created the problem were then put in charge of solving the problem. Who else could?

In economic theory, "moral hazard" is the term for a situation in which a party has insulated itself from the financial consequences of its decisions, resulting in a lack of financial accountability. In the aftermath of the mortgage crisis, moral hazards were discovered all over the financial sector of our economy. Yet how and why were they allowed? Where were the accountability and oversight when they were needed most? Such mismanagement of our economic institutions is yet another example of the failure of ethical leadership to check and prevent the exploitation of professional privilege.

There are other issues that must be brought into a discussion of appropriate accountability and moral responsibility with regard to our applied economic policies and philosophies. Neither consumerism nor "the market" is a universal ethical philosophy that is able to elicit the moral behavior some seem to expect. Capitalism is an economic philosophy that has many constructive and beneficial merits. Furthermore, capitalism and free-market economies are perhaps the best tools yet discovered to create the means necessary for the levels of socioeconomic flourishing we both need and desire. But left alone, capitalism, like any economic, social, political, or religious system, is incomplete and can become twisted toward evil if not maintained within a robust moral framework through which we can hold ourselves and our societies accountable for holistic ethical living. As one basic example, capitalism has nothing to say, for instance, about forgiveness. This is not unique to capitalism. No economic policy or philosophy can sustain unilateral application to every area of human life. Unfortunately, this seemingly simple fact is too often missed in our business and economic schools today. What has now replaced ethics and virtue in many of our schools of business and economics is the somewhat idealistic belief in the benefits of competitive markets. It is now argued that competition alone can reliably be trusted to weed out the "bad apples" in the common basket of consumer "goods." This is a huge assumption that has not been consistently proven. Other negatives concern the greed and self-centered desire for personal advancement that tend to be inherent in the competitive drive for individual glory and power.

Where is the blessing of God to be found in the level of human competition that breeds so much avarice, ruthlessness, and contempt that the entire global economy teeters as a result? We need well-trained, well-versed, moral, and ethical Christian economists to guide and direct the cooperative nature of healthy, progressive, innovative, and virtuous marketplaces. When enveloped in a larger ethos of mutually benefiting relationships, competition can manifest a form of cooperation that leads toward increasing levels of excellence. Again, competition, capitalism, and free-market economies must all be subordinate to an overarching ethic of general welfare, common flourishing, and moral courage that stands above our theories and policies. Our leaders must shepherd us toward the Psalm 23 perspective of life. Attaining a life without want and deprivation requires us to rethink our contemporary assumptions and their far-reaching connections to what have become somewhat sacrosanct political and economic dogmas that tend to blind us to their full effects.

PUBLIC ACCOUNTING

When situations such as the economic crisis of 2008 arise, we have come to count on a steady stream of defensive "spin" maneuvers by a host of "experts" attempting to justify various actions as "necessary." What the public tends to perceive almost instinctively in such cases is that the rationalizations presented have no commonsense applications in any other "normal" area of human life. In fact, we see these "experts" as offering an endlessly complicated, nuanced, and esoteric explanation for their actions and motives in hopes of escaping accountability. Such examples are often highlighted on evening news programs. We are very familiar now with the image of an "expert" sitting behind a long conference table in front of a microphone, giving wide-eyed testimony before a congressional panel or oversight committee. We listen closely to the sound bites, trying to make sense of the words with only fleeting success. Too often, we simply turn off the TV, shrugging our shoulders and shaking our head, firm in the knowledge that in every other "nonprofessional" aspect of our lives such "nonsense" is understood as harmful, if not clearly immoral, and punishable by law.

What is seldom if ever asked in these situations is why the mentors of the person called to account—economics professor, college football coach, high-school principal, parent, uncle, business partner, and pastor—aren't called to testify about their responsibility for this person's actions as well? We seldom admit to the series of leadership failures that led an individual, and perhaps through that individual a country, down the path of destruction and despair. Can we imagine a "This Is Your Life" kind of Senate hearing in which all those who had a role to play in someone's collective failures were brought to testify regarding their roles, relationships, and duties? Of course who would be left unaccountable? Instead, we tend to place blame on a lone individual as a means to avoid, or at least limit, the net of accountability and liability. Nevertheless, we collectively either thrive or fail as a society only if our societal leaders, all of them, are accountable for their spheres of influence and moral character. The weak links will fail us every time. Ignoring this reality will not make it go away.

For Christian leaders, spokespersons, and professionals, the nature of accountability is focused exclusively on correction and redirection of the kind provided by a good shepherd. The rod and staff give comfort as they guide the wanderer back into the green fields and refreshing waters that provide life and sustenance. Likewise, accountability is not primarily a matter of inflicting punishment or shame. Rather, it is the natural response of a loving God and a responsible leader to protect and defend those entrusted to their care in appropriate ways. If accountability, both legal and moral, is not asserted in the situations we have described above, leadership and professionalism will become synonymous with the abuse of, and the license to neglect, the need to protect the public interest and general welfare. Such distortions of the leadership function and its effects on common flourishing are a many-sided phenomenon that produces grave consequences for the quality of life in any society. The consequences far outweigh specifically moral questions and are a major issue that requires understanding in order to discern precisely what a modern society is and how it functions either well or poorly.

In summary, the number of societal leaders today who possess enough of the "Golden Rule" character to wield the power that is unequivocally linked to their skills and knowledge are significantly fewer than those who possess only an understanding of "professional ethics." Policies and laws with obvious double standards only sap credibility, authority, and confidence from our leaders in crucial areas of public and private life. This can and must change. In light of the definitions we have offered thus far, we must inquire whether we are willing to accept the limits of professional ethics and their lack of ability to properly protect the public from the inappropriate actions of unscrupulous leaders. Perhaps this is why "being for hire" must be eliminated from leadership positions altogether, a subject we will deal with in more detail in a later chapter.

ANOTHER WAY, ANOTHER LIFE

Despite the difficulties we have discussed, it remains very possible, and even laudable, to approach the subject of ethics from a view of leadership roles and responsibilities as opportunities solely devoted to pursuing and achieving goodwill and flourishing for an entire community. The overarching idea Maxwell argues for is that becoming a "Golden Rule" kind of person allows one to actually will and achieve what is ethical and good for all concerned. It is this stance, he proposes, that creates the best chance for success in any profession or vocation, especially business. Although there might be some special concerns about how to appropriately put the Golden Rule into effect in a particular situation, the conditions and context should never require that the demands of the Golden Rule be set aside. A "Golden Rule" form of servant leadership requires devotion to the practice of one's chosen field as a way of being a good person and pursuing good ends for oneself and others. This is precisely what Jesus had in mind for leaders in every area of life. Yet such an idea actually requires no official religious identification at all.

In total, the well-being, common good, and flourishing of every free society rest in the hands, minds, and hearts of moral leaders. It is by and large in the key leadership positions of our society where the expertise and knowledge required for common flourishing are found. Christian leaders of all stripes and spots must begin to consider how the ideals described as the fruits of the Spirit can and must infiltrate the organizations they lead. One of the most basic of business axioms is, "What gets measured gets accomplished." This is also why many business leaders understand a budget as a moral document. If this is so, how can a corporation's bottom line measure not just profits and losses but also the degree to which peace, kindness, and patience are in increasing supply? How can human resource divisions begin to implement employee care strategies that seek to increase the degree of joyfulness in their job-satisfaction ratings? Included in such a charter must also be the customers. How can we assure that our businesses are taking the best possible care of their customers' holistic well-being? Is it unimaginable that love can actually be a corporate or institutional value? Is there a law against declaring love of one's neighbor (instead of the colder and more distant language of "mutual respect and appreciation") in a vision or values statement? What could be the result if love was actually articulated as a measurable objective for both employees and customers? Love isn't proprietary to a religious creed or worldview. Most people are "pro" love whether they actually experience it or not.

POLITICAL INFLUENCE

Finally, it is not just in the corporate arena where courageous moral leadership and accountability must be rekindled in our societies. Here we must also address a key misunderstanding regarding the roles and responsibilities of Christian political leaders, who offer and demonstrate another way for life and living. This misunderstanding lies in the idea that Christian virtues and character can or should be hidden from public view and are of no significance for how the world runs. One can, in this view, be exactly the kind of person God intended, yet have no transforming effect or influence on any social concerns. Of course this would include but not be limited to governmental action. We suggest that few statements venture farther from the truth. The Bible, Christian history, and careful observation all attest to the fact that the Christian movement in general, and specifically during the period of the first century, drastically and intentionally transformed its world. However, today study after study shows that the character and lifestyle of ordinary Christians in North America does not differ significantly from those of non-Christians. *Christianity Today* reported on a study conducted by the Barna Group that compared Christian to non-Christian life-styles. The director of the study, David Kinnaman, summarized his findings with this sad analysis: "The respect, patience, self-control and kindness of born-again Christians should astound people, but the lifestyles and relationships of born-again believ-ers are not much different than [those of] others."[7]

This fact—as awesome and tragic as it sounds—effectively closes the door on the good number of Christians and Christian leaders who really are profoundly different. When faithful fol-lowers of Christ are routinely dismissed as oddities, then Chris-tian virtue is eliminated from any serious consideration in public life and order. This has two unfortunate results: it works against the well-being of society and erodes the confidence of those steadfastly devoted to the purposes of the God.

A part of what emerges from this picture is the usual assump-tion within a secular society that religion has no relevance to government, business, economics, education, or any other social realm. The truth of the matter is that the character of Christ lived out as the "good life" does transform our world, including in ways that affect the public welfare. These facts can be seen in the testimonials of those who have actually attained the flourish-ing they seek and have guided others to the same. Whether this is the experience of the majority or even a growing minority is irrelevant.

THE PROPHET

Of course disciples of Jesus are not to *dictate* governmental or other large-scale policies. This is as unnecessary as it is futile. Christian faith does not elevate anyone to a position to do so, and that is a good thing. We will discuss this again in a later chap-ter, but disciples of Jesus are in a position to *address* public issues that affect all citizens, and not just those of a particular "flock" or political action committee (PAC). Not every Christian leader, whether clergy or laity, should engage in this important work, but many should. The well-being of our neighbors and our loved ones is at issue, and love dictates that we speak the truth, as best we can, to as wide an audience as we can humbly access through various means to communicate our hope and confidence in God. Again, this represents the well-established prophetic role in a biblical picture of life. It is a role Jesus engaged in and, though certainly not for everyone, for those called to and gifted for this task it is essential and invaluable work.

One effect of living in a free, open, democratic society is that all individuals in positions of power, governmental and other-wise, fall in some form or another under the constant scrutiny and accountability of the public they serve or partner with. Therefore wise, loving, qualified, and courageous Christian lead-ers must offer their perspectives on how these services and part-nerships are to proceed. Who else is to do this? Who else can accomplish such a task while keeping love, joy, and peace at the forefront of their motivation?

Human beings execute government. As political philosopher John Dewey understood so clearly, all human beings tend to drift in the direction of self-interest within these structures. This often coincides with a natural leaning or gravitational pull in the direction of the world and the desires of the flesh. What should be accomplished for good and how our judges, legislators, civil servants, and professionals discern the good cannot be left up to them alone. Context, if not mere egotism and group identity, has traditionally and historically overwhelmed even the best intents and purposes. That is where the prophetic voice must rise to the fore and be heard in political, religious, and social conversations.

It is the sad mistake of many Christian ministers and leaders to suppose that they can or should carry out this duty only within the confines of their local church or denomination. Jesus speaks to the world about everything that really matters in life. It is our responsibility to follow him and be with him in this difficult, delicate, and crucial work. Therefore, any leader walking humbly with God and seeking justice and mercy may be one called by God to carry forward his truth. The role of the prophet is not one exclusively set aside for those ordained as clergy. Only God chooses his prophets. But the veracity of their message is to be discerned against God's words and ways, since it is his truth they are to carry.

One perhaps controversial example of where the prophetic role becomes especially necessary in our contemporary context is found in the area of government assistance. We are considering here those situations and circumstances where the government accepts or seeks to increase its responsibility of providing "welfare" for the people. Of course in some measure it is perfectly good and right that our government provides assistance programs. But if and when the "good life" has come to mean that the government accepts full responsibility for securing a comfortable life for citizens who receive "entitlements," such a condition must eventually implode. This is now occurring in our generation. Deficit spending is inevitable and uncontrollable when those in positions of power cannot and will not say "no."

A "no" in such circumstances may, but need not, cause a great deal of pain and harm for some people. There is no doubt that for many this could create a tragic situation. But neither individuals nor governments can live perpetually beyond their means, with continuous deficit spending and no plans for recovery. Economist John Maynard Keynes, a great sponsor of deficit spending, was often told that "sooner or later" Britain would have to pay off its debts. His reported reply was, "Sooner or later we will all be dead."[8] Well, that is certainly true, but shortsighted. Too easily forgotten is the fact that the bill for the funeral is left for others to pay. Not offering even a "sense" of how to go about prioritizing our spending, reducing overspending, and seeking means of debt reduction is simply madness. It is a madness driven by the desire for gratification now, whether we can afford it or not. This willingness to ignore the obvious is only evidence of the blind hope that somehow, somewhere, someone will work it all out.

Balance must be achieved, prudence valued, priorities set, and discipline applied graciously and wisely. Who has the will to engage such complicated, multifaceted, politically and culturally contentious, yet vital matters of public policy, all with love, joy, and peace and equal measures of knowledge, expertise, and courage? If not moral prophetic shepherds and disciples of Jesus, then who? Who understands and can apply the historically revealed wisdom of scripture, variously applied down through the ages to beneficial effect in any number of contexts and cultures, to the contentious contemporary issues of our day other than disciples of Jesus? Who has this knowledge? Today, by God's grace, the prophetic voice is still heard, albeit too often from platforms far afield from the confines of the local church. Contrary to popular belief, the prophet is not primarily interested in the debauchery of sin, but is instead moved by God's shepherding love of his sheep to avoid sin's devastating effects. Moral servant leaders must be willing to articulate grace-filled positions through the crucial, yet seldom appreciated and often marginalizing, role of prophetic witness.

MENTORING

First, when considering other key tasks in the ongoing transformation of Christian leadership, a few brief suggestions and observations are in order. One such undertaking will require accepting the challenge of apprenticing and mentoring future leaders with the intention of positioning them in arenas of influence throughout every aspect of society. Such tutelage must include the development of a character that will allow the individuals to play a role in public leadership that guides others in the direction of wisdom, not just toward securing a position and advancing the interests of particular supporters. The goods our leaders seek must be available for all. This is what makes it the "common goods." For Christ followers, this necessitates identification of servant leaders modeled on the greatest Servant of all. It is only through such servant leaders that a society or government can take on the qualities that will ensure the achievement of the good life. One cannot bypass this with dreams of a "system" that will do the job on its own. Christian leaders must continually stress and model servant leadership qualities, so that they are developed in others called to Christlike leadership positions within every arena of public life. We must emphasize that this is a *holy* calling, a calling of being set aside or setting oneself aside for a specific and invaluable service.

Too often our most experienced and successful Christian leaders, those with a wealth of experience and wisdom, are not mentoring or seeking mentees who can and would benefit from a sustained period of relational engagement. Author and speaker Bob Buford is one who has been a positive pioneer in this way. Taking the lead from his mentor Peter Drucker, Buford regularly gathers professionals from various backgrounds and vocations with the express objective of helping them discover and achieve their full potential as leaders in and for the kingdom of God.

One of the common hurdles for mentors and mentees is hesitancy. Insecurity may cause a potential mentee to assume that a mentor may not have the time or interest to invest in the relationship. Conversely, a mentor may be hesitant to assume a prospective mentee would value and appreciate the experience and insight the mentor has to offer. Therefore, they remain silent, and the relationship is avoided. This must change. Discipleship and mentoring are intentional endeavors, engaged by overt and not covert action. Therefore, after appropriate and prayerful consideration, mentors and mentees must be willing and able to court one another with a graciousness and confidence that comes from the certain knowledge that they are mutually benefiting siblings in God's family plan. Our churches can become a wonderful gathering and assimilating point for these mentoring relationships. But they will not happen on their own. Effort is required, which we can confidently expect God will accompany with his grace.

These mentoring relationships for Christian leaders are vitally necessary, because leaders in crucial positions of influence can only survive and thrive when the hand of God is moving along with them. This is the power of grace to accomplish in and through our lives what we could never accomplish—or even imagine—by ourselves. But that is just another day at the office for those whose actual citizenship lies in the heavens (Phil. 3:20). We should explicitly assume the reality of such a life and, if we are in a position of leadership, count on it, along with our mentors who journey with us in our discipleship setting. As mentors we should do what we can to help such leaders gain and sustain positions of influence where their judgments and examples can make a difference. Again, this is never about stacking up influence or hoarding power. The full intent is to seek positions of substance in order to substantially bless others. In the economy of God, the natural consequence of blessing is to beneficially affect the common good.

WISDOM

Second, astute Christian leaders must make a point of knowing what is actually taking place in our world. This means some will need to take on the role of investigative reporters and journalists who organize their operations around this vital vocation. These messengers must go into our world and go out of their way to become informed through personal interactions with leaders in social, political, religious, and economic matters. Here Christian academics and specialists must come to their aid. As John Dewey foresaw, in a democratic form of governance, being properly educated and informed is essential for a responsible citizen.

This is more difficult today than ever before. What is now called "journalism" has for the most part degenerated into a branch of entertainment, and fewer and fewer journalists endeavor to responsibly inform the public on matters that deeply impact our lives. Again, this task is not for everyone, but some need to minister to the public welfare as Christians devoted to telling the truth and enlightening the public, so we all can wisely engage the essential situations of our lives. This is largely what being a "light" means. We are not speaking of creating specifically "Christian" news programming or television stations with a certain sociopolitical bias. Instead, we are suggesting that Christians enter into existing media institutions to take a stand as truth tellers offering wisdom and perspective to the world.

The increased lack of interest in and decreasing value of higher education are aspects of a multifaceted problem. Certainly not everything sold as education is actually beneficial or worth the high cost and debt accumulation that now is part and parcel of the educational experience. Further, there are many well-developed and beneficial portals outside the formal institutions of learning through which people can develop their minds and intellectual capacities. A library card will do wonders—but it's got to be used. Unfortunately many libraries are being closed for lack of funding. Yet we must ask at what cost do we sacrifice wisdom for _____ (fill in the blank)?

What is becoming more predominant in our information age is the lack of ability to discern wisdom and truth in the avalanche of opinion dressed up as fact. Astute leaders must remain lifelong learners about God, his Word, and his ways in concert with the movements of our world in economics, politics, religions, ideologies, and ever-changing worldviews. Leaders should stay abreast of multiple sources for opinion and not rely on only those who wear a familiar jersey. Community colleges should be full of Christians staying abreast of our world, both as teachers and students. The anti-intellectualism of the past needs to be buried there.

RAISING UP HEROES

Third, contemporary leaders today must appropriately accentuate, even laud, the lives and actions of moral and ethical heroes among us. Changing our cultural climate regarding morality and ethics will not be automatic, nor will it come as a result of a clever parlor trick. Meaningful change comes through sacrifice and dedication. Human history is brimming with the gallant acts of saints and heroes that enable us to measure the depth and breadth of what moral courage and honor can inspire. These stories demonstrate the level of sacrifice and degree of devotion to truth that are necessary to forge a new vision of life. They continue to capture imaginations, hearts, and minds across the globe regardless of social, cultural, and economic variations.

A saint or hero is one who to a significant degree chooses to forgo or to risk forgoing the enjoyment of goods or even necessities, perhaps life itself, for the sake of advancing the good of others. Sometimes our heroes even sacrifice for more abstract goods such as truth, justice, or beauty. Such persons are the ones who illuminate by their lives the true nature and worth of moral goodness. Their lives and choices transcend the normal activities of those who manage an ordinary, uninspired level of decency.

We desperately long for heroes, and from an early age we imagine ourselves as someday being worthy and capable of the same kind of amazing feats and character. Jesus is the greatest hero of all. This can and should be debated. Even so, he is and has remained the hero of so many of our celebrated heroes across time. One has to seriously inquire about, or perhaps even do an empirical, quantitative study on, the number of individuals who heroically gave their lives in sacrifice for the greater good who also placed their faith and assurance in Jesus as their hero.

The German theologian Dietrich Bonhoeffer was one such hero. His wonderful shorter works and letters from his time in the concentration camp are well beloved for good reason. However, we lose the full strength of his heroic life if we overlook the depth of his moral theory based on the life and teachings of Jesus. He took a stalwart stand against the Nazi regime, which based its moral theory on something very different from the teachings of Jesus. Bonhoeffer's stance cost him his life, but his heroism resulted from the power and reality of the truth he discovered in the risen Christ, who directed him toward right and away from wrong regardless of the forces set against him.

Even still, few children, even those from Christian homes, "dress up" like Jesus and go trick-or-treating on Halloween. This must change. Why? Because Jesus is seldom regarded as a heroic individual who with courage and moral integrity chose to live and die for the ultimate good of all humanity. We must begin to inquire why our educational institutions—our universities, both Christian and secular, but above all our local churches and seminaries—still resist bringing their best critical thinking to bear on the teachings of Jesus and their ensuing traditions as a field of moral knowledge in and through human history.[9]

Today, we must ask whether we believe it good or even possible for everyday heroes to be found outside the realms of first responders, soldiers in battle, or schoolteachers and administrators who gave their lives in a school shooting. These heroes deserve our admiration, to be sure. Yet history reveals that there was a time when this was absolutely the norm for many more areas of societal leadership than just a precious few. And perhaps this was exactly the expected norm for early leaders in democratic governments, those of both ancient Greece and our own American republic. Sacrifice was assumed and relied upon as an essential quality of a democratic citizenry in order for a liberated society to even survive, much less flourish.

Again, the circumstances of the Nickel Mines tragedy is a case that points to the kind of moral courage and heroic character we seek. Several victims attended the killer's funeral. Monies were even collected within the Amish community and presented to the widow and her three children. Vengeance and wrath were ignored. There was no attempt to use the tragedy as a political hot button. This deeply religious community understood that pardon and mercy do not excuse the wrong but are instead the first crucial step required to move toward hope. These Christians are heroes, discovered in the worst of conditions, while also bearing witness to the world of the best of what human beings can become. This is moral leadership.

We must ask if this can or should be a model for other victims of similar tragedies to pursue. Can we imagine Jesus's words of forgiveness being applied to an unthinkably heinous act? The Christ followers of Nickel Mines could. And when they did, the world stood in awe.

If and when our society begins to ask these essentially Christocentric questions, our leaders must be prepared to provide guidance. When they do, our moral foundations can regain a solid footing so they can withstand the storms of contemporary life, and perhaps as a result little boys and girls might even want to be like Jesus again. Can we imagine a time in contemporary life when a little girl decides that when she grows up, she wants to be a doctor, like Jesus? Or a little boy who wants to be a police officer, like Jesus? A schoolteacher, like Jesus? This is a realistic and attainable goal.

This is precisely the vision social theorist John Ruskin, writing in 1860, describes in a wonderful piece that illuminates his understanding of the high calling of the modern leader.[10] Ruskin argues that there are "five great intellectual professions" necessary for the success of any "civilized nation":

The soldier's profession is to *defend* it.

The pastor's, to *teach* it.

The physician's, to *keep it in health*.

The lawyer's, to *enforce justice* in it.

The merchant's, to *provide* for it.

He appends to this list: "And the duty of all these men is, on due occasion, to *die* for it." The soldier is to risk death "rather than leave his post in battle"; the pastor, "rather than teach falsehood"; the physician, "rather than leave his post in plague"; the lawyer, "rather than countenance injustice"; and the merchant? We will leave that for a later chapter.[11] The main point is that leadership is a moral calling that elicits an ethical duty to seek the good for those who are led. Ruskin defines, in specific terms, how each of these specific vocations can and must be engaged from the perspective of a good and noble shepherd. The goodness and graciousness of God demands and offers nothing less.

"LEVEL 5" LEADERSHIP

Much of what has been discussed over the past five chapters is encompassed by Jim Collins's definition of a level 5 leader.[12] For those unfamiliar with Collins's research, between 1996 and 2001 he and a group of twenty-two research assistants combed through mountains of data on 1,435 Fortune 500 companies asking one primary question: Can a good company become a great company, and if so how?[13] The result of that study left him with eleven companies that displayed seven common characteristics, one of which is level 5 leadership.[14] Collins defines a level 5 leader as one who "sit[s] on top of a hierarchy of capabilities and is, according to our research, a necessary requirement for transforming an organization from good to great."[15]

There are four lower levels of leadership in Collins's leadership pyramid. Level 1 is defined as a Highly Capable Individual who "makes productive contributions through talent, knowledge, skills and good work habits." Level 2 leaders are Contributing Team Members who "add to the overall group effectiveness by working constructively with others to meet common objectives." Level 3 leaders are Competent Managers able to "organize people and resources toward the effective and efficient pursuit of predetermined objectives." Level 4 leaders are Effective Leaders who "catalyze commitment to and vigorous pursuit of a clear and compelling vision" while stimulating the group to higher standards of performance. Level 5 leaders are able to coalesce all of the lower levels of leadership development and blend these traits with a deep personal humility and an intense professional will. "They routinely credit others, external factors, and good luck for their companies' success. But when the results are poor, they blame themselves. They also act quietly, calmly, and determinedly—relying on inspired standards, not inspiring charisma, to motivate."[16]

Collins goes on to describe level 5 leaders as those with an unwavering commitment to excellence and a devotion to mentoring superb successors. As a result, Collins suggests these leaders are able to "build enduring greatness" in both their organizations and in those they lead. It is exactly these kinds of leaders, devoted to both effectiveness and Christlike character, who must come to the fore in each of our social institutions today. This must become a primary objective of our Christian educational institutions and churches. We must refocus our efforts on developing each of Collins's leadership qualities in those who are discipled in our churches and our universities to lead well. The world is watching and waiting.

After laying this foundation for moral servant leadership, we can now move on to the more specific issues of moral thought itself, for it is only when we as leaders are able to discern what is good that we can then develop means to achieve good for our communities and ourselves. From there the following chapters will discuss how leadership and moral knowledge combine in the more specific areas of education, law, medicine, business, economics, politics, and ministry.

These areas of public life are meant to be repositories of knowledge, providing our leaders and professionals with the expertise and insight required to be deemed competent in our society. Our leaders must have and wield knowledge and authority within their field of expertise and also know how to perform their duties honorably and ethically within their fiduciary relationships to others in each of these critical social spaces. Thus, moral knowledge and moral character are as inescapable as they are necessary. What moral knowledge is, where it is attained, and how it is maintained and transferred into every institution and service throughout our societies are the subjects we must next pursue.

MORAL LEADERSHIP

Discussion Questions for Chapter 5

1. What "fiduciary" relationships do you currently have in your life? Are any of these relationships officially defined by the state or the church? How do you understand your "fiduciary" relationships with regard to your ethical and moral behavior?

2. Do you believe that a good person would perform leadership functions better than a bad person regardless of role? Does good character make one more competent, or does morality have little to do with effectiveness? Provide support for your answers.

3. The ethical dimensions of servant leadership demand the willingness of self-sacrifice when pursuing common flourishing. How has self-serving leadership hurt your organization in the past? In what ways has the self-sacrifice of a leader enhanced your community for the greater good? How has lack of moral courage cost you in your profession? What were the circumstances?

4. In nearly every segment of society, we have seen leaders who lack moral character remain very proficient and well rewarded

in their particular profession. How do we teach, train, or lead others when immoral leadership is rewarded and even praised?

5. According to Willard and Black, "The well-being, common good, and flourishing of every free society rest in the hands, minds, and hearts of moral leaders." Does the Golden Rule have the power to achieve what ethics training has been unable to in the workplace? If so, in what ways?

6. The key tasks of a moral servant leader include preparing, mentoring, and apprenticing future leaders. Who within your sphere of influence are you seeking to influence as a mentor? In your experience what is the biggest hindrance to establishing effective mentoring relationships?

7. The moral leader has three duties: (1) mentoring, (2) remaining wise in the ways of the world, (3) celebrating and emulating the moral courage depicted in the lives and actions of heroes. Of the three, which requires more of your attention?

8. *Exercise:* Do you have a trusted friend, peer, or colleague with whom you can be authentic and transparent regarding the crucial and often sensitive areas of your life? If not, make a list of those who are trustworthy, have a proven ability to maintain confidences, and are able and willing to speak the truth to you in love regarding your morality, your choices, and your leadership. Choose one, and make plans to establish that relationship this week.

CHAPTER 6

Moral Knowledge

The fear of the LORD is pure, enduring forever; the ordinances of the LORD are true and righteous altogether. More to be desired are they than gold, even much fine gold; sweeter also than honey, and drippings of the honeycomb. Moreover by them is your servant warned; in keeping them there is great reward.

PSALM 19:9–11

IN THE PREVIOUS discussion on leadership and its overwhelming importance in our contemporary setting, we discussed the critical nature of moral direction and personal integrity in the lives of our leaders. Thus, it is natural to now discuss more completely what morality is and isn't. This may not be the topic that initially grabs readers' attention or interest. Let us be clear on this point: until and unless we have a lucid understanding of moral knowledge and its virtues, we will be left spinning in the wind, personally and collectively.

Today, morality is an area that few in secular society or education—and increasingly in the religious arena—are willing to discuss. That morality and ethics are subjects increasingly left out of the general education requirements of our schools, both public and private, elementary through doctoral levels, has left us largely bereft of the basic logical faculties required to see how essential moral thinking is for life and living.[1] But moral distinctions, decisions, evaluations, and judgments are exactly what ordinary human beings must constantly employ in their activities and responsibilities of everyday life. We simply cannot and should not avoid wading headlong into such a crucial part of human existence for fear some may disagree or feel imposed upon. Certainly that is not the aim. But we cannot let fear dictate our response. Great discernment, humility, and graciousness are required with reference both to one's own moral standing (a touchstone for all moral theory) and to others' (where morality is employed with much less clarity and assurance). Grace and humility are fundamental necessities in moral discourse, because discerning moral behavior, both personally and corporately, is one of the most difficult yet crucial aims of communal life dating back to the earliest tradition of moral reasoning beginning with Socrates.

It is our lack of attention to and concern about morality and ethics that have cost us incalculable amounts of time, treasure, talent, and lives. Therefore, we can and must refocus our minds and hearts back onto the "good" aspect of the good news. We must realize that what is good is also what is moral. Many philosophical inquiries into morality and ethics over the millennia have tried to understand, define, and implement what God revealed in the Torah and Jesus came to display: namely, the news of the availability of goodness. We can understand, define, and live moral lives. We can pursue and live in the truth. We can reform our wills and societies in ways that allow us to feast on the fruits of love provided in communion with God's Spirit, but we must first be willing to at least give a moment's attention to these subjects. Our task here is to simply put the spotlight on these subjects in an effort to rekindle the necessary good thinking and discussion on the subjects of goodness, righteousness, and their attendant virtues.

A HORSE IS A HORSE, OF COURSE, OF COURSE, UNLESS . . .

Unfortunately, as will be discussed in more detail in the following chapter, the progression of modern philosophy, its effect on contemporary education, and the resulting shifts experienced in societal discourse have made the task of engaging moral instruction and insight more difficult. A fairly straightforward example of this phenomenon can be seen in the great difficulty experienced in coming to agreement even on the most simple and basic of definitions of things and events around us. When under pressure from special interests or merely from historical drift and inattention, the accurate description and classification of almost any "thing" in society can now be called into question. Many readers may not recognize this at first, but it is no longer widely believed that moral knowledge can be expressed through language. Conversely, it is now widely believed that language can be used as a means of constructing reality. These two beliefs are primary factors behind the continuing efforts to redefine and call into question key social and political institutions. The assumption that language itself alters the social consciousness and experience of reality is frequently behind the desire to engage questions such as: Is there something called "right"? Does evil exist? What is a "family"? What is a "marriage"? What is "love"? What is "justice"? These are but a few of the many concepts up for redefinition again and again in political and social life.

Frequently, conventional "wisdom" requires shifting and correcting. Slavery, women's suffrage, and apartheid are a few areas where concepts such as freedom and equality were appropriately redefined. Such change is significantly beneficial when the prevailing definitions, understandings, or descriptions being reconstructed are replaced with or adapted into "new" understandings that shift us toward things as they actually are. For example, an accurate understanding of political equality was not being applied to women before the suffrage movement. Therefore, any definition or understanding of "equality," specifically between the sexes, that allowed for the lack of voting rights for women was both inadequate and erroneous. Thus the change moved society toward a proper understanding and application of gender equality and freedom.

However, if definitions are changed away from things as they actually are, two results are likely to occur. First, definitions that do not represent things as they are will not have a clarifying effect, but only create or increase confusion. Second, as a result of this confusion and ignorance, individuals and societies as a whole suffer because their errors and lack of knowledge keep them from properly discerning their surroundings.

We've taken the time to make this observation for one crucial purpose. What an "X" *is* cannot be determined merely by an intellectual movement to adapt our terminology or social definitions of things around us—as a matter of choice, power, or popular convention. Words and descriptions do not *make* an "X" what it is. However, words may, can, and should properly *describe* the qualities, relations, and features of an "X." We can and should continue to better clarify all the different aspects of what an "X" actually is. Our research and study must continue to probe these matters to good effect. Nevertheless, labeling a water glass a hammer doesn't change the fact that a water glass is what it is and a hammer is what it is. We are free to call anything we want an "X," and we can certainly be wrong and thus be corrected in our labeling. This is all a part of learning. But the effects and reality of what "X" actually is, good or bad, despite our valiant or malevolent attempts, will generally pay no attention to whatever definition, terms, or words we eventually settle on. "X" is what it is, a fact we will quickly discover if we attempt to drive a nail into a board with a water glass.

It may seem odd, but such statements and the realism behind them are not thought well of today, especially when considering the subject of morality. This becomes especially obvious when we see that definitions, meanings, and classifications are now believed to be matters solely left to choice, interpretation, or power deployment. Even so, here we want to say that the divisions and distinctions between an "X" and a "Y"—or for our purposes here, right and wrong—are not matters of social convention or even pure choice. This would require a "constructionist" view of reality, especially social reality, according to which everything "is" a matter of how it has come to be either thought about or labeled. In such conditions linguistic constructivism, relativism, and pluralism are sure to follow. Each too often ends only in a whirlwind of debate and dialog with little action or progress toward determining right from wrong and good from evil. Perhaps this is the overarching goal.

Yet for the political aspects of life, such paralysis is disabling and even deadly. When constructionism goes too far, as we have seen occur over the past few decades with several court decisions, we begin to come perilously close to losing our firm grasp on the crucial differences between a water glass and a hammer. Such movements require a work of fiction to achieve their end.

This is now the primary atmospheric condition overtaking our universities today, a problem we will turn to shortly. Debate on these issues is healthy and beneficial, but only if there is the possibility of moving beyond hard skepticism or cynicism toward a beneficial goal and means of accomplishing our most essential objective—finding this thing called truth.

WHAT IS TRUTH?

Connected to the questions mentioned earlier is perhaps one of the oldest human questions: What is truth? Highly paid and well-educated philosophers or scholars might think such a question impossible to answer. We could consider the suggestion of philosopher Francis Bacon, who quipped in the opening of his essay on the subject that Pontius Pilate asked the truth question of Jesus, but didn't stay around long enough to get an answer.[2] Not many of us today can afford such a luxury.

First, contrary to popular belief, the nature of what we call truth is very obvious and simple to understand. Truth is not an enigma. Part of our problem lies in the idea that truth is endlessly philosophical and deeply mysterious. We must dispel such a myth. A statement is deemed to be true if what the statement either claims or refers to is accurately represented.

In practice this is easy to demonstrate. When someone makes the direct claim, "My car is white," we know precisely how to determine whether or not this statement is true. We inspect the car. Without getting into esoteric conversations about "whiteness" or "carness" or the many interpretations of ownership suggested by the term "my," we can fairly quickly determine if this statement is true. If the person's car is white, then the statement accurately reflects the reality it refers to and is therefore a true statement. As a result we find that truth is amazingly identical wherever and whenever it is discovered and therefore can be discerned in indirect ways as well. This is not to suggest that truth is always directly verifiable, but truth is routinely encountered when ideas are confronted with actual reality.

We learn very early about the truth. We do this to survive, but also to flourish. It is not true that we can fly off a rooftop if we flap our arms like a bird. Children learn this early on, which is largely why children know how serious it is to be lied to. They also learn very quickly how to manipulate their world by lying. The fact that no human being ever had to be taught to lie is testament to the obvious and essential nature of truth. Even from an early age, the truth is indispensable for us if we are to endure even the simplest situations we encounter.

Second, reality is totally unmoved by what we believe or claim about it. No statement has ever been made true or more true simply by having someone believe it. Try it. We can and often do hold deep, core beliefs. We can even get some friends to believe with us. Or we could start a political or religious movement. None of this will change the color of the car. Of course we can change the color of the car, but we don't do that by believing; we do that by acting. We are not able to change reality simply by believing, but belief does have an effect on how we perceive reality, even if our perceptions may not in fact match up to reality. That is why positions conveyed in statements such as, "True for me," are so destructive.

Conversely, authentic belief requires the willingness to act as if what is believed is in fact true. Truth is based on evidence and therefore is unyielding to one's professions or propositions regarding the truth. Reality is unmoved by either our representations or our misrepresentations of it. The masses cannot change truth. This is crucial to understand in a liberal democracy. Having the majority rule may be the best means of settling disputes. It certainly is beneficial to have the majority agreeing, especially in circumstances where the government is required to pay for the consequences of being wrong. In such circumstances it may be more efficient to have many people on the same side of an issue. Yet we must not conflate consensus with the truth. Truth is unbending to either the majority or majority opinion about it.

Truth is a gift God instilled into creation so that we can properly engage reality. In this way truth is like aiming a rifle. If our aim is right, or true, then we are able to hit the target. Likewise if our ideas and beliefs are true, we are empowered to engage with the reality of our lives. This is a very simple concept that only very bright people can confuse for us. It is a tragedy that truth, as it has come to be known today, is often considered enigmatic, unrecognizable, or even relative. Unbelief in truth encourages both hopelessness and arrogance. Neither can be endured for long when engaging the most important things in our lives.

MORAL THEORY

In short, our thesis on the role of morality in society argues that *only an appropriate moral realization in the lives of our citizens and their leaders can make possible a good society under modern conditions.* Consequently, to understand truth related to human good, the good will, and the moral or good person, we need to set forth a few very basic tenets of moral theory. For the sake of clarity on "what morality is all about," we have listed the most basic moral distinctions. Any lucid theory on morality can be formulated only after distinguishing between the characteristics inside the categories of good and bad, after which we offer a few comments about the idea of professional ethics as a pursuit of the good and moral life.

Again, we refer back to the four classic questions of ancient philosophy, two of which are: What is the good (moral) life? How does one become a good person? The first basic distinction that falls within any adequate discussion of the moral life concerns moral *actions*. These are the things we do that are classified as either right or wrong. Additionally, moral actions can be classified as obligatory (things we must do if we desire to do good) and praiseworthy (those things others recognize as good for all). The second basic distinction of moral life concerns moral *persons*. Here persons are considered moral or immoral by determining which qualities and features make up a good person and which make up a bad person. There is also a discussion in moral theory regarding those qualities and features that make up not only a good person, but also a great person, a saint or hero.

Within these categories of actions and persons, moral theorists begin to consider all the details and interrelationships in which morality or immorality exists. This requires the establishment of logical truths such as:

1. A *right* action is one that is not wrong.

2. Alternatively, an action is right if it is the *kind* of action a good person could or would characteristically do in specific circumstances.

3. A right action is not necessarily praiseworthy. It is (most likely) right, and not wrong, for you to have lasagna with green peas for dinner this evening. But it is not morally praiseworthy, unless there are some very peculiar circumstances involved.

4. A *wrong* action is one that you have a *moral obligation* not to do.

5. There is a moral obligation *not* to do something, if doing that thing would diminish your goodness as a person.

6. There is a moral obligation to *do* something, if failing to do that thing would diminish your goodness as a person.

From the abbreviated descriptions above we can see that a key moral distinction must be made in determining what a morally good person is and is not. This is the question that captures our interest, because it is only through such a distinction that our moral pursuits can be clarified. Again, we cannot engage all these important issues here. But for the sake of our interest in societal leadership and the common goods, we offer the following propositions as positive descriptions of what leadership ethics must contain, if we are to provide the quality of well-being and flourishing our communities both pursue and long to achieve:

1. A morally good person is one who is committed to preserving and enhancing—in an appropriate order of importance—all the various "goods" (individual aspects of "the good") over which he or she has influence. This includes pursuing one's own moral goodness as well as the well-being of others.

2. A morally good person is one who cultivates understanding of the various "goods" of life (by education) and the capacity

to reason clearly about those "goods" and about the conditions necessary for their preservation and enhancement.

3. The good person is a thoughtful person who seeks to be informed and who is, though not in an overly sentimental sense, a person animated by love. Thus, being a good person is always first a personal choice and achievement.

4. A good person is one who arranges life in such a way as to become morally upright and who seeks out and implements the means for remaining so. Becoming and remaining a good person does not just "happen."

5. A good person is one who effectively cares for him- or herself and those who are close. This is the principle of proximity.

6. A good person is someone who can be trusted.

Such persons, we might say, are of the sort who deserve assistance and support (whom it is wrong not to support) and are also worthy of emulation. We routinely admonish and encourage our children to be "like them," and often others naturally desire to be so. These kinds of people are role models or heroes. We naturally or instinctively want our leaders to be morally good persons. Simply consider the discourse around any of our elections.

The general factors that enter into being a good or bad person are called *virtues* and *vices*. Most basically, good persons have weaknesses; for example, they may not be very wise or may exhibit habits like laziness. Likewise, some basically bad persons have moral strengths; for example, a brutal person may also be courageous. Unequivocally we must say that "being" morally good or evil is a question of *degree*. Typically only media creations or fictional characters lie at the far ends of the spectrum. Few of us ever meet someone who truly belongs at either end of the scale. Still there are, in fact, thoroughly good persons and thoroughly bad persons, though few are perfectly good or completely bad.

Morally bad persons are those who intend, have set their minds and bodies in the direction of, destruction of the various "goods" of human life or those who are routinely uninterested in either the presence, maintenance, or proliferation of the essential "goods" necessary for life and living. Evil persons are those who cultivate and sustain malicious thoughts, feelings, and intentions and "naturally" act according to them. Evil persons are committed to the diminishment, even the obliteration, of essential human "goods," to the point of life itself. Less evil, but still bad (not good), are those who do not take care of or enhance the "goods" of human life under their influence.

Many leaders tend to be desperately afraid of being thought a "goody-goody" or other schoolyard names such as "Boy Scout" or "Miss Goody Two-Shoes." Somehow they fear being thought too obtuse or irrational if they are considered a "do-gooder." Yet for all the petty resistance that exists in our society to being good, the overwhelming desire to find saints or heroes remains a constant theme in contemporary life. Our entertainment venues are full of this language. Sports franchises, movies, and television shows pump out "heroic" stories one after the other, even to the point of using animated cartoon figures to satisfy the hunger for heroes. (Teenage Mutant Ninja Turtles?)

Last, the morally good person is a *thinking person*. Moral persons are conscious of the diverse deliberate states that make up the mental life and endeavor to develop and maintain a growing knowledge of the various "goods" of human life and their conditions and relations. They have factual knowledge, are able to form logical connections, and have the ability to engage in hypothetical judgments and entertain conclusions on the basis of established premises and propositions. Contrary to philosopher Friedrich Nietzsche's critique, one need not be a genius to be a Christian.[3] Yet one must bring one's full mental faculties and abilities to bear on these matters.

In total, a moral person is a *person of character*. Moral persons have the capacity to shape and uphold long-range or lifelong commitments that pursue good. People are not morally good by accident, but by a choice, an act of the will, that has settled into their character. This is the choice to live as persons who are intent upon advancing the various "goods" of human life with which they are effectively in contact. The reverse is true of morally evil persons.

Settled intention, or disposition, is the fundamental locus of moral character. This is deeper than a single act of the will, which can change or waver. Character is more consistent. It is this type of intention, worked into the substance of one's life, that forges over time a moral identity. And it is the moral identity of persons that naturalism would have to account for, if it were to successfully accommodate the moral life and ethical theory.[4]

What must be investigated briefly here, but will be engaged more practically in the chapter on education, is whether our academic programs of study and training that focus on the finer points of morality and ethics, religious or secular, have in fact created individuals who are more morally sound and ethically behaved. There is good to be found in theoretical and philosophical training on the marginal effects and aspects of ethics, and we can learn from our "lifeboat" games about how we think and prioritize our understandings and biases.[5] Whether all our philosophical training in moral and ethical theory has been effective in producing a will that is good, or a good person, remains empirically unconfirmed and unvalidated. We do not have to know what people would do in a "lifeboat" situation to discern whether they have developed a will that seeks the good. It may be helpful and insightful to see what they may do in such a hypothetical situation, yet such extreme conditions do not necessarily bring to light their moral judgment at all; rather, their reactions may reflect compassion, the desire for approval, or even some other clever way humans can negotiate these matters. Within the academy broadly, it remains sufficient to have a respectable awareness of human "goods" without becoming a good person who effects the good, through good actions, produced from a will set on the good. This must change if we have any hope of forming good societies.

For Jesus, the good person is the person who is appropriately concerned about and committed to the well-being of others (Mark 12:31; John 13:34–35). The bad person is one who is intentionally destructive or indifferent to the well-being of others (Matt. 15:18–20; John 3:30; 7:7) The right act is the kind of act that is characteristic of the person who is committed to the well-being of others (Luke 10:25–37). Admittedly, the moral statements listed in the points above deserve and require more elaboration, but the objective here is to demonstrate how these moral truths capture the essence of Jesus's teaching. Yet they cannot be based on themselves. It is very nice to have a moral theory, but how does it actually work in creating a good life?

CHAPTER 7

The Common Goods

In the world it is called Tolerance, but in hell it is called
Despair, . . . the sin that believes in nothing, cares for nothing,
seeks to know nothing, interferes with nothing, enjoys nothing,
hates nothing, finds purpose in nothing, lives for nothing, and
remains alive because there is nothing for which it will die.

DOROTHY L. SAYERS

FROM THIS FAIRLY technical description of moral theory, we can move now to better describe and envision how
morality works, or doesn't work, in the practical areas of personal
and public life to form or run afoul of *common goods*. This term
has returned to the forefront of our thinking and conversation to
beneficial effect. Yet in dealing with this term we need to beware
of the overwhelming desire to define in great specificity the word
"good." This is impossible. Thousands of years of philosophical
inquiry have yet to fix this essentially contested concept. This
will be discussed again later, but it is important to say here that
we can know and experience *a* good thing or event and people
who represent significant aspects of "goodness." In this way we
can implement strategies and systems to pursue "common goods."
Yet we can never fully comprehend or define *the* good anymore

than we can comprehend or fully define God. Full comprehension of an all-encompassing, total, and unmitigated "good," at least in this life, will elude us.[1]

We can and must, however, seek "goods." These are things and qualities that represent, illustrate, and point us to what *the* good is *like*. "Goods" are those noble, virtuous ways of acting and being in both individual and communal life. This absolutely includes many activities and objectives within business, economics, politics, law, medicine, and religious life. Such "goods" are also accompanied by "ways" and "means" of "being" and "behaving" that will result in benefit to both others and ourselves.

An example of these "goods" would be generally encountered in displays of patience, wisdom, honesty, reliability, credibility, honor, expertise, and the like. These are "common goods" simply due to the fact that these aspects or qualities of life carry both individual and collective decency with them and will therefore work effectively for the benefit of everyone who engages and applies these goods in community life. Such benevolent customs and practices are examples of "good," and they are also things that manifest goodness.

Truth and morality are inexhaustibly connected. For centuries, societal leaders and thinkers have recognized the irrefutable need to preserve moral leadership in order to maintain thriving communities. As an example we can contemplate the importance of truth, morality, and "goods" in the works of Plato, Aristotle, and Augustine. Each in his own way argued for the necessity of moral clarity and thought its pursuit was a worthy end in itself. Aquinas makes this point well:

> The first precept of law is that *good is to be done and promoted, and evil is to be avoided*. All other precepts of the natural law are based upon this; so that all the things which the practical reason naturally apprehends as man's good belong to the precepts of the natural law under the form of things to be done or avoided.[2]

Or perhaps we could consider a more recent contributor such as Henry Sidgwick. As one of the premier British ethical philosophers of the Victorian era, Sidgwick, with his "maxim of Benevolence" (for "maxim of Benevolence" read "motto of goodness"), articulated perhaps some of the clearest understandings of how and why societies must achieve the "goods" they seek. He writes, when in a community, "each one is morally bound to regard the good of any other individual as much as his own, except in so far as he judges it to be less, when impartially viewed, or less certainly knowable or attainable by him."[3] Sidgwick goes on to incorporate justice and prudence in this crowning maxim as well.

Even so, arriving at a set of "common goods" remains a complicated and increasingly contentious negotiation. What is "common" and what is "a good" are approached from diverse points of view and with different expectations. The various solutions, cultural contexts, sociological values, religious perspectives, and ethical standards within the many proposed solutions to the question of what is goodwill eventually, with enough time and attention, produce a philosophical framework within which "goods" can be understood and defined. When such paradigms come to fruition and are eventually applied, few aspects of human life will become more catalytic or revolutionary, for good or ill.

THE VIRTUES OF TOLERANCE, UNDERSTANDING, AND GRACE

After describing the ways of understanding moral persons, moral actions, moral intents, and common goods, we can begin to better recognize that all contemporary secular forms of life are—despite dismissals to the contrary—teaching and embodying a version of morality that is as rigorous, dogmatic, and potentially shame-centered as any religious form. One only need run afoul of a secular form of morality to feel its wrath and condemnation. As a case in point, consider the demonization that occurs on both sides of the abortion issue. It is widely recognized by those "outside the Beltway" that a majority of our political "discussions" today amount to little more than two groups standing in condemnation of one another. We can call this "condemnation engineering." This is the process of using condemnation to control people through their fear of disapproval.

In contrast, Jesus teaches and demonstrates that we can disagree and not condemn. Condemnation and judgment are two separate mental and emotional activities. Morality is central to human existence in any era, but these issues are at times extremely difficult to navigate in contemporary life. Jesus offers us a light to guide us in both discerning what is best and navigating our disagreements. He entered human history as the unqualified greatest teacher of the human race in the area of right and wrong. He gives us truths that can successfully guide our lives, so that we are not so starved for knowledge that we must search the cosmos for it. To drink from this spring of truth, we must only admit that we have wandered far from what counts as knowledge and from what authority it precedes.

In disagreement and discord we also follow Christ's example of seeking peace, of being slow to anger and quick to listen. Additionally, concepts such as acceptance and tolerance—religious or otherwise—find significant support in the teachings of Jesus. These are important topics in contemporary life. Toleration of others is part of what was lost in the rise of secular morality, which coincided with an increase in negative attitudes toward Christian virtue in the academy and government. The fact that Christians are regularly thought to be close-minded, dogmatic, and intolerant is certainly justified in some cases. Yet this attitude is also highly ironic, since the very tradition of tolerance in the Western context is accentuated in the Christocentric worldview. Just a simple count of the tolerant societies in the world today gives some clue as to the power of the applied moral teachings of Christ and their benefit to the world. If self-professed Christians are being aggressively and consistently intolerant, they are certainly not emulating the example of Christ or the traditions and teachings of Christianity. Much trouble and confusion about these matters can often be attributed simply to mislabeling. "Christians" are often not Christlike. However, this lamentable fact should not impugn Jesus or his teaching on tolerance.

Tolerance is a twofold notion for Christ followers. The first aspect deals with a genuine interest in the truth, which requires an authentic willingness and ability to engage differing points of view on a variety of subjects. The second aspect involves moral character. We must become the kinds of people who can develop beneficial relationships and hold meaningful conversations with those who maintain views that are different from or opposed to our own. We must be able to value and love people as they are, whether or not we agree with their views or choices. Above all we are interested in their good and the goods that will contribute to their flourishing. If we only gather and discuss our views with those who agree with us on primary matters, then tolerance is never an issue. Tolerance is only in play in the midst of discord. Today the only socially permissible level of intolerance occurs when engaging those perceived to hold intolerant views. Thus, our current definition of tolerance includes permission to be selectively intolerant of the intolerant, which of course means to have no tolerance for them at all.

This is a predominant irony in our culture, especially between liberal and conservative Christians. This game is played out on the global stage and only diminishes the credibility of the Christian message. Being loved and accepted by God is the primary means of engaging any meaningful acceptance and tolerance of others. Grace and tolerance are not only about managing our anger in disagreements. For Christ followers, grace and tolerance are a state of being. Reasonable disagreement is a primary means through which we can practice the discipline of submission that builds authentic tolerance, humility, grace, patience, and appreciation of those around us who are not like us. It is essential to establish such appreciation and tolerance before engaging the task of describing and pursuing the common goods.

A GOOD PERSON IN A GOOD SOCIETY

Looking back for a moment, we can perhaps now better understand why moral goodness is so crucial to God's pursuit of world transformation. It is not until we are able to understand what good is, and is not, that we can begin to grasp how the need for common goods is inextricably linked to how we understand and discern the moral qualifications in the actions and motives of a good person. How are our leaders to be held to account for pursuing the common goods? What ends do we desire for our vocational objectives? These are matters of great importance for us. We are in constant interaction with and dependent on leaders as clients, citizens, colleagues, and even fellow leaders. What do we expect of one another? What can we expect? What should we expect? What can we hope for?

What is necessary, what is possible, and what is unacceptable are all moral questions and also subjects about which the scriptures, including the teachings of Jesus, hold specific unique and essential insights. However, it is only after we as individuals develop an understanding of both the responsibilities and opportunities of moral knowledge that we can begin to create a vision for what personal and public life might be like when the kingdoms of this world conforms to the kingdom of our God and his Christ. The gospel of the kingdom of God provides answers to these questions. What else does? Does communism? Does socialism? Does democracy? Does the university, the justice system, the military, the business community, or even the religious community routinely offer an explication of what is moral, good, and best in a manner that is not only articulate but also attractive? Where does the beacon of righteousness shine in our society? Where can one find that city on a hill that acts as the magnetic north for our moral compass?

Of course there are deeper questions that naturally lead us closer to the crux of the matter at hand. Where do we go to get the kinds of people we can trust with the power and knowledge required to lead? How are these kinds of people developed? Where do they come from? What vision of the future do we desire? Where do our leaders develop their vision of what is good and right? As discussed earlier, we live in the wake of the reality that professionals and leaders are in fact too often not who they should be, who they must be, for the common goods to be pursued and achieved. Too many of our leaders are simply not the kinds of people who can lead well. Are we prepared to change this? Where would we start? The answers are perhaps not as complex as the changes such answers will necessitate.

A GOOD WILL

We have thus far engaged the issues related to moral theory and the plural forms of the common goods. Now we must discuss the goods with which we have personal experience and engagement. These are the good things we can do. In order to begin such a discussion we must pursue the idea of a personal "good will." This is a subject upon which Jesus focused an incredible amount of his teaching, for he knew, and the Pharisees demonstrated, that knowing good was not sufficient to produce a heart set on good. Likewise, a significant misstep of ethical theory beginning in the turbulent period of the early 1960s has followed the Pharisaical line of reasoning. As a result, most moral pursuits today almost totally neglect even the concept of an individual will trained to pursue either good or ill. Of course this has tragic consequences for sociopolitical issues, many of which are primarily concerned with human goods. Yet contemporary moral theory will not lucidly come together if it remains focused only on political or communal interests and origins. Social issues and individual moral commitments are inexorably linked. Jesus understood this and therefore taught that the essential concern for any movement with designs for transformation must begin, but cannot end, at the epicenter of moral practice, the individual human will.[4]

The will is not a dreamy affair concerned only with some notion of utopian virtue or self-centered fulfillment. In general, when our thoughts and words about such ideas remain at the ethereal level of abstractions, we nearly always defeat our cause. As British philosopher F. H. Bradley clearly understands in his treatise "My Station and Its Duties," leaders and professionals are almost always, but not quite totally, willfully concerned about the entire moral atmosphere in which they play a single but essential role.[5] In the midst of human goods (those things beneficial for humanity that enable them to thrive) are those persons who demonstrate a will set on the good.

It is active caring and concern for specific goods, pursued in word and deed, that characterize a will that is good. Such a good will is centered on intentions and actions that pursue the good of other human beings as well as its own. Hence, one's own good will is a human good. Good people, who will the good, are good for all people at large. This is what philosopher Immanuel Kant terms the moral "perfection" of the self.[6] Clean water, safe living and working environments, opportunities to learn, play, and labor, committed family and community interactions, and so on, all make the list of specific human goods. But each of these finds its genesis as a result of engagement with particular human wills set on and pursuing these good things.

The will, the desire or motivation to advance the goods of human existence, both individually and corporately, is always connected to the motivation to find out how to do "good" and then apply that knowledge properly. When one actually wills the end, then one must also will the means. Therefore, understanding what goods we affect, their circumstances, and interconnections is a prerequisite for the realization of any authentic pursuit of a good will and good character. Thus, truth, knowledge, thoughtfulness, and prudence are themselves human goods that can and should be engaged for their own benefits.

THE IMPOSSIBILITY OF SEPARATING LOVE FROM CHRIST

The traits that encompass a good will are crucial to the development of one's own moral self-realization. Reason is elemental to developing a good will, but reason alone is not satisfactory, nor is rationality the end.[7] The virtue of love, an authentic *agape*-level acceptance of others, is the ultimate attainment in Christian moral living, but it is impossible without an eternally forgiving and merciful Christlike example. Therefore any move to extricate Jesus from the foundations of morality is a significant barrier to moral change.

There has developed an almost industrial-sized effort to place morality on some factual basis other than the divine person of Jesus. This is even true now in some of our local churches, which have chosen to abandon the seemingly divisive claims of scripture about the person and works of Jesus in hopes that certain aspects of his teachings will be enough to stave off social decline and despair. His teachings about community, love, forgiveness, generosity, rebirth, and so on continue to be celebrated and well received. Therefore, attempts have been made to implement these realities through social structures and political processes of various kinds. We can now state that such attempts have been and remain demonstrable failures. Reinventing a better broken wheel is never a success. There is no feasible means of setting the teachings of love of neighbor, charity, tolerance, and so forth on a basis of fact different from one that is inseparable from Christ himself. In short, we fail to effect change because, apart from a resurrected Christ, we do not possess the means to do so.

The entire point of morality is to restrict and guide individuals and groups by preventing—saying no to—desires that are wrong and inappropriate. There needs to be a basis of power and authority from which these statements can be consistently referenced so that they can be applied. Otherwise, there is no confident means through which a society can actually begin to produce and train the kinds of people who actually are willing and able to live moral lives individually and corporately. We often hear that society cannot legislate morality, when in fact morality is exactly what we can and should legislate. What we cannot control through legislation is the power over the will. Transforming or even controlling the human will takes a tremendous amount of power, more power than any society or form of government has yet manifested or employed.

TRANSFORMING OUR MORAL LIFE

This brings us to the crux of our discussion on moral theory and its connection to God's mission of transforming our societal structures in ways that conform to his benevolent will. We must find the means by which we can actually engender the good we desire and seek. Thus the crucial questions become: Where does this power to change the will come from? Where is moral courage to be summoned from? Where are we to catch a vision grand enough and wide enough to absorb the disappointment, subservience, submission, and sacrifice that are so often required for morality to reign?

Such power can only be found and utilized in the love and grace of a good God acting through the Spirit of his risen Son, in and through his people. Such moral courage comes from understanding the function and purpose of Christ in human history as an undeniable, unconquerable force of redemption and blessing *to the entire world*. Such hope can only be found in light of an eternal destiny that gives one sufficient room to believe in the plan of God to finally and ultimately work out good in every circumstance. Without these foundational understandings of power, courage, and hope, the good news of the moral knowledge of God will struggle to become applied in people's hearts and minds, and very few people will ever be able to love themselves, their neighbor, or their spouse or child, much less a competitor or enemy. It is only within the sufficiency of relationship with the Triune God that a reservoir of loving sufficiency, power, courage, and hope exists to transform our world.

How do we routinely develop a society of individuals who are brave, honorable, loving, moral, and ethical? Where do we find self-sacrifice, courage, devotion, and integrity in our societies as a whole? Who is responsible for the department of goodness and courage in our cities? Where is the division of mercy and integrity in our government? Where are the training centers and degree programs for moral knowledge and character? Who offers a diploma in prudence and virtue? Where is there a master's degree in faithfulness? Such certifications can only be offered when there are university administrators, professors, and teachers of every discipline who themselves value and demonstrate a level of mastery regarding the sustenance available in God's kingdom. Then such leaders can critically and unashamedly lead students into the body of moral knowledge that exists in the teachings of Jesus. How do we alleviate the famine of moral knowledge in our world? We employ it ourselves, and then we model and teach it to current and future generations of leaders, assessing our progress and techniques along the way.

To summarize, our society will come no closer to being able to distinguish right from wrong if our morality is founded strictly on theory and not reality. For moral principles to be effective, they must be based in the real world and connect to our daily lives and relationships. If our morals are merely social constructions and ethical theories that are never firmly attached to real-life events, then such theories will never be able to sustain the authority required to change behavior.

One of the most fundamental and dogmatic illusions of modern secular society is found in the idea that we can train people to be ethical without grounding those ideals in reality. Morality cannot be based solely in politics or any other social arrangement. Moral living rests entirely on the human will. What the grand social experiment of American democracy has proven is that moral behavior demands the self-sacrifice of individual human beings. And the real moral heights that we celebrate in human life surround those events and individuals who are willing and able to sacrifice all, in love and service, for the greater good. These are the kinds of heroic moral leaders the people of our world are dying to emulate.

CHAPTER 8

Illuminating the Good Life

Despotism may govern without faith, but liberty cannot.
How is it possible that society should escape destruction if the
moral tie is not strengthened in proportion as the political tie
is relaxed? And what can be done with a people who are their
own masters if they are not submissive to the deity?

ALEXIS DE TOCQUEVILLE

NOW WE CAN connect the propositions and positions offered earlier regarding the responsibilities of leaders and the moral courage necessary to lead in appropriate ways with the essential moral issues of our daily lives. If we as Christian leaders are to begin to understand what is good and right for our own lives, and then for those who are given to our care and responsibility in our families and vocations, we must readopt the proper devotion and respect for the Word of God—not as a self-righteous hammer of condescension toward others—but as a means through which we can be "transformed by the renewing of our minds so that we may discern what is the will of God—what is good and acceptable and perfect" (Rom. 12:2) and thus follow the Spirit of God as he guides us in navigating the increasingly complex moral circumstances within our contemporary society. This will require pastors and teachers of scripture to step up their game, as we often say. Very little of what we understand or receive today as scriptural teaching is actual instruction. More commonly, contemporary parishioners only receive a certain amount of preaching. We must remember that teaching and preaching are not the same offices or responsibilities, something we will come back to toward the end of this chapter.

In order for the kingdom of God to proceed and overwhelm every corner of our globe with love, light, and power, our understanding and application of Christian leadership must be reformed by Christian leaders themselves. Therefore it is appropriate now to suggest some practical suggestions about how Christian leaders can and should consider their calling to model the light and life of God's empowering kingdom in their realms of influence. To summarize, we have suggested that testing two major factors would be required in order to successfully demonstrate the presence of "a good life." Again, each of these factors requires God's active participation and is therefore only partly subject to human direction and control.

The first factor is the prevalence within the population of a certain range of individual moral character. The second factor required is that our social and political arrangements, practices, and institutions manifest these same moral characteristics. Good people are necessary building blocks of good societies. In both of these circumstances, the role of leaders, professionals, and spokespersons remains paramount. For instance, honest governmental or business agencies that pursue honorable intentions and means must be guided by those individual leaders and professionals who maintain the character to enact and provide moral direction. No autonomic systems of legislation or oversight will suffice.

Focusing on the first requirement, the good life, both individually and collectively, only emerges from the prevailing characteristics and actions of the particular persons who make up a population. The particular person is primary because only individuals are capable of action. Corporations, organizations, and institutions can only function as a direct result of the work of individuals asserting their will. As a result, the order or disorder in any dimension of society, under ordinary circumstances, is entirely a function of what individuals intend and are prepared to carry out. That such propositions and explanations are often shunned by social scientists today are matters to be seriously considered and pursued.

The social structures and processes in which individuals are immersed and have been formed will in turn largely determine what individuals become willing and prepared to do. This is so regardless of whether one is thoughtful, informed, or self-motivated to think critically about one's own life or who one follows, learns from, or is corrected by. Therefore we must have leaders and teachers that challenge our individual and collective habits of thought, feeling, and action in order to enable the public to do much more than simply react in knee-jerk fashion to their surroundings. We always have to take into consideration, when reflecting on the good life, both the characteristics of particular persons and the social contexts and structures that actually influence people to do what they do.

Still, it is the actions of particular persons—and the character traits that those actions express—that directly constitute whatever wisdom (or foolishness) we may find exemplified in a given context. So it becomes imperative to look briefly at those particular individual characteristics that work favorably toward the development of individual and public well-being. Here we note that such foundational characteristics are also essential for *any* decent form of human existence. The list of these characteristics can be collected from almost any of the great thinkers in human history, from the East or the West (e.g., Socrates and Confucius), because these attributes are so important for human life. Yet in approaching these issues from a Christian standpoint, we will take our list from the New Testament.

THE ETHICS OF THE FRUIT OF THE SPIRIT

What might a moral society look like? In his Letter to the Galatians, the apostle Paul lists the primary components of what he calls "the fruits of the Spirit" and contrasts them with "the works of the flesh." The list includes love, joy, peace, patience, kindness, generosity, faithfulness, gentleness, and self-control. "Against such things," he says—with a sly bit of humor, no doubt—"there is no law" (5:22–23). Such attributes are "legal" directly due to the foundational role each plays in building strong and beneficial relationships that contribute to human well-being in general.

Take these key aspects of "goodness" out of human life, and you are left with a condition that few would find endurable, much less desirable. Here "the works of the flesh"—"fornication, impurity, licentiousness, idolatry, sorcery, enmities, strife, jealousy, anger, quarrels, dissensions, factions, envy, drunkenness, carousing, and things like these" (Gal. 5:19–21)—provide the exact negative counterpoint to the fruits of the Spirit. We can say confidently that a glance at our daily or hourly news programs suggests these conditions, in varying degrees, are prevalent within most cultures around the globe. Such conditions also contribute heavily to—or make inevitable—the rash of foolishness that manifests in outright wrongdoing and evil that we routinely experience all around us.

Just consider the list of "the works of the flesh" and imagine what they presuppose and what they produce for public life. Now compare that image to one based on "the fruits of the Spirit." Such comparisons should allow us to better understand the stark differences in the consequences of each. Again, one need not be religious or Christian to grasp, witness, or experience the differences in form and substance between these two contrasting lists and their corresponding results. We might even want to engage a quantitative or qualitative research project on such a phenomenon.

A life structured around and animated by the fruits of the Spirit will be one in which personal relationships, which are central to human well-being, are strong and beneficial to everyone involved. That is why we call the elements demonstrated by the fruits of the Spirit "foundational." Let us think briefly about a few of these foundational traits, considering love, joy, and peace from the viewpoint of the general welfare of the public.

Love, of the *agape* variety, is goodwill in action. To love something or someone is to act or be poised to act for the good of that thing or person. Love of neighbor is a disposition to act for what is good for those closest to us. If you see harm coming to them, you act to deflect or diminish the harm. And if they need some good thing, you do what is reasonably in your power to supply it. In the larger social, governmental, or economic setting, those motivated by love do what they can to establish and sustain arrangements and practices that will benefit everyone or as many as possible. They will oppose institutions and practices that hurt the public or fail to provide what is good and helpful. Thus, all leaders, professionals, and spokespersons devoted to love would be simultaneously committed to common goods.

This is why each vocation is considered a "calling." As individuals and leaders form or join organizations or societies, their objectives would not be directed toward self-seeking gain. Instead, these groups would be "called" to "higher" ends, such as service to their profession or their clients, customers, and neighbors, and not for personal prosperity alone. Those motivated by love at the public level will care for the public, because they care for (love) the people who make up the public.

Joy is a positive outlook of hopefulness based upon a pervasive, overall sense of well-being. Joy, like love, has a "feeling" component that is pleasant. Yet joy, like love, is not a feeling. Joy maintains a positive posture in life that assumes that good *will* be supported and eventually triumph over any apparent obstacle. Therefore, joy is fully compatible with the experiences of pain, disappointment, or sorrow, because joyfulness always takes a wider view of circumstances and works with hope to expect good to prevail. Joy enables patience, faithfulness to commitments, and the all-important ability to defer instant gratification. Joy gives one the ability to say no, or perhaps a very firm "not yet," to the immediacy of desire. Both responses are evidence of joy's ability to overcome the tyranny of the urgent, since one is joyful with the present state of affairs, whatever that may be. The bearing of joy on the good life should be obvious. It is indispensable to steady contentment and perseverance in any task. Joy liberates from the demand or temptation of immediate satisfaction, which resists waiting for what is good or best. Accordingly, joy is the best platform from which to make any sound investment.

Peace, or *shalom*, is a kind of rest that comes from bedrock confidence in the holistic, universal provision of what is necessary and good. Hymnist Horatio Spafford offers one of the best descriptions of the effects and sources of peace: "When peace like a river attendeth my way, when sorrows like sea billows roll, whatever my lot, Thou hast taught me to say it is well, it is well with my soul." Consequently, a person of peace does not attack others and faces attacks by others with calmness and without rancor, since there is an assured knowledge and experience of abundance. Such a one is neither hostile, suspicious, nor "touchy" to the point of offense. The wisdom that springs out of a life from above, says the Letter of James, "is first pure, then peaceable, gentle, willing to yield, full of mercy and good fruits, without a trace of partiality or hypocrisy. And a harvest of righteousness is sown in peace for those who make peace" (3:17–18).

THE EFFECTS OF LOVE, JOY, AND PEACE
ON COMMON WELL-BEING

Can we begin to imagine what a society, nation, or world, even a neighborhood or family might look like that has been transformed and revolutionized by an effluence of God's permeating good will and *shalom?* We must. These few remarks, we hope, will make clearer the role the fruits of the Spirit play in any public pursuit of human flourishing and well-being. It is not necessary here to discuss each additional element listed by Paul in the fruits of the Spirit. Others have done so and continue to do so with great clarity and benefit. When we add all the fruits of the Spirit together, including patience, kindness, generosity, faithfulness, gentleness (or moderation), and self-control, there comes into focus a grand design for a uniquely different kind of person who would naturally be set apart from ordinary human beings.

Just a moment of reflection will illuminate that the well-being and flourishing such leaders would promote for others in the natural course of living their lives would dramatically influence the social, economic, and governmental arrangements they are involved in or lead. Those in whom these characteristics are well developed and who simultaneously abstain from "the works of the flesh" will tend to be capable of being at home in their context and of supporting themselves and others. By contrast, one can observe that people caught up in a life *not* devoted to love, joy, peace, and the rest of the fruits of the Spirit are often, by their own admission (with the obvious allowances for exceptions), lacking in their experience of the good life.

Bringing light, love, joy, peace, and truth is not a new task for the people of God. The scriptures are of inestimable worth in discerning both what has and what has not worked well in our attempts at creating a shining "city built on a hill" (Matt. 5:14). Forming and manifesting the kingdom of God in and through his people has always been at the heart of what God expects his children to achieve as a gift to the broader world. It is the people of God, wherever and whomever they may be, who have the task of exemplifying confidence in the nature of God and his ways. According to Jesus's understanding, this is what a witness must be able to faithfully embody. Witnesses "are" much more than they "do." The task for those who are disciples of Jesus is to prayerfully consider what our unique context requires and then provide testimonials to specific circumstances of how God's loving, powerful, and grace-filled ways may be best manifested in and to our world. This is the essence of Christlike leadership.

It is the properly attained and applied mastery of the special knowledge and character of Christ, incarnated by leaders, spokespersons, and professionals who are baptized into a dual fiduciary relationship to Christ and neighbor, that is also the means and end of the great divine conspiracy. This is why trustworthy leaders are so essential to: (a) the establishment and achievement of the general welfare of our society; (b) manifesting what the common goods are; and (c) providing accountability for how our world either suffers or thrives as a result of the motives and actions of those in key leadership positions.

THE GOODNESS OF GOD IN THE SCRIPTURES

This is where the scriptures become an essential and catalytic tool for human life and our pursuit of flourishing. It is also important to admit to a few additional assumptions. First, one certainly does not need to be a Christian or even religious, as the term has come to be used today, in order to benefit from the engagement of the topics of truth and morality. As with any claims to knowledge, including moral knowledge, whether made in the realm of religion, science, philosophy, or any other field, the propositions and arguments made in the scriptures should be able to be tested and verified on their own merit by those who come to them with the desire and willingness to find the truth. It is specifically for this reason we have chosen to accept and apply a Christocentric worldview. We find in the revelations of God—as evidenced and experienced in nature, articulated in the scriptures, and most specifically manifested in the teachings of Jesus—a body of knowledge that can and should be validated on an appropriate basis of fact and experience.

Second, without engaging any specific doctrines regarding what the scriptures may or may not be, we propose that the Bible, in all its forms, can be trusted to reliably and consistently *guide us into a life-saving and beneficial relationship with God in his kingdom.*[1] Yet belief in claims about the Bible is not a prerequisite to engage the knowledge the scriptures provide. If in fact there is knowledge and truth for life and living within the scriptures, its claims about itself should be required to stand up to the appropriate tests and measurements of all knowledge claims before presuming any level of authority over the situations, circumstances, and potential solutions offered to the issues we face today. Here no exceptions to this high standard of credulity need apply. Only a fair and unbiased hearing is required. No quarter should be expected or necessary.

As an example, even a passing engagement with the Psalms, for instance, will provide inquisitive readers with a plethora of specific claims and instances of practical theological and moral knowledge about the good and righteous (moral) ways of God. The book of Psalms makes this point in its very first stanza:

> Happy are those who do not follow the advice of the wicked,
> or take the path that sinners tread, or sit in the seat of scoffers;
> [2]but their delight is in the law of the LORD,
> and on his law they meditate day and night.
> [3]They are like trees planted by streams of water,
> which yield their fruit in its season,
> and their leaves do not wither.
> In all that they do, they prosper. (1:1–3)

What the writer is discussing here is the moral life that comes through delighting in and routinely contemplating (or bringing before the mind) the teachings and wisdom of the LORD.

A much longer and more detailed description of the moral benefits of God's Word and truth comes in Psalm 119. Its 176 verses are a testimony to how human life and living will be blessed, prosperous, and flourishing if and when we "walk in the law of the LORD" (v. 1). Verse after verse extols the benefits of living in and applying the precepts, testimonies, statutes, commandments, judgments, words, ways, law, wonders, ordinances, discernment, and knowledge that come exclusively from God's bountiful and gracious love and wisdom, which he generously gives to all who seek him (James 1:5). Therefore, discussing morality is in fact discussing the nature of God's law and truth, which Jesus famously suggests is found in him: "I am the way, and the truth, and the life. No one comes to the Father except through me" (John 14:6). What Jesus is saying explicitly and confrontationally to a Jewish audience very familiar with the Torah is that in him, through him, the life the Torah describes and highlights is available. He is what the Law and the Prophets point to as the fulfillment of the righteous life of God (Matt. 5:17; 11:13; 22:40). In that way, Jesus should be seen as the perfect embodiment of morality. This is why his teachings, specifically the Sermon on the Mount, dovetail perfectly with the ideals exemplified in Psalm 119.

Here we must say something briefly about the connection between biblical illiteracy and the growing lack of moral knowledge in our world. There has been an overarching sentiment within many fundamentalist or conservative circles that "fighting for the Bible" must be funded by esoteric claims regarding inerrancy and inspiration. It should be recognized that these are important and worthy debates, for there has been a tendency throughout human history to eschew the more problematic texts that bruise people's feelings about themselves. As a whole the scriptures routinely espouse inconvenient ideas that oppose the ways in which individuals, societies, or institutions, including at times the church, may want to express themselves or pursue certain priorities. Therefore, the conservative end of Christian belief has resisted attempts to anthropomorphize God or to adopt interpretations of scripture that cast God in a role more befitting an idol with human attributes and attitudes. As a result, conservatives have a tendency to blame "liberal" interpretations of scripture for the immorality that has grown in our society.

In more liberal circles, postmodern hermeneutics and linguistic games of literary deconstruction have effectively created a situation in which any and all interpretations are deemed valid, since nothing concrete is believed to be referred to in the text itself. People get to say whatever they want to say about what they believe a text refers or doesn't refer to. One wonders how teaching is even possible in such a situation, for what knowledge could there be at all, if it is all "relative" or "contextually contrived."

There are many important causes and effects in these issues. However, for our purposes here, we suggest one of the primary effects of the growing epidemic of biblical illiteracy in both the liberal and conservative circles is the lack of awareness that God has given the world a rich repository of moral knowledge in the scriptures. And this demonstrates the kind of life available to those who actually put their trust in the realities that lie behind these moral truths. While the liberal mind disparages any claim to "moral truth" and thus tends to ignore the scriptures as such, the conservative mind remains unaware of the knowledge it claims to respect. Either way, illiteracy and moral ignorance are growing on both fronts.

We are not speaking of religious moralism here or its deadening cousin, legalism. The ability to focus one's attention on immorality, especially in others, or to condemn others or their voting record by proof-texting isolated scripture verses thought to settle a moral dilemma in one's favor is one thing. In contrast, what the scriptures routinely demonstrate is an assumption that knowing what is good and moral is helpful to a specific end. That end is the ability to become a good person, who routinely is empowered by God to do the good and right thing in everyday life. In such people moral superiority and legalism are rarely a problem. Psalm 119 can be comprehended in no manner other than as a reflective testimony about applying the moral knowledge attained in the revelations of God's precepts, decrees, and truths, not as a tool of condemnation, but as a means of discerning right from wrong, good from bad, in order to flourish, as a gift from the very hand of God.

THE LOST OFFICE OF MORAL TEACHER

We will only start this discussion of moral teachers here and continue it more fully in the next chapter, but as a lead-in we suggest that what is typically lost in the scriptural illiteracy argument is that those within the conservative camp tend to lead lives that are just as unrighteousness as those of any "liberals" they choose to point a finger at. Perhaps the sins are different, but only in application, not degree. Nevertheless, biblical literacy is on the decline in both the conservative and liberal camps, although neither party seems to recognize it within its own faction, and with illiteracy, the loss of moral knowledge is increasing as well. For conservatives, the priority of teaching the Bible simply is not what it once was. Sunday school classes, for both children and adults, are now thought of as an artifact of a bygone era. Perhaps we have forgotten that these classes were initially created at a time when it was no longer politically acceptable for the Bible to be taught in the public school system. Therefore "schools" on Sunday that focused on the Bible were created to supplement the increasingly secular public educational system. It is no surprise, then, that as Sunday school curriculums and Christian education in general have increasingly fallen out of vogue even in the most conservative "Bible-based" denominations, there is a parallel demise in scriptural literacy in general. The Bible simply is not being taught.

Some may argue that many conservative "Bible" churches still focus on exegetical preaching and are therefore still Bible-centered in their vision and values. However, here are a few points to consider. First, even consistent exegetical preaching is a very different exercise than intensive contextual study of the scriptures. Second, the academic discipline of biblical studies is just as significant and robust as any other field. Finally, the skill of teaching itself is a very different discipline, with a different expected outcome, than the preaching event, a fact that the church catholic once historically recognized, but that is now losing cachet. Taken from this point of view, it would seem that few contemporary local churches are prepared or endeavoring to both actively study and teach the scriptures.

We need be careful here. Certainly, the scriptures are accessible to any who put their minds and efforts to the task. Nor is it beneficial to create a class system that further separates the clergy from the laity. However, the knowledge of the scriptures and their concepts is not usually something that can be picked up without some concerted effort. The intentional pursuit of historical and contextual interpretive insight requires, at a minimum, the assistance of some educated guidance and instruction. A number of very good written and online aids today make the Bible more accessible and user friendly than ever, with good effect. However, it may be that in our contemporary attempts at making the scriptures increasingly accessible, we may have unintentionally lowered the competency bar to the point where inadvertent ignorance is passed off as proficiency to lead others. One would think it awkward for an economist to be employed to teach a course in Greek philosophy, or vice versa. However, it is often widely assumed that the Protestant application of the "priesthood of all believers" dogma gives those with little, if any, formal training the "right" to lead a Bible study group when we wouldn't accept such a lack of credentials in any other meaningful activity in our lives.

Small-group formats offer wonderful opportunities for prayer, support, and fellowship, which are keys to developing community and individual discipleship. However, if adult small groups are now the accepted means for critically engaging the scriptures, who is to call whom to account if expertise in the knowledge of the scriptures is missing from the group altogether? There is simply no replacement for well-informed and educated teachers of the scriptures. Those who are called and gifted with the ability to teach among us are a necessity for our congregations to function properly as the body of Christ. We must reconsider how to develop and utilize these integral ministers of the Word, supporting their education as a necessary means for developing their skills and achieving the blessings they are meant to bestow on those they serve.

In summary, in order to consider the kind of transformation required for individual and corporate flourishing, we have attempted to demonstrate what we mean by good, what a good person is, and what qualities must exist in the good society we seek to develop. We have described how we can come to know these things as good or bad, as they are on an appropriate basis of fact and experience. Only then can our leaders and professionals begin the process of developing mastery and expertise in order to steer us appropriately and be held to proper account for directing their services and expertise in ways that achieve our overarching welfare. To not engage in this essential task is to start a journey of a thousand miles with no destination in mind. We will certainly arrive somewhere, but exactly where we land will be a catch-as-catch-can enterprise. Surely our lives, our loved ones, and our communities deserve better.

All of the moral discourse within our nation and its various communities today demands that we develop an understanding of moral theory before we present any specific moral distinctions. In a pluralistic, relativistic, constructivist, postmodern or late modern world, our investigation of morality and ethics as actual realities has become increasingly fragmented and marginalized. Much of this fragmentation stems from the direction our universities and colleges have taken on the subject of knowledge and the concern over being cornered by concepts such as "truth."

Whether we like it or not, our societies work on the assumption there is something to the ideas of truth and reality ("We hold these truths to be self-evident . . ."). So we must at least engage truth and reality in ways that are honest and transparent.

Finally, we have argued that when we reengage the scriptures with this mind-set, we can begin to better probe such questions as: What is moral? What is good? What makes a good leader? These are central points that must be properly understood in order to grasp how the kingdoms of our world can become the kingdom of our God and of his Christ. We must be clear about what this means and how it can become a reality for us. This vision can only begin to take shape when leaders of the kingdoms of this world, in economics, finance, education, law, medicine, business, politics, the sciences, and the arts, willfully place their lives and spheres of influence and control under the reign, the rule, the direction, the lordship of Christ. What will result is a realization of the ethics and goodness of life and power under the guidance and with the provision of a good and loving God. This has been understood for centuries as the pursuit of the "common good." How a leader can and should pursue the common good is directly tied to the nature of what a leader is.

In the next few chapters we will explore, as case studies, different venues where God's leaders are called forward to act in the ways we have spoken of generally in the previous chapters. Our hope is that all leaders will gain insight into their own area of concern by reading about specific venues of involvement.

Our educational systems are the first area we will direct our interest. Teachers, with their essential skills and intellectual foundations, have and must continue to hold one of the crucial leadership roles in our society. The teacher is accountable for transferring knowledge from generation to generation. If the knowledge of the past and the discoveries made in our time are to benefit coming generations, it will be as a result of the dedicated talents of our teachers, both inside and outside the church.

It is the primary opportunity and responsibility of our educational institutions to employ, train, and equip teachers for this key responsibility. Therefore the next chapter will continue our discussion of the critical leadership functions our educators provide within our communities. It is to the unique calling of these crucial men and women that we next turn.

MORAL KNOWLEDGE, THE COMMON GOODS, AND THE GOOD LIFE

Discussion Questions for Chapters 6 through 8

The past few chapters on moral knowledge, the common goods, and the good life present several questions that have become increasingly important in our relativistic world. The authors ask important questions such as: "Where do we go to get the kinds of people we can trust with the power and knowledge to lead us? How are these kinds of people developed? Where do they come from? How do our leaders develop their vision of what is good and right?"

1. To better consider each of these questions, draw four columns on a piece of paper or whiteboard and place one question at the top of each column. Below each question list the potential answers to it. See if there are any overlapping answers.

2. We live in a world that often has a difficult time distinguishing truth from "truthiness." Some have even described our times as the "age of post-truthfulness," when the redefinition of terms, manipulation of language, and marketing strategies for characters, products, and services leave us thinking fantasy is more important than facts. We have learned to be skeptical, because it seems all systems and persons of power have a manipulating agenda. In that context, what is the impact of trust when there

is confusion about truth? How might this condition affect you and your organization's attitudes, behaviors, beliefs, and participation as a member of a larger community?

3. Willard and Black believe that "truth is a gift God instilled into creation, so that we can properly engage reality." Why is the statement, "It may not be true for you, but it is true for me," so destructive in our thinking? Give examples.

4. One of the more essential duties of any leader is to accurately assess reality. What is necessary for us to assess reality correctly, both as an individual and in team settings? In what ways do our organizations get into trouble by not accurately assessing the realities we face?

5. According to the authors, the scriptures advocate that "the good person is the person who is appropriately concerned about and committed to the well-being of others." In contrast, "a bad person is one who is intentionally destructive or indifferent to the well-being of others." Think about the events and people discussed in the news. Can you list two or three people who might fit into these definitions? How did these individuals become either a good person or a bad one? Do we know? In what ways were truth and morality or deceit and immorality connected or disconnected in each event?

6. Toleration is one word that has been redefined in secular morality. A tolerant person, according to Willard and Black, has an authentic interest in the truth and the moral character to have genuine conversations with those with whom they disagree. By that description, is our society becoming more tolerant or less so? In what ways can our local churches and Christian leaders seek ways to be more tolerant when engaging some of the moral tensions in our world?

7. The authors argue that the power to transform individual lives and social structures must be accomplished through a good God acting through the Spirit of his risen Son in and through his people. Do you agree or disagree? If you believe Christianity is not prepared or does not intend to engage this kind of transformation, what ideas, past or present, do you think can transform both individual lives and social structures? Which Christian endeavors to transform both individual and social structures have failed? Why do you think they failed? Which Christian endeavors have been successful in transformation? What made the difference?

8. Besides the activities included in a weekly worship service, in what other ways are you or your congregation receiving moral training in the scriptures? Do you find that your church is more knowledgeable about the Word of God or less so over the past five years? What factors do you believe led to the change?

9. *Exercise:* Meditate on Galatians 5:19–26 and then memorize it. Ask yourself the questions: Why did God create me specifically? What can I hope for? What causes me to strive for more power or want to protect the power I already have? If I live by the Spirit and manifest the fruit of the Spirit, how might my life and my relationships be different?

CHAPTER 9

Knowledge and Education

*Enlighten the people generally, and the
tyranny and oppression of body and mind will
vanish like evil spirits at the dawn of day.*

THOMAS JEFFERSON

V ERY SIMPLY, THERE is one social institution whose primary responsibility is the maintenance and proliferation of knowledge. This duty lies with our educational institutions. Education is foundationally devoted to knowledge, its acquisition, and transfer. Today, a majority of our educational institutions are endlessly tethered to some form of state, local, or federal governmental system. This has been in large measure due to the financial requirements of our educational systems. However, there is a more basic reason why governments are interested in education. A society must have a collective base of knowledge and wisdom at work inside its primary institutions in order for those institutions to both understand and pursue what is good and best for all concerned. This is in part why there are multiple interested parties in the muddied field of education. What our children learn or do not learn today is the primary determiner of the future of our society.

131

Hence, if the object of knowledge becomes endlessly confusing and unapproachable for the majority of people who rely on the services our educational systems provide, then formal education and its benefits will begin to drop on our list of social priorities and eventually fade into oblivion. This currently appears to be the situation in which we increasingly find ourselves. However, the demise of knowledge and its foundations does not at all lead to the demise of the desire for education. We are always receiving an education. The question is: What is that education and from whom are we learning?

Evidence of the unyielding hunger for knowledge can be found in the rise and popularity of individuals like Oprah Winfrey and her collection of quasi-philosophers, thinkers, perceivers, speakers, and spiritual gurus. She is surely a well-meaning woman who has helped many people and who appears to be very devoted to seeking wisdom. We should realize that each of the various tenets offered by her assorted "experts" and the full force of the industry surrounding her personality are routinely focused on the one vital human question of how we as human beings should live. She is attempting to bring knowledge of the world and of life down to the street level in order to teach people how to go about living the good life. This is a noble endeavor.

Some the questions we might ask of Oprah and her experts as well as of all our educational institutions are: How do we know that you know what you are talking about? By what authority do you claim your knowledge of how to live life to the fullest and best? More specifically, what is it about you that gives you the specific authority to teach others on these subjects?

Before we can even begin to discern all the various answers that might be given to these questions, there are more primary, foundational understandings that must be attained. First, we must come to a basic understanding of what knowledge is and where authority comes from. Then we must come to an understanding of how the very ideas of knowledge and authority have changed in our day, after which we can clarify any confusion surrounding who to believe and what to believe about knowledge itself. The result will, we hope, restore the authority of our leaders and teachers and allow them to shoulder their rightful responsibility of instructing current and future generations in the best ways and means for attaining common flourishing in every area of society.

KNOWLEDGE LOST

The previous chapters presented several questions: Where do we go to get the kinds of people we can trust with the power and knowledge required to lead? How are these kinds of people developed? Where do they come from? Where do our leaders develop their vision of what is good and right? In our discussion on leadership we pointed to the lamentable fact that too few of our professionals and leaders today are the kinds of people we need them to be in order to pursue and achieve the common flourishing and holistic prosperity we require. We then argued that if we desire to change this pattern, we must overcome the hurdles surrounding the lack of knowledge that causes our world to struggle with discerning right from wrong, even though very few individuals or leaders today would blatantly admit to such a deficit. There is a long, documented history and progression of thought in Western civilization over the past four hundred years that has allowed the field of leadership and morality to become an essentially contested arena. Although we cannot go into all of this history here, we will focus briefly on the results of this progression in contemporary forms of education.

The simplified, straightforward answer to why knowledge is a contested concept in our educational institutions today comes in two parts. First, we do not know the difference between what is right and what is wrong, because right and wrong are not concepts and differentiations that are routinely accepted by an increasing number of leading authorities in our educational institutions charged with teaching and conveying such wisdom. Second, the primary reason why our educational authorities do not teach right and wrong as knowledge is that we have accepted a definition of knowledge that only allows what is empirical and quantifiable to qualify as knowledge. Empirical data is data one can sense with the eyes, hands, ears, and so on. Quantifiable data is data that can be measured or counted in some methodical way.

This shift in the definition of what constitutes knowledge is a relatively new phenomenon. The increasing belief that all knowledge and truth are "relative" first grew from a progressive degradation and then a nullification of the idea that a body of verifiable knowledge exists outside the "hard" sciences. As a result, we now live in a period when any knowledge claim, in any subject area, unless it is included in the "hard" or physical sciences, is considered invalid until proven otherwise. Therefore, anything that cannot fit into a beaker, slide under a microscope, be measured by a scale of some sort, or be dissected into smaller and smaller pieces is suspect. This includes things like God, love, grace, knowledge, forgiveness, morals, ethics, virtues, wisdom, joy, peace, patience, and so forth. All these nonempirical realities were separated from the "hard" and discernible world of "science" and relegated to the exceedingly "soft" realm of "faith." For many scientists, "faith" is now a code word for the opposite of knowledge.

A quote from a professor of philosophy at Harvard University in 1901 gives us some indication of how educators thought of ethical and even religious knowledge at the turn of the past century:

> Ethics is certainly the study of how life may be full and rich and not as is often imagined how it may be restrained and meager. Those words of Jesus . . . announcing that he had come in order that men might have life and have it more abundantly are the clearest statement of the purposes of both morality and religion, of righteousness on earth and in heaven.[1]

Can we even imagine someone in such a prestigious, secular academic position stating the same today? Why is this the case?

Up until the end of the nineteenth century, in most European societies there remained a clear body of unscientific, nonempirical knowledge that was accepted and taught at the highest levels of education and culture. University courses actually taught moral principles and discussed what was right and wrong; tests and exams were even given on determining right and wrong on moral subjects. In the United States, prior to the end of World War II, the Ten Commandments were still widely assumed to represent knowledge of right and wrong. This is why they were found routinely chiseled into courthouse columns or placed outside school buildings or in other public venues. We can be thankful that God saw fit not to give Moses knowledge of something like the multiplication tables or the strict energy–mass equivalency equation $(E = mc^2)$. If God had revealed such knowledge, is it possible that we would now not be able to teach it in our schools today? Perhaps God is wiser than we give him credit for.

AD HOC ENGINEERING?

A primary way to demonstrate how the very idea of knowledge has been lost in our educational systems is found in the differentiation made between "scientific" knowledge and the knowledge gained from subjects in the humanities. Very often undergraduate philosophy, psychology, or sociology students are invited to consider a few select moral and ethical theories offered by thinkers of the past, then asked to create their own moral, social, or psychological theory, and then instructed to apply this uniquely constructed hodgepodge to a hypothetical topic. Often the lone delimiter of this assignment is that the theory not "hurt anyone."

Such an exercise would never even be considered in the "hard" sciences. It is a recognizable absurdity to imagine a professor of mathematics, physics, chemistry, or engineering inviting a room full of freshmen—with all the elements and equipment at their disposal—to "invent" their own scientific theory—without hurting anyone. "Constructing" an artificial theory in chemistry or physics is a fool's errand. One certainly does not want to drive one's car over a bridge built according to ad hoc engineering principles. As creative as our architects and engineers can be, they still must use basic, proven scientific principles in their work. Unfortunately, the same sort of grounding is not a priority in many of our humanities courses.

There are commonly accepted and justified means for determining facts, for instance, about whether and why the number five is larger than the number four. For millennia children around the globe have acquired this knowledge when taught to them by others who have themselves learned it from other knowledgeable instructors. Even at a very young age, perhaps even before formal education, children know and accept this knowledge and its basis of authority. Such knowledge is so fundamental that if children do not yet know about numbers, they cannot even discern their ignorance until this knowledge is developed and has matured. Therefore, we expend great effort and spend significant amounts on the resources to make sure our children acquire this knowledge as quickly and effectively as possible. And we have measurements, in law, to assure this factual knowledge is passed appropriately from generation to generation.

Likewise, it is just as perilous and absurd a task to construct morality ad hoc. Neither a bridge constructed by "relative" engineering nor a society applying "relative" law or medicine will stand for long. Therefore, attacking the basis on which knowledge stands may allow people to avoid being held responsible—or found guilty of hurting someone—as a consequence of having done "what they wanted to do." But tragedy will eventually rule the day. Our educational institutions are duty bound to eliminate such ad hoc moral tragedies as diligently as possible, and for centuries they did just that.

Since there is no longer a standard or recognized authority by which right and wrong can be determined, what we have generally been left with is the arena of human emotions, or feelings. We are still allowed to have feelings or strong opinions about what is right or wrong, better or best. But no standard exists by which we can make a claim to *know*—in the same way we *know* that the number five is larger than the number four—what is right and wrong. There is no means of examining or grading people on the accuracy of their interpretation of a sonnet or piece of literature, like the standards we would impose on a geography or algebra exam.

Thus, gurus and celebrities are left as our guides and teachers for everything outside the realm of the "scientific." We are sure our celebrities would likely not build very sturdy bridges, manage our nuclear-power plants effectively, or be well entrusted to transplant human organs. Why then do we assume they possess any other form of beneficial knowledge outside their areas of expertise and are therefore credible to teach and instruct us in these matters? Primarily because we have lost the ability to think critically and settled for entertainment instead of enlightenment. We simply don't think these things through, because we have not been taught to think very well. This is a primary task of our schools. Teaching our children both what to think and how to think about the issues and subjects of our world should be equally valued and tested in our state and federal assessments of learning. Critical-thinking skills cannot be sacrificed or traded for a "good" mark on a statewide standardized test. Too much is at stake. Educators must reclaim this distinct difference.

KNOWING KNOWLEDGE

Unfortunately, many of our universities are not helping these matters. Despite all the philosophizing about nonfoundationalist epistemology in our late modern or postmodern world, there are enduring secular attempts today to find a new basis or *foundation* from which to credibly teach and lead. For the most part this task has been farmed out to our universities. Unfortunately, what we often find there is a tangled web of theories and debates. Currently university courses in ethics and the like are largely surveys of different perspectives and there is no clear agreement about which can, or dare we say should, be applied.[2] Any moral foundation tied to a religion is routinely eschewed. As a result the moral need of concrete existence, the need of any people to plainly know what is good and right in order to experience the reality of the common goods we so desperately need and seek, continues to elude the general populace.

This is why professional educators at all levels are crucial to the prosperity, flourishing, and proliferation of good in our communities, of any size and shape, throughout the world. Educators are paramount in furthering the proliferation of knowledge throughout every level of society. Although every educator is important, a special obligation is held by educators in our universities and colleges, which are dedicated to higher learning. This is primarily due to two key factors. First, today most professionals both seek and receive degrees from institutions of higher learning. Second, nearly all of our educators employed throughout our various educational systems are taught how and what to teach from those in our universities and colleges. Therefore, what we must engage here is how leaders within the various fields and levels of our higher educational system can appropriately lead their institutions and constituents, namely students, toward their own good and, by implication, the good of all.

What is it that educators are to accomplish? Again, education is primarily concerned with the effective transfer of knowledge. This knowledge is not only what we call "head knowledge," although there is some of that. We need to learn our multiplication tables and historical dates. Yet those who originated what we now call the academy thought of knowledge as something quite different from a collection of factoids regurgitated on multiple-choice tests. Knowledge *of* something is very different from knowledge *about* something. For ancient philosophers knowledge was essential to the ability to navigate the world, to live and thrive in it, since the possessor of knowledge was empowered to accurately engage the world and its conundrums as they actually are in reality. Thus there remained a palpable desire for intimate awareness and experience that is inherent in the quality and type of knowledge the ancient philosophers and teachers both sought for themselves and endeavored to convey to their students.

The ancient understanding of holistic knowing that includes experiencing the impact of knowledge on the learner is largely bypassed in our academic pursuits today. Theory rarely if ever leads to practice or application. As a result our contemporary society is mystified by, even cynical about, knowledge and has an increasingly difficult time understanding what knowledge amounts to, much less how to attain and discern knowledge of ordinary life, the nature of human beings, or the world.

Let us clearly state that knowledge is *the capacity to represent things as they are on an appropriate basis of thought and experience*. Knowledge is not present when someone makes a correct guess. Also, the presence of a mound of accurate data or evidence does not in itself constitute knowledge. Two conditions must come together in order for knowledge to exist. The first is accuracy (representing things as they are), and the second is having appropriate thought and experience upon which one's conclusion (representation) is based. When these two factors are present, knowledge is attained.

Additionally, knowledge is fundamental to responsibility, and responsible action must be based on knowledge. We want and need our professionals and leaders to *know*, not just guess rightly, about what they are doing. And we also understand that in an overwhelming majority of cases such knowledge does not come by inspiration. Such knowledge is acquired through learning the appropriate means through which thought and experience can develop.

With regard to making knowledge claims, the subject matter itself, not the theory being applied, should determine what kind of thought and experience are appropriate for any subject in order to represent it well. Many subjects, including moral ones, can be brought before the mind with clarity and understanding, even though we cannot see, taste, or smell the qualities that make up morality or measure them with a ruler or thermometer. We can measure their effects. This is why the definition of knowledge given earlier does not include sense perception or quantification. It only references accuracy of thought and experience, which can include, but is not limited to, methods of empirical research and quantification. We can and must continue attaining whatever knowledge is possible using scientific methods. However, these methods simply are not the only, and sometimes not the best, methods we can employ.

Here is a key observation: any theory of knowledge that rests solely on empirical and quantifiable justification is itself a self-refuting theory. The claim that empirical knowledge is the only source of knowledge about the world is itself not empirically veri-fiable. In other words, the very type of knowledge this theory produces is of a nature that cannot be determined or quantifi-ably measured by the method itself. For example, consider some-thing as simple and majestic as a monarch butterfly. We can and have empirically validated and measured most of the features and characteristics of that wonderful insect. There is more to learn, but scholars and researchers have gathered significant amounts of knowledge on this subject.

The primary point to highlight here is: Where does this knowledge exist, exactly? Is it "alive" or contained somehow in the symbols of language that make up our books and journal articles? When we read about or listen to lectures on butterflies or watch the butterfly in its environment, where exactly does this knowledge come from, and where does it go, how does it exist? Is this knowledge collected in our brains? If so, where exactly is this knowledge in our brains? Can we isolate it in the combinations of synapses? Is it to be found in the left side, the right side, or the frontal lobe? Can we point to it, see it, touch it, hear it, or even smell this knowledge? Can we prove where human knowledge of the butterfly physically or empirically exists at all? Or perhaps if we could find this knowledge, could we measure this elusive bit? Exactly how big or wide or deep is the knowledge of the monarch butterfly quantitatively?

In fact, none of these questions have been answered, which demonstrates how the complexity of knowledge itself continues to elude a physicalist theory of knowledge. All "hard" sciences confidently assume (by faith?), but never empirically prove, the "soft" essence of knowledge itself. Thus an empirical theory of knowledge does not use its own method to validate its claims.

AN EXAMPLE FROM HISTORY

Here it is important to look at an example of this gradual development within the various disciplines in our universities. Take for example the discipline of history and the ways some historians have dealt with the issues of moral knowledge. We can admit that much of what is routinely taught about history doesn't seem to matter very much. Too often the overt focus on memorizing specific dates on a calendar tends to deaden our interest in the subject. But a very crucial part of history can be discerned when we focus our attention on the historical events of our past that consistently threaten our national ego or identity.

For example, take the historical question of what happened at Wounded Knee. Consider what occurs when we reflect on more than just the facts, dates, and characters in that event, but look closely and critically on the reality of that tragic massacre. Or perhaps we could reflect on the burning of Atlanta during the Civil War, or perhaps we could contemplate the misrepresentations told by government officials regarding the Gulf of Tonkin incident. Each of these events potentially threatens particular viewpoints regarding whether these events were "good" or "bad" and whether good or bad resulted from them.

The reason these events tend to threaten the national ego is that *they have the power to call into question both our individual and social identity*. What comes into focus is whether these events reveal "us"—as Americans, Northerners, or whatever group you choose—as good people. Thus, the way we view history reveals something that is also true of morality. Moral issues also threaten the ego or identity.

Looking at the ways in which historians classify and analyze historical events is crucial, because it reveals one of the deepest needs in human existence. Every human being needs to be thought worthy of affirmation and esteem. Validation and proper appreciation of who we are and what we achieve are necessary in forming a strong and healthy love of self. Even children instinctively know that validation—being fully appreciated and valued—must be honest, accurate, and more than mere "talk." Empty praise is experienced as nothing but vanity and is thus counterproductive to the authentic affirmation the ego strives to achieve. What we instinctively know is that empty validation is useless. Therefore, we need to be worthy of the acclaim we receive, both individually and collectively. Determining whether our actions are noble, right, and moral is paramount for attaining the worthiness we desire. Morality and ethical distinctions are therefore inexorably linked to our deep longing to be found worthy of the validation we require.

This is just one simple example of how *moral knowledge* is inexorably linked to the *factual knowledge* in the subjects we engage with in our educational institutions. No doubt there are innumerable other examples within the fields of athletics, art, economics, medicine, law, literature, and so on. Theodore Roosevelt is reported to have said, "To educate a man in mind and not in morals is to educate a menace to society."[3] The point is that engaging these moral and ethical questions is impossible unless there is a willingness to make a determination of what is good and what is not. Such a foundation is increasingly in danger in our contemporary educational environment.

THE COURAGE TO TEACH
RELIGIOUS EDUCATION

Attempting to fit the previous definition of knowledge into our current educational climate is sure to cause a significant degree of angst. This is due to the bifurcation of knowledge and the degradation of moral knowledge that are pervasive within nearly all of our educational institutions today. Therefore, contemporary teachers require a significant degree of strength of character, and even courage, simply to utter a claim regarding moral knowledge. This is particularly true for many Christian teachers.

In rough terms, over the past several centuries the Christian church has lost the credibility and authority to make knowledge claims, because some of its claims were in fact inaccurate: for example, claims such as the earth is flat or the earth is the center of the cosmos. Meanwhile, scientific knowledge, which is highly empirical and quantifiable, although subject to inaccurate interpretation, progressed rapidly. Eventually scientific research began to replace the authority of the scriptures and the church to describe reality. There are many other reasons for this, some of which have been discussed in other works.[4] Here we will specifically engage only the results of this phenomenon.

Perhaps the most notable result is the wide assumption that the Word of God or God's moral authority has been superseded by other forms of secular knowledge. Christianity's foundation of knowledge is unapologetically relegated to a religious substructure. In an increasingly post-Christian, secularist society this fact provides a "target-rich" environment for educators who want to critically deconstruct Christianity's moral opposition to the unfettered liberation of the human will. What complicates this issue is the inconsistent manner in which secularist educators determine the authority or field of knowledge upon which their critique will be based. The field of mathematics is deemed to hold an uncontested body of knowledge. The fields of theology and religion are not thought to contain bodies of knowledge. We have to understand why this is the case if we are going to effect any degree of change.

There are two primary reasons why religion, and Christianity in particular, is not thought to offer or represent a body of knowledge. First, religion in the university system is studied primarily as a sociological phenomenon. Researchers might investigate why people are involved in religion, what the religious say about their religion, what they claim to receive from religious activities, why they believe religion is beneficial, what their religion inspires them to do, and so on.

It follows, then, that from a secular social-scientific perspective, when considering, for instance, a statement such as the Apostles' Creed, researchers would rightly point out that many Christians recite it on a regular basis. Perhaps they might discuss its historical significance and even indicate what believers say is significant about the creed. However, there would be no consideration of or investigation into whether the Apostles' Creed was actually true. This is a significant and often overlooked aspect of social-scientific research. If in fact the Apostles' Creed can be determined to be a statement that does not contain knowledge and truth, or if such a question is simply ignored and left unanswered, then all of the ethical systems that rest on the teaching of Jesus and have undergirded much of Western civilization can be overlooked as well. If something like the Apostles' Creed is in fact a true statement, then there is a huge body of knowledge behind it that would establish an appropriate moral basis from which our society could proceed.

Again, what is odd about this situation is that there does currently exist a commonly accepted method for discerning the knowledge and authority for determining many aspects of life. There is a means to determine that five is greater than and not equal to four and how to build a bridge. However, these simple examples using knowledge of math and engineering are not assumed to work when applied to other knowledge claims in our universities. Think of all the debates on various social, economic, and political matters, many of which are related to deeply personal issues of marriage, sexuality, family, or even taxation and immigration. These issues are clearly no longer thought of in the same terms we use to think of math or perhaps even history. In fact, it is surprising to many in our younger generations that there was a time in human history when morality was conceived of and taught in concrete terms. Despite these transitions, we still find ourselves in the unending predicament of discerning what the right thing to do is, what we should teach and model to our children, and what we should hold ourselves and others accountable for with regard to right and wrong.

FAITH AS KNOWLEDGE

In order to begin the healing process between the realms of science and faith, the subject of religion as a social, historically developing institutional reality must be championed again in the university system. Hence our universities, both secular and faith-based, must reconsider the notion of whether religion, as a field of study, maintains a verifiable and beneficial body of knowledge. We do not suggest a redevelopment of the current curriculum of religious studies as a sociological phenomenon alone. Instead, we argue that religions and their claims must be approached again and tested on their own terms regarding all their claims about life and living in order to determine if and which religions convey viable understandings of reality. To do this well, two key tenets of religion must be understood.

Religions propose and place confidence in the existence and effects of another realm or world. This alternative or other realm is held to be uniquely different from the natural, sense-perceptible world experienced in earthly life. Also, religions hold to the belief that this different realm retains a claim both on the natural world and on us as human beings. Furthermore, human beings are also able, and sometimes required, to make claims on this alternative realm through the application or engagement of certain religious responses and activities (rituals, prayers, sacrifices, etc.).

Combined, these two seemingly simple and straightforward tenets of religious thought produce various worldviews, each of which works to illuminate a comprehensive vision for human existence. Very soon, as a religious worldview spreads, a people or community can form around its shared values, partly due to the way in which individual and corporate identity are discovered. This leads to equal measures of purpose and destiny. These values also tend to convey some form of moral conduct that shapes how those in these communities care for and treat one another. Therefore, in these ways, religion addresses universal, identifiable, measurable, and deeply experienced existential realities of human life.

There have been several attempts to curtail if not eliminate religious thought in American education over the past two centuries. Increasing levels of secularism along with ideologies such as Marxism, Darwinism, Nietzsche's nihilism, and Freud's form of humanism, among many others, all in some manner argued that the progression of knowledge would eventually eliminate the "illusion" or "opiate" function of religion. Yet, despite increasing resistance to religious worldviews, specifically during the nineteenth century, religion in some form or another has maintained overwhelming dominance in even the most intellectually advanced cultures. Today religion has retained a degree of importance in private life, while simultaneously being intellectually disowned by the majority of our academic, political, and artistic communities. Such disavowing is demonstrated in the ways the media routinely handle religious issues as they are encountered in political, social, and familial areas of life.

The power of any religion is directly tied to the profundity of human needs with which it engages. This allows religions to do both great good and great harm. As Christopher Hitchens and the New Atheist crowd are so expertly able to point out, many horrific events and much harm have resulted from misplaced religious fervor or insanity.[5] What this group often fails to address, however, is the nature, existence, and origination of the existential void that human beings continually seek to fill through religious life.

THE PROBLEMS OF CHRISTIAN EDUCATION

It is crushingly true that there is a tragic history of harsh religious moralism, legalism, and condemnation that has created oppressive structures that seek to justify immorality under the auspices of both religion in general and Christianity in particular. We must admit and confess that religion, including the Christian religion, has routinely used violence, fear, and shame as destructive forces in families, in communities, between groups, and even in nation-states.

What is vital to understand is that Jesus's ministry dealt directly with and uncovered the destructive underbelly of ignorance, arrogance, legalism, and moralism in religious life. He knew all too well how religion could serve as a destructive and oppressive force by making negative distinctions between people in ways that cast them out simply for noncompliance or nonconformity, with no regard for their needs, abilities, or knowledge. Jesus routinely takes outcasts and accepts them, reestablishes them, reaffirms them as valuable and worthy of his love and attention, after which their desire to follow his truth-seeking example is often fanned into flame.

Similarly, a primary objective for Christian educators and

a major task of professional pastors, if not the foremost task, should be the wholesale elimination of condemnation and anti-intellectualism from the local church. The media routinely highlights those local churches and their ministers who are con-demnation "machines," articulating robust confidence in their religious legalism and narrow-mindedness. If Christian under-standings and knowledge are to offer widespread benefit to our society, Christians must take it upon themselves to wisely articu-late an alternative narrative to this story, so that productive con-versation, influence, and blessing can occur.

Unfortunately, many non-Christians take their cue from the ongoing negative effects of moralism and religious ignorance, both historically and in contemporary life. Sadly, due to the sig-nificant "public relations" problem Christians have developed in society, some local church leaders have conceded to the growing misperception of Christian knowledge and faith, backed away from healthy dialog on the issue, and elected instead to push cer-tain political agendas, while maintaining strong *feelings* about the way life should go. But they resist standing as people who make knowledge claims that would enable their communities to benefit from distinguishing the differences between right and wrong.

If we as educators move in the direction of repentance and seeking truth, whatever that requires, it is possible to return to the knowledge traditions that have nourished the world for cen-turies. But this will not happen simply by inviting people to sit down and talk about morals and ethics. Morals come to us through traditions that have long established histories and expe-riences from which we can learn and grow. Therefore, the follow-ing are a few first steps that could put us in a position to revamp our knowledge traditions:

Christian educators can work to alleviate the harsh, shame-based judgmentalism that marks so much moral teaching and replace it with teachings that give life, hope, and grace.

Christian educators can give their full, critical, and honest effort to comparing, measuring, and discerning which traditions and teachings are *most* life-giving.

It is only *after* discerning the reality, effect, consequences, and the costs and benefits of a tradition that Christian teachers can and should assign authority to its tenets.

This strategy is not unique. We require people in all walks of life to demonstrate their ability to perform tasks—to work on our cars, do our taxes, or perform surgical procedures, for instance—before we give them authority over these tasks. The same is true for our moral responsibilities. True authority comes from those who have a firm grasp on reality and can demonstrate that fact.

For instance, educators can look at the life and philosophy of a man like Friedrich Nietzsche, who has come into higher regard as of late. We can look at his self-proclaimed "anti-Christ" or un-Christ philosophy and see what it has to offer and the results it produces in the lives of people who apply it. Or perhaps we might consider a world religion such as Buddhism, one of the world's great religions, which offers profound understandings of human dynamics in the Four Noble Truths and the Eightfold Path. Educators need to study and understand these human constructions as well as Christianity in order to compare and contrast them by the standards of accuracy and integrity. This needs to be done in every generation. This is part of learning. Therefore it is essential to have professional educators who are well trained and supervised when we engage these ideas.

When we do, there is nothing to fear from such investigations, since God is most certainly with us when we are actually *seeking the truth*. Ironically, the very intellectual movement that formed nearly all of the Western universities stems from the Judeo-Christian tradition. This was in large measure due to the idea that Christianity carried a vital body of knowledge that the world could engage and apply to good effect. Such intellectual inquiry has been done for millennia, can be done today, and needs to be done continually, prior to handing over the moral authority for guiding our lives. When we do this, as Jesus instructed us to do in "counting the costs" (Luke 14:26–33) or "doing our homework," we can be confident, but not arrogant or haughty, about the fact that *rightly applied* Christianity, when honestly compared with other religious or philosophical worldviews, in full view of all its flaws in application and interpretation, has a valid historical track record for producing the most beneficial and positive moral and ethical system for human life the world has yet known.[6]

This does not at all mean that other traditions have nothing to offer. There most definitely is much that is valuable and beneficial in many non-Christian traditions and in secular teachings. And Jesus is the sort of person who would want us to have the very best of everything—wherever it comes from—despite its "wrapper," shall we say. There is no contradiction in such a position. Likewise, neither is there anything untoward about humbly acknowledging that something is good and true even though it is a product of one's own tradition.

For instance, we can wholeheartedly celebrate the moral teachings of Jesus in Bonhoeffer's work *Ethics*.[7] Yet there is no benefit in breaking one's arm patting oneself on the back. There are many egregious wounds to atone for in the Christian tradition as well as in all religions. We must be thorough, critical, and reflective, which includes self-critique and self-reflection as well. When we are—if we also choose to be humble and fearless—history demonstrates that the teachings of Jesus on these matters hold their own.

TRAINING CHRISTIAN
PROFESSIONALS AND LEADERS

Now a word of special importance to Christian colleges and universities. As mentioned in the chapters on leadership, it is the responsibility of the "experts" who occupy positions in education—and specifically *Christian* higher education—to prepare those who choose this prophetic ministry to the church, nation, and world for effective execution of their special tasks. It is reasonable to expect that leading a divine conspiracy will require journalists, writers, artists, and scholars to carefully, accurately, and courageously expose the follies of our social institutions in government, business, religion, art, economics, engineering, medicine, law, finance, security, and education. This is where our Christian universities play perhaps the central role, if administrating the common flourishing is to occur in any meaningful way. Christian educators and scholars must begin to reconsider their specific area of study, their discipline, in light of the reality of Jesus and the characteristics required of citizens in his kingdom. Educators must ask what knowledge and skills our students will need to enter their world, as citizens of the kingdom of God and disciples of Christ, with the express intent of bringing common flourishing and benefit to those they either employ or serve. Can we imagine a day when our students create a business or open a practice and the fish symbol that shows on their business cards means more to nonbelievers than to believers?

Another significant issue on the topic of business and business leaders centers on the educational institutions in which our business leaders and professionals acquire their training. Business schools need to recognize and adopt into their academic programs the overwhelmingly accepted fact that personal, financial gain alone is not a sustainable objective that will continually provide meaning and significance in one's life or career. The university education has evolved into a training ground of higher employment opportunities, upward social mobility, and increased wealth. These are not vices in and of themselves. However, a Christian education should bring these motives and drives in line with the overarching mission of God to develop servant leaders and shepherds who are first seeking the benefits and blessings of others. It is important for schools, universities, and professional societies or training centers that influence and equip our current and future leaders to grasp and exemplify the unique reality and calling of the Christian professional. The university is the training ground for this essential character development and maturation.

When our students accept the call of a servant leader to further the cause of Christ, it is time to begin considering how they can escape the strictly Christian subculture in order to shine their lights of truth into the dark places in our world. This will take great care and wisdom. But this will also require just as much focus and attention on formation of Christlike character. Where and how is the Christian university or even the seminary assessing the increase in their students' ability to love their neighbor, live in peace, and express joy in all conditions? Christians who graduate from our universities must have attained infinitely more than the "credits" required to graduate. They must also be the type of individual *worthy* of the trust the public places in them as leaders and professionals. They must have more than knowledge of the good, the right, and the ethical. They must become good, righteous, and ethical people. What are the advantages of a so-called Christian education? What is the value of the esoteric body of knowledge specific to the Christian worldview and tradition if not to demonstrate, in any and every area of study, Christocentric answers to the four basic human questions mentioned earlier? This is the task of Christian higher education, and one that must be revived if the project of developing Christian leaders who are capable of leading toward the kind of *shalom* we all seek is to "bless the nations."

THE WORK OF CHRISTIAN INTELLECTUALS

Beyond the boundaries of our responsibilities to teach and train future generations of leaders, there is also a unique and invaluable position in our society for Christian intellectuals, who are often housed and supported in our educational institutions. There are several unappreciated advantages to the academic life, and to education, for Christians. Both faculty and students on the university campus often feel defensive regarding their Christian faith. First, there is no reason to be defensive. In fact, there is every reason to be appropriately proud of the Christian worldview. It is essential that Christian scholars and students in higher education be proud of and admire Jesus as an intellectual giant. Jesus would be today, and he was in his day, perfectly at home in any academic environment we could imagine. When we get past the Sunday school images and the cultural adaptations that melt away in what philosopher Paul Ricoeur describes as breaking free from the first naïveté,[8] which education plays a critical and beneficial role in allowing, then we can see Jesus as the genius he really was. It is essential for educators and students to realize that there was no one more at home in the halls of learning than Jesus of Nazareth. Once that mental shift occurs, then Christian intellectuals can begin to realize their beneficial position.

A second often overlooked advantage for Christian intellectuals is that they know why they are pursuing knowledge. Disciples of Jesus do not attempt to acquire knowledge in order to attain power or privilege or as a means to stroke the ego. Such clarity is a wonderful gift. Nor are Christ followers out to simply "make it big," in worldly terms. There is no desire or need to impress others. Nor is there a motive to make one's mark on the world, as that has come to be known. For Christians, all these self-centered motivations are as attractive as a two-by-four in the eye. Instead, Christian educators and students are simply in pursuit of God and learning of his ways in the world. Of course there are some utilitarian benefits, which are good and right in themselves. But this is not the purpose of acquiring knowledge. Instead, Christian intellectuals are there to serve the greater good in any way possible. And God is there to bless, encourage, and equip them to do that work to the best of their ability for his purposes and glory.

Finally, Christian intellectuals are advantaged in the pursuit of knowledge by the very fact that Christianity itself is a grand set of ideas based on a person. These ideas are profoundly simple yet world-changing. Christianity has and does compete at the very heart of every intellectual, philosophical, religious, political, scientific, and artistic inquiry. Jesus is very comfortable in the realms of Confucius, Joyce, Einstein, Monet, and Marx. Why? Paul says that in Jesus "are hidden all of the treasures of wisdom and knowledge" (Col. 2:3). This is who we must take into, or reintroduce and reintegrate within, our universities if we too want his knowledge and wisdom. Again, we reiterate here that Christian knowledge is good, and it is good for us, all of us. To categorically eliminate Jesus from the institutions of learning is to abjectly ignore this fact. Nor are Christian teachers and professors required to stand idly by as this continues, although at times we have participated in the segregation of science and faith. Faith integration programs in Christian educational institutions are a testament to this history. Nevertheless, Christian educators can and must remain humbly confident in their understanding of Jesus, to the point where they are willing and able to look their students in the face and propose that mastery of their field will remain elusive until they understand what Jesus has to offer on the subject.

The prophet Amos foresaw the problems in our educational system today and described them for us in stunning detail. It is no mistake how precisely we face what Amos faced within so many of our social structures and relations in contemporary life:

> The time is surely coming, declares the Lord God, when I will send a famine on the land; not a famine of bread, or a thirst for water, but of hearing the words of the LORD. They shall wander from sea to sea, and from north to east; they shall run to and fro, seeking the word of the LORD, but they shall not find it. In that

day the beautiful young women and the young men shall faint for thirst. (8:11–13)

As an answer to this famine of knowledge of the wisdom of God, consider the words of Jesus:

> "Why do you call me 'Lord, Lord,' and do not do what I tell you? I will show you what someone is like who comes to me, hears my words, and acts on them. That one is like a man building a house, who dug deep and laid the foundation on rock; when a flood arose, the river burst against that house but could not shake it, because it had been well built. But the one who hears and does not act is like a man who built a house on the ground without a foundation. When the river burst against it, immediately it fell, and great was the ruin of that house." (Luke 6:46–49)

> Then Jesus said to the Jews who had believed him, "If you continue in my word, you are truly my disciples; and you will know the truth, and the truth will make you free." (John 8:31–32)

We live in such a time as Amos predicted, when the Word of the Lord, the Logos of God—which can be understood as ultimate reason, rationality, logic, or the true depiction of ultimate reality—is not presented, recognized, or appreciated in society. One can find it if one looks, but the acknowledgment of the Word of the Lord is predominantly missing within the educational systems, venues, and institutions of public life.

Christian leaders in education must reassert, in appropriate, open, creative, and intelligent ways, how and why Jesus can be trusted as a source of knowledge who understands and has mastered the nature of history, anthropology, psychology, aesthetics, religion, and any other subject we care to engage with him. He is alive in all these arenas of intellectual life. Christians do not need to come into their fields of study at an angle. They simply need to seek to do good work—writing good poetry, composing good songs, taking good pictures, making good movies, painting good landscapes, engaging in good research, building good buildings, and so on. They don't write Christian songs, or compose Christian poetry, or do Christian research. They simply do good work and that is Christian work at its best, because Jesus is good and the testimony of good work done in concert with God's grace is unmistakably beyond what they could have accomplished by their own talents alone.

There is no reason to be bullied into a corner. Strength of character to face opposition can and will come from a settled understanding of the facts of Christian history, the reality of the risen Christ in his people, the function and purpose of Christ in human history, a view of eternity that gives one sufficient means to believe in the goodness of God, and the experiential knowledge that Jesus was the smartest person who ever lived. If these realities do not remain a vital part of what we learn, dwell on, and understand as true and good in our minds, it will be impossible to sustain any meaningful sense of ethics or moral behavior in our pursuit of truth and wisdom in our field of discipline. The consequences of this are now predominantly evident throughout most of Western civilization, the ultimate result of which is the inability to proclaim right from wrong, correct from incorrect, good from bad.

When our society is bereft of a theory of knowledge and becomes dominated by desire alone and the power contests that arise from such a condition, who better but the devoted students and teachers of a humbly brilliant rabbi can offer hope? Jesus brought the words of life, light, and love to a lost and broken people living day to day under the boot heel of the greatest, most advanced civilization of its time. And looking around, he said to all who had ears to hear, "Reconsider the way you live! Rethink what you've been thinking. For now the kingdom of God is available to you" (Matt. 4:17, paraphrased). Christian educators must think deeply about how that invitation pervades all arenas of human life and study.

Our society, today and in the future, rests in the hands of leaders who are proficient experts in both manifesting and passing on all the knowledge and truths from previous generations to future ones. There is no more sacred and essential calling. We desperately need a great Teacher, who is also a Good Shepherd, to teach us and lead us toward accomplishing these tasks. This is exactly what Jesus came to provide.

KNOWLEDGE AND EDUCATION

Discussion Questions for Chapter 9

1. Share with one another your educational or academic experience. Did you attend secular educational institutions, public or private, or were you in a religious educational setting? Do you think that the transfer of knowledge in your discipline and other subjects would be any different if you were to have received a different form of education? Give reasons for your answer.

2. Was your educational training aimed more toward helping you develop a skill set for a future career or toward developing your ability to "navigate the world" with the wisdom to engage life as it really is? If your education was primarily career-based, who helped you navigate the world with wisdom? Which teachers assisted you in navigating the world and what were their greatest qualities?

3. Willard and Black state that moral knowledge is inexorably linked to factual knowledge. Do you agree or disagree? Give reasons. What current issues in our society are creating tensions when people attempt to determine what is good and what is not? How has this affected your organization or congregation?

158 THE DIVINE CONSPIRACY CONTINUED

4. The authors argue that stubbornly holding on to inaccurate traditions and dogmas has caused the Christian church at large to lose much of its authority as a reliable source of knowledge within our secular society. What are the implications of this shift of authority in both secular and Christian educational institutions? Do you agree or disagree with the notion that there is a specific body of Christian knowledge?

5. Christian higher education implies that students should receive a Christian perspective on or understanding of every field of study. This is often called "faith integration" within the academy. Do you believe subjects like art, engineering, mathematics, or marketing can be taught or conveyed in ways that integrate Christian faith into the curriculum? Why or why not?

6. What if anything is wrong with the argument, "All I need to know is in the Bible"?

7. *Exercise:* Read through the Apostles' Creed:

I believe in God, the Father Almighty, Creator of heaven and earth.

I believe in Jesus Christ, his only Son, our Lord. He was conceived by the power of the Holy Spirit and born of the Virgin Mary. He suffered under Pontius Pilate, was crucified, died, and was buried. He descended to the dead. On the third day he rose again. He ascended into heaven and is seated at the right hand of the Father. He will come again to judge the living and the dead.

I believe in the Holy Spirit, the holy catholic church, the communion of saints, the forgiveness of sins, the resurrection of the body, and the life everlasting. Amen.

Do you believe these statements, or do you "profess" belief in these statements? What is the difference? Is there anything in these statements you do not believe? If so, why? What knowledge and truth does it contain for you, your faith community, and the world? How does this claim of truth and knowledge speak to the natural world, human beings, and the world to come?

CHAPTER 10

Economics and Politics

It is not our affluence, or our plumbing, or our
clogged freeways that grip the imagination of others.
Rather, it is the values upon which our system is built.
These values imply our adherence not only to liberty and
individual freedom, but also to international peace, law,
and order, and constructive social purposes. When we
depart from these values, we do so at our peril.

SENATOR J. WILLIAM FULBRIGHT

T HUS FAR WE have discussed the range and effect of moral
and ethical leadership required to lead a divine conspiracy to
overwhelm the systems of our world with good in the crucial area
of education. Now we must engage the leadership responsibilities, opportunities, and challenges in the arenas of economics and
politics. We are joining these two areas for one simple reason.
In the majority of our contemporary forms of liberal democracy,
some form of capitalism or free-market philosophy remains the
more dominate and widely supported economic and fiscal platform. Therefore, especially in the West, political freedom has
increasingly come to be indelibly attached to financial freedom.
In so many ways, both are, for better or worse, inseparable in
contemporary experience and thought. Therefore, it seems appro-

161

priate to discuss what an economy is and can be in concert with what the political arena must pursue, since there are significant overlapping interests and challenges in both political and economic life.

Further, we will consider what an economic and political vision would reasonably consist of in light of God's vision of *shalom*, life without either fear or want, which currently remain two of the most motivating and dominating aspects of contemporary economic and political existence. Here we will engage the subject of the nature of liberty in our current economic and political climate, the call to stewardship, the necessity of moral leadership in a representative democratic form of government, and finally the unique differences between a purely secular version and a Christocentric understanding of a thriving society.

LIBERTY

Liberty, or freedom, is a gift of God to humanity. Therefore we can call freedom "a good" and those things that perpetuate, protect, or instill freedom also can be considered good or beneficial. In comparison to other forms of governance and economic systems, political democracy and economic capitalism tend to promote human freedom. This is a verifiable reality that is demonstrated and evaluated in the facts and circumstances of the world around us. Of course there are many varieties of democracy and capitalism, some of which are practiced or applied in ways that work against human freedom. Yet on the whole, in full view of all their setbacks and pitfalls, liberal democratic governments and capitalistic economies tend to provide better standards of holistic living and human flourishing than the current alternatives.

As a result, over the past three hundred years there has been an overwhelming social revolution surrounding individualism that has dramatically shifted the ideals and means by which our

Western democratic forms of government are conceived of and operate. A significant part of what lies behind the inability to have a basis for public knowledge of moral truth discussed earlier is a direct result of the unmitigated, obsessive drive in the Western consciousness for liberty and freedom. The Western ambition to be free has become the ultimate virtue in modern history. A significant aspect of that enterprise has coalesced with individualism. What was once the "right" to life, liberty, and the pursuit of happiness has now been interpreted as an edict enabling and protecting one's "right" to do what one wants. What has evolved in this modern sense of liberation is the expectation that "no one has the right to stand in my way or thwart my will by telling me I'm wrong." Thus, a deep resistance has been built in the liberal mind-set against others imposing "beliefs" about right and wrong on "me," especially if it inhibits or limits "my personal desire, or 'right,' to do what I want."

Of course this has little or nothing to do with liberal or conservative political views. We are using the term "liberal" here in the sense used in the sentence, "The United States is a liberal democracy," meaning a form of government founded on the principle of "freedom for all." Consequently, doing what one wants to do has come to be thought of as an unrestricted good. To test this thesis, visit any third-grade classroom in the United States and ask the children to respond to the question of whether or not everyone should be allowed to do what they want to do. In unison they will all scream, "Of course!" To such a blinding obsession, commitment, and empowerment of personal freedom, the constraints of morality, which unapologetically restrict this view of personal freedom, can't hold a candle.

As another thought experiment, think about life in Singapore, for example. This is not a "free" country as we think of political freedom today. And because it is not free (liberated), the government has no difficulty telling its citizens what will be enforced as right and wrong. As a result an overwhelming percentage follow along. So the point here is not that Singapore is a shining example of morality or a democratic form of governance. It is not the case that eliminating freedom increases morality. This is impossible, since freedom is a virtue. The point is that freedom and morality are often at odds, especially if the human will is not set on achieving a moral end. However, if the human will remains set on achieving moral ends, freedom and morality become interdependent, since the moral will cannot pursue worthy intentions without the freedom to do so.

In addition to the concepts of freedom and liberty, any discussion of our social governance must include our economic concerns. Several Christian parachurch organizations and nonprofit foundations have sprung up that are deeply concerned about the moral foundations of prosperity and the economic structure of our society in general. These groups are too numerous to be listed here. Yet many are doing crucial work in reconsidering our Christian understandings of global economic, political, and social issues. Clearly, such research, thinking, and planning must be—if they are to lead to a flourishing life for individuals and groups through our economic and political systems—guided by an appropriate vision of what is good and right in these key areas.

This is precisely due to the inescapable fact that economic, political, and social systems are inherently moral realities. We must remember that democracy and capitalism, for example, are not automatically good social structures and institutions. These systems are good only if those persons who govern, use, direct, and support the proliferation of these systems are good as well. By this we mean that, among other things, these systems will not be successful for the beneficial purposes of society, government, and the individual unless those who create and oversee the mechanisms by which these systems function intentionally incorporate basic moral values into their undergirding structural integrity. Only then can our governmental and economic systems spawn appropriate, beneficial goals and means of attaining those goals for the public welfare.

STEWARDSHIP

God certainly maintains great interest in all human enterprise. The scriptures support the concept of understanding economic, social, religious, and political responsibilities as that of *steward-ship*. Stewards work both for God and for the benefit of everyone involved. One difficulty for us in contemporary life is the limited use of our words and a lack of understanding regarding their historical definitions and reach. This is true for our current use of the words "economy" and "steward," and therefore it is critical to distinguish and more accurately define each.[1]

Our economy is a much more sophisticated phenomenon than we are often led to believe. Economies are much broader and deeper social systems than what we typically hear about on the evening news regarding the number of jobs lost or gained, the increase or decrease in interest rates from central banks, the level of taxation, or the degree of consumer confidence in any given quarter. An economy is holistically defined as the system in which the "goods" and "services" that human beings—within a certain location—regard as necessary for life and living are created and exchanged.[2] This includes, but is not exclusive to the interest and scope of influence related to our governments.

Another misconception about economic matters is the idea that economics is limited to money matters or governmental fiscal policy. Though today there is a tendency for the news media and political leaders to focus on these topics, in fact economists pursue questions such as how people live together; what is regarded as acceptable housing; how we think about and practice education, warfare, or national security; and the freedom needed to live our lives and make essential decisions on a multitude of social, famil-ial, and personal issues. These and many other activities involve some exchange of goods, services, protections, legal agreements, and relational arrangements, all of which amount to much more than money, fiscal policy, or trade agreements between nations.

Economists are in a crucial professional leadership position in our world today and stand in a unique position to offer us information much more valuable than the direction the stock market will likely take over the next fiscal quarter. As a society we should look to the field of economics to assist us in grasping a broad vision of what "rules and customs" we consciously and often unconsciously apply in our family life, communities, nations, and world. Such "insider information" is both necessary and wonderfully beneficial.

Additionally, a major objective in free (liberal) democratic societies such as the United States has been for individuals, families, and groups to attain and maintain the liberty required for self-determination. Such independence has historically been tied to and included self-supporting economic sufficiency. This is why economic freedom—living independently of outside resources—has become increasingly tied to political freedom.

Obviously there will be those who require assistance from the community and are dependent in some ways for their well-being or "welfare" on others. To respond to this is the nature of mercy. Acts of mercy attempt to ameliorate the exceptional tragedies of life that overwhelm people's resources, both material and spiritual. This is not a state to which we aspire, and so often we can become increasingly vulnerable to abuse when overcome by our circumstances. With those who are literally "at our mercy," great attention and care must be given to every act of kindness in order to protect and encourage the return of dignity and love of self that can become so easily disoriented in the pain and suffering of loss.

We make this point here simply to illustrate how the classical idea of an economy includes complex interactive ends and processes that require proper (intelligent) arrangement and direction. Such oversight and care are contained in the New Testament concept of stewardship. Following the principles of modern stewardship is also necessary for both economic and political leaders as they discern the priorities and fiscal policies that work for the good of the economy, which then impacts the common welfare of individual participants. These are matters of judgment that require wisdom and experience in order for our social systems to work best. Once again we see how wise discernment is essential for making sure that our social organizations, most especially our governments, are seeking everyone's advantage rather than furthering the bureaucratic ends of the system as a whole.

An economy, whether global or local, has many connections and relations. The diversity of modern economies is staggering. Interests and expertise are many and varied. The components are as diffuse as the production and distribution of the energy required to power our utilities, to the behavior of the local credit union, which is connected to a worldwide monetary system, to the laws we enforce or ignore, to the transportation systems of our highways and airports, even to the institutions of higher learning that set the course for the skills and education required to engage all these issues in the first place. All of these topics and areas of economic and political life carry their own special delicate and esoteric considerations that together create the environment in which we attempt to live and prosper as individuals and families, from generation to generation.

WHEN CITIES CRUMBLE

Thus leadership ethics, competency, and moral courage are inseparable qualities in our economic and political leaders. When these qualities are lost, there is often a plague of suffering and loss that is staggering in scope. It may seem odd, at first, to consider the analogy of addiction as a means of describing what occurs when economic and political leaders fail in these responsibilities. However, at the individual human level, the case of the addict provides a simple illustration of what can occur when there is a massive failure to wisely and intelligently govern, prioritize, and subordinate individual desires for the person's best interests. We know and experience that such failures, as painful as they may be, are unfortunately not limited to the individual. The failures of addiction are regularly witnessed all around us on a global scale as well. We routinely see and feel the effects of the costly consequences of imprudent and unwise decisions in individuals, but also in groups, economic sectors, and nations. When an entity, whether public or private, becomes obsessed or consumed by an idea, motivation, or desire that disrupts our economic and political systems, chaos eventually overtakes the order necessary to protect the range of values and needs that characterize the well-being of a population.

This was the case at the middle of the past century with Fascism and Communism, but it also can happen within capitalist contexts as well. The nineteenth-century "robber barons" are a case in point. Perhaps some may even consider the financial meltdown and mortgage bailout as equivalent examples. That political, economic, and financial analysts consider boom-and-bust cycles predictable and normative and that elected officials seem impotent to reverse the damage their decisions and policies affect only highlight the presence of a binge-and-purge mentality, which is indicative of the very addictive behaviors of instant self-gratification, consumerism, greed, and lust for power and position that are threatening to overwhelm our local, state, national, and even global economic and political systems.

DEMOCRATIZING GOOD?

The democratic ideal, starting from its earliest days in ancient Greece through the ages down to our present circumstances, is both a beautiful and a problematic means of governance. It is beautiful because it considers the individual will worthy of determining the direction and objective of corporate life. Democracy is problematic precisely because of the potential for individuals to utilize their power of self-determination in social and govern-mental decisions toward self-destructive ends. Thus, from the earliest discussions regarding democratic ideals, leaders under-stood such power must be regulated by moral constraints. Listen-ing to the running commentary on current political affairs today, we get the impression that democracy and mobocracy are inching ever closer, appearing at times to be identical twins.

How democracies are to function properly in the labyrinth of mass freedom is where the early twentieth-century political phi-losopher John Dewey starts his query. How does a democratic society pursue and achieve a culture where truth, beauty, and goodness are of premier value? Dewey's context is crucial to his conclusion. Written in 1927, *The Public and Its Problems* came at a time when the Unites States was a deeply troubled society with worse times just ahead. Progressivism, for which Dewey was something of a prophet, was struggling to solve harrowing social situations still left unresolved after the Civil War. Great adapta-tions and the effects of modern industrialization produced amaz-ing advancements, yet with them came hard economic and labor conditions and a massive influx of European immigration.[3]

Dewey realized what lay at the heart of classic American lib-eralism, or the focus of a liberal society: the need to ensure that all its citizens are equally free to realize their potential.[4] This specifically required the release of the individual from the bonds of the outdated restrictions and requirements of existing institu-tions. What follows is the obvious dilemma of determining and defining *which* individuals are to be released to realize exactly *what* potential. Obviously not all potentialities can be realized. Burning a flag may be at the margins of acceptability for some, but setting off a bomb is not. Some capacities are inconsistent with or contradictory to others. Some individuals or groups only realize their potential at the expense of others. How are these conflicts mediated? There is a difference between realizing com-mon well-being and fulfilling a desire to "have it my way." People often desire what is not good and, as a result, can reduce or even destroy their own potential.

It is at this point that Dewey's concern with the "eclipse" of the public becomes relevant. How is the public to perceive what is happening, and what is best for a social system of the size and dimensions we now experience? Dewey concluded that the "Great Society" had not yet developed into a "Great Community." So how is the public to be enabled and encouraged to act wisely on its own behalf? This is the perennial—and currently unresolved—problem of any democracy.

The issues are further complicated by conflicting concepts of liberty or freedom that turn out to underlie three quite different ideas or beliefs about democratic citizenry:

I am "free" only if no one is "telling me what to do" or preventing me from *doing* what I *want.*

I am "free" only if I am actually able to *achieve* what I *want* to achieve.

I am "free" only if I am able to *achieve* what is *good*, and that which is most conducive to the fullness of my life or the realization of my potential toward the highest and best result.

Philosopher T. H. Green has famously described this third version of freedom as "a positive power or capacity of doing or enjoying something worth doing or enjoying, and that, too, something that we do or enjoy in common with others. We mean by it a power which each man exercises through the help or security given him by his fellow-men, and which he in turn helps to secure for them."[5]

TWO VIEWS OF SHALOM

In modern democratic societies the economic and political systems, traditions, and practices, at whatever level, *must* be evaluated by reference to the freedom to pursue human flourishing or well-being; and it is at this point that serious issues have arisen for Christian leaders, spokespersons, and professionals in dealing with current social, economic, and political issues. For students of Jesus and his teaching, what is understood as a revolution of goodwill and the good life is often radically different from the distinctly non-Christian or strictly secular points of view on human flourishing and progress.

It is not an easy matter to characterize such "natural" conditions of well-being or flourishing or the point at which one passes into and out of the myopia of materialism. This makes it difficult, but not impossible, to conceive of arrangements, in what we today think of as "the economy" that would secure, or tend to secure, a population in such favorable conditions. It is easier to work from the other end of the scale, where people clearly lack well-being and certainly are not flourishing; and that is what we nearly always do. Franklin D. Roosevelt—who formulated for government attention much of what is treated today as "welfare"—spoke of a large population in the United States of his times who were ill-housed, ill-clad, and malnourished. These dire conditions, which in many cases are clearly identifiable, require immediate remedies. Surely some reasonable action can and must be undertaken with regard to these bare necessities required for human existence for those unable to maintain them for themselves. In his eleventh State of the Union address (January 11, 1944), FDR proposed such action.

It came in the form of a "second Bill of Rights" that would undergird "economic security, social security, moral security" for all. "Essential to peace is a decent standard of living for all individuals," Roosevelt declared, and "freedom from fear is eternally linked with freedom from want."[6] In spite of strong opposition from some at the time, FDR held that a country should extend guarantees of minimal social and economic security to all its inhabitants. Americans supported creating such a "safety net," which included "a useful and remunerative job," fair (legally regulated) business practices, a decent home for every family, adequate medical care, protection from the economic fears of old age, sickness, accident, and unemployment, and a good education. Eventually the language of a "net" transitioned into a "right" or an entitlement, which is the common terminology today. All this would, at minimum, provide a framework for a flourishing life—a life of well-being—*without God*. This increasingly explicit secularism (legal, social, political) of the last half of the twentieth century might be reasonably seen as a natural expression of the "discovery" that general human prospering can be provided for in strictly human terms.

We especially want to reject the idea that there is this relatively self-contained system called "the economy" or "the state" that runs on laws that can be discovered by clever people and manipulated in such a way that the system produces human well-being (general welfare) all by itself. There is no invisible hand, divine or otherwise, that winds the clock of an economy or government that can be trusted to produce exactly what we want the way we want it. Some seem to think that if we tinker with the economic/governmental vending machine long enough, if we can produce the right legislation or the right experts in positions to guide governmental action or inaction or shift emphasis into one area from another, we will eventually be able to create the appropriate "conditions" and out will pop our intended aim. Of course there are endless propositions for how to tinker the "right" way. Some argue for low inflation with fair and mild taxation, others emphasize care for the needy, while still others create program after program offering great opportunities for upward mobility. Yet all of these interest groups preach that prosperity will flood the land and people's pocketbooks, if and when their specific proposals come full circle.

Yet such God-less, or secular, answers to the questions of political governance and economic flourishing in a democratic state are precisely the problems significant philosophers and thinkers such as John Dewey, Jean-Jacques Rousseau, C. B. Macpherson, John Mill, and John Stuart Mill have spilled much ink over. Each in his own way wrestles with the idea of American democracy and how and where it is supposed that the "people" should rule. Again the question that remains at the forefront for consideration here is: What is the best thing to do? What is the good we should pursue as a society and how can Christians add unique perspectives and wisdom to bring this about?

The assumption from the experience of the United States of America is that (a) the better society is one that provides the greatest amount of freedom or liberty to its citizens, and that (b) the society that provides the greatest amount of liberty to its citizens is one that supports and defends democracy. Here the term "democracy" refers to the appointing of officials of the state—and possibly of other social groupings as well—through periodic elections, mandated and enforced by the will of the *demos,* the public. It is presumed that the individuals standing for office (officials) are voted for (or against) on the basis of the public policies they intend to implement if empowered by the majority. Therefore, the democratic answer to governance is to place this responsibility onto the shoulders of the masses to express their will through the vote. As a result, the franchise[7] of suffrage (voting) lies at the heart of democracy, although "just" voting leaves much still to be determined and is part of the reason why democracy has acquired a fairly tumultuous reputation.

The language of philosopher Thomas Hobbes about human "felicity" pretty well captures the difficulties in the secular, American democratic proposal for human flourishing. He states that the happiness "of this life consisteth not in the repose of a mind satisfied." Instead, for the modern citizen, "Felicity is a continual progress of desire, from one object to another, the attaining of the former being still but the way to the latter."[8] And the more one gets, Hobbes acutely observes, the more one strives to

secure the possession of what one already has. As a result he finds
a general inclination within all humanity: "a perpetual and restless desire of power after power, that ceaseth only in death."[9] The
verifiable accuracy of Hobbes' description of humanity's broken
condition should at least cause us to pause and think more deeply
about the inherent hazards of directly combining a "restless desire
of power after power" with the ballot booth. However, for the
democratic secularist, there is simply no other acceptable foundational means of pursuing corporate well-being and flourishing.

It is at this point where Dewey's perspective of American
democracy becomes so crucial. In the context of pre–Depression
era American life, Dewey argued the public could not see itself
or what to do about its problems. Again this is an age-old issue,
since no human beings have ever possessed the answers that
solved their own problems. For Dewey's generation the public
problems were many and varied. They faced high unemployment,
a failed educational system, and no health care for the majority of
people. All of these issues depended, then as now, upon a full and
proper examination of the facts of the situations at hand. Dewey
knew it would not be helpful to pursue these issues from ideolog-
ically driven platforms of established opinions (i.e., conservative,
liberal, etc.), where interest group–sponsored legislation favors a
particular beneficial outcome for interested parties.

Dewey argued the primary problem of the public was found in
the essence of those consequences that calls the public into being
in the first place. He understood that all the facts and circumstances that create public problems lie deeper in the social fab-
ric than those who are charged with producing solutions to these
problems can either understand or articulate.[10] Furthermore,
the "state" is a body of rules and officials that exists to care for
the interests of the public. The "essential problem" for the public is generated by the very existence of government. Somehow,
in a democracy, the public is to appoint leaders to discern and
then overcome, through processes and arrangements, the means

by which these same individuals will prevent themselves from "advancing their own interests at the expense of the ruled."[11] This disastrous irony creates an almost impassable "barrier to effective democracy," because of the "impossibility of perception of consequences by the people affected and communicating about them."[12] In summary, Dewey suggested the first problem was that majority rule and self-governance do not ensure good governance. Democracy is only good if the public is good. If self-interest and selfish desire rule the public will, how can the common good or general welfare be assured?

Surely we need something less unstable than human desire on which to build either our lives or our societies in seeking the level of flourishing indicative of life under the direction of a good and loving God. Desire, whether of an individual or of a group, is variable, conflicted, limitless, and routinely deceitful. It does not remain the same, but is highly volatile and therefore unpredictable. Then there are always desires, in the individual or group, that are incompatible and given to competition and domination. Desire also, as Hobbes insisted, never comes to a final rest in satisfaction. "More" is always desired. The moving sands of desire are deceitful because they promise rest in satisfaction "if only" or "only when" more of what is desired becomes attained. Such is the nature of the endless spiral of covetousness.

We have encoded constraints to pure desire in our laws. However, we have witnessed for centuries now how even the Constitution changes under the impact of the desires of interest groups and sophisticated theories of linguistic meaning that are no longer constrained by old-fashioned logic. Once even the shadow of good has faded, nothing is left but the drive to win, and the desires that "win out" will rule the day, and with them whatever consequences follow. Similarly, the morality of our laws is disappearing under the impact of desire. Nietzsche accurately prophesied the "will to power" motivation would grow and flourish long before it institutionalized itself broadly throughout the Western cultural consciousness. Even the Judeo-Christian "shadow" is now on the verge of disappearing as a public resource for legal morality.

The writer of James understands this tension as well when he asks, "Those conflicts and disputes among you, where do they come from?" The answer: from the pleasures and lusts hidden in unbridled desire (4:1–2). As T. S. Eliot recognized decades ago, the secular mind is "looking for a system so perfect that we will not have to be good."[13] But such a system is not going to rise from nothing. There is no autopilot "answer" of that sort for the problems we face today. Spokespersons for Christ and those leaders who are disciples of Jesus, in every area of our economic and political systems, need to repeat the poignancy of Eliot's insight often and with emphasis. Only then can we deal realistically with the human condition. A "good life" requires much more than favorable economic or political conditions, because such a life is most certainly not accomplished as a result of human ingenuity.

A CHRISTIAN PERSPECTIVE ON WELL-BEING

After briefly considering some of the key difficulties of pursuing well-being from a strictly secular point of view, we now must consider a scriptural understanding of these subjects as a counterpoint. Of course there are many non-Christian viewpoints other than secularism, but perhaps nothing accentuates the Christian perspective in contrast to other worldviews weighing in on these matters more clearly than Jesus's illustrations of the "blessings" and their corresponding "woes" (Matt. 5:3–12; Luke 6:20–26). Well-being (in its upper levels, flourishing) for secularists or nonbelievers is routinely conveyed as the satisfaction of natural desires received mainly through the body and social relationships. Moreover, this satisfaction is to be achieved through normal human abilities, applied in a community. "'What will we eat?' or 'What will we drink?' or 'What will we wear?'" mark the range of individual objectives Jesus mentioned (Matt. 6:31) for those (the "Gentiles") who do not find or situate their life in the kingdom of God. Of course the natural desires of the "flesh" are considerably more complicated than this brief list might suggest. The apostle John in his First Letter clarifies what makes up the "world" (socially/historically organized human abilities) and its intensive desires (2:16). John lists the world's priorities in terms of "lusts" (NASB, KJV, RSV). These compulsions include the "lust of the flesh" (the will to satisfy bodily appetites), the "lust of the eyes" (the will to covet possessions of others and be perceived in a favorable light), and the "pride of life" (the will to power, domination, or ascendency over others).

These and other thoughts and desires of the same sort make up what Paul calls "the mind of the flesh" (Rom. 8:6) and "the works of the flesh" (Gal. 5:19). Paul's basic conception of the "flesh" here is that of a life lived entirely by means of unaided human powers and intelligence. To be "well-off" in this sort of life is be humanly secure in the satisfaction of the desires that rule one's existence. To "flourish" under these conditions would be to satisfy more of these desires in ever increasing degrees. In contemporary life the secular vision of well-being has taken the mind of the flesh toward a materialistic end. In a capitalist system, consumerism becomes the delivery method for the materialist addiction. The apostle Paul's assessment of the materialist craving resulted in the stern warning that death and corruption were certain to follow (Rom. 8:6; Eph. 2:3; Gal. 6:8).

The secular conceptions of well-being and the common good are noticeably different from the traditional view of human flourishing in history, throughout the scriptures, and in the literature and practices of the Christian church through the ages. The Christian view of human well-being and flourishing necessitates the action of two *nonhuman* elements. The first requirement is the actual *presence* of a living, acting God in human life, both corporate and individual. The second is awareness of and dependence on the *provisions* (including material provisions) that come from God, that originate outside of the limits of normal human efforts and/or natural events (Phil. 4:19).

The connection of these two elements is conspicuously and abundantly touted in both the Hebrew and New Testament accounts of God's dealings with humanity. Again, one of the most helpful discourses on these aspects of God's care is found in Psalm 23. The opening words of the psalm, "The Lord is my shepherd, I shall not want," express the two essential elements of the flourishing life in the biblical and Christian view: the presence of God as overseer, protector, and guide, which results in the utter lack of any unfulfilled need. Taken by itself, however, this psalm may give a false impression of the well-being that comes with life in God. Other passages in the Bible describe a life of well-being that does *not* include such a heavy emphasis upon the abundance of material provision. These passages better clarify the adequacy for human well-being of God's presence and care, even in circumstances where desirable provisions of the usual sort are indeed in short supply or even totally absent. Habakkuk 3:17–19, previously referenced in Chapter 2, is one such example. In fact, much of Israel's history after the reigns of David and Solomon, which includes the ministry of Jesus and the first-century church, stands in contradiction to the "name it and claim it" message that is now part and parcel of much of mainstream Christian teaching and preaching.

Although cases of well-being during periods of extreme deprivation are covered, the scriptural texts usually present a life in which people have adequate material provisions while remaining freed from greed and the obsession with material goods—"freed" because of the presence of the kingdom of God "at hand" and always in action. Jesus's summary statement on this is found in Matthew 6:33: "But strive first for the kingdom of God and his righteousness, and all these things [including material needs] will be given to you as well" (see also Josh. 1:8; Ps. 1). This is a point made repeatedly and applied in numerous ways in Jesus's teaching and in the lifestyle he himself lived and taught to his disciples.

God's intent for us, according to Paul, is that our leaders should rule well and "that we may lead a quiet and peaceable life in all godliness and dignity" (1 Tim. 2:2). Contentment with what one currently has in the active presence of God becomes a major emphasis in the New Testament writings. Paul's astonishing statements in Philippians 4—especially given the harsh conditions in which he found himself at the time of writing, which continued for most of his ministry—expresses the understanding of and attitude about "flourishing" that was part of the disciples' way of living in the earliest phase of the Christian movement and continued through most of the following century. Paul said:

> I have learned to be content with whatever I have. I know what it
> is to have little, and I know what it is to have plenty. In any and
> all circumstances I have learned the secret of being well-fed and
> of going hungry, of having plenty and of being in need. I can do
> all things through him who strengthens me. (4:11–13)

Elsewhere Paul states, "Of course, there is great gain in godliness combined with contentment; for we brought nothing into the world, so that we can take nothing out of it; but if we have food and clothing, we will be content with these" (1 Tim. 6:6–8). Yet again the New Testament tells us: "Keep your lives free from the love of money, and be content with what you have; for he has said, 'I will never leave you or forsake you'" (Heb. 13:5).

We suggest here that a scriptural perspective on the good life, experienced in a public setting by ordinary people under normal conditions, would allow individuals to engage in productive living (with a job), with adequate resources to meet the basic needs of life, with reasonable assurance of physical security, and with a reasonable hope for attaining familiar human objectives, given appropriate application of their talents, thoughts, and efforts. Generally speaking, individuals abiding in such circumstances would be able to lead useful and happy lives, finding contentment with their lot, even though those lives might be far from perfect. It is unwise to suggest that a condition of the good life is the attainment of—or even the opportunity to—"make it big" as we say. Though of course some might do just that. Nor should we expect that people could flourish without appropriate, intelligent effort or without the assistance of individuals around them (family, friends, acquaintances) who willingly contribute to their lives.

The key issue at hand here is that, in such a situation, the "good life" can be enjoyed while many wants and perhaps some needs go unsatisfied. Utopia is not the objective, despite what political campaign advertisements and product marketers try to fool us into believing—the passage of a particular piece of legislation or the purchase of a particular brand of electric razor or cleaning solution will not create some sort of total bliss. While these things might make some contribution, it is crucial to understand that the environment required for the "good life" is not something that can be acquired or manufactured that easily.

The basic characterization of the teachings and witness of Christian history reveals a certain radical independence from the drive to satisfy those natural desires on which the secular perspective of well-being rests. Still, the overall outlook of Jesus, Paul, and the Bible on "secular" human values is not one of rejection, but of subordination. The material goods Roosevelt sought to provide during the Great Depression, such as food, housing, and clothing, for example, are not rejected from a godly life, yet they do not and shall not control us. The same is true for all "natural" desires and their satisfactions. We are neither to serve "mammon" nor to fear material wealth, power, and possessions. Instead, we are to use them as tools for good ends in devotion to God (Luke 16:9; 1 Tim. 6:17–19).

Moreover, such a state of well-being is only possible for those who have sources of supply and contentment *beyond* what is attainable by human efforts alone and hence are free of bondage to any government, policy, economic downturn, or financial boom. The material conditions of life are simply included in all the other "things" that shall be added to us after we have sought "first the kingdom of God and his *dikaiosune* (the ability to both know and do the right thing)" (Matt. 6:33).

Consequently, flourishing without God compared to flourishing with God, or even simple well-being in the two cases, yields two very different versions of "success." For both secularists and Christians, "success" is the label used for a positive evaluation of human arrangements and activities, especially those that make up our economy. One might think that Christian spokespersons, out of mere love of God and neighbor, would desire to be deeply involved in understanding these two versions of human flourishing and in having a say about the wisdom or foolishness of various economic plans and practices or socially prevailing political attitudes and institutions that might come up for consideration. Christians must be involved in the discussions and debates that determine what measures are used to best define what we call "success."

Even still, we must realize and concede that flourishing, despite our best intentions and plans, is not something that can be produced *for* people generally, though some provisions for "general welfare" can and must be made. The general welfare can be destroyed through the application of foolish policies and actions just as easily as a hurricane rips over a storm wall. But flourishing is also essentially a matter of the character of the people involved. Augustine says in his *Rule:* "Those who have the strength to lead simple lives should consider themselves the richest of people. For it is better to be able to make do with a little than to have plenty."[14] What an idea! The character of people in a population is hugely determinative of precisely how well-off they are and therefore whether or not their society flourishes.

Some dimensions of general welfare or flourishing can perhaps be quantified and dealt with abstractly and externally. It remains essential to realize that two people in the same material conditions may not have an equally "good life," be equal in welfare, or experience the same quality of well-being. This is due to their attitudes and understandings and especially their human relationships. Two lives identical in material wealth may remain quite disparate as far as human flourishing is concerned. Fifty dollars in the hand of an intemperate or ignorant person is *not* equal, as far as overall flourishing is concerned, to fifty dollars in the hand of a wise and virtuous person living within a network of sensible friends and relatives. Perhaps the disparity grows as the dollar amount increases. A "safety net" is one thing, and a "net" in some measure might be provided to a population so long as the money or credit lasts. However, well-being, or a flourishing life, is quite another thing and cannot be handed out, provided, legislated, or mandated to anyone in general.

We hearken back to the biblical role of the prophet as one that must be reconsidered within contemporary political life when seeking to envision our world in a way that God's good will can be done on earth as it is in heaven. Christian leaders and spokespersons should always be learning from these prophetic experts in every area of life, wherever and however they surface. We must be willing and able to gain the appropriate knowledge and insight from these wise and courageous individuals despite their sociopolitical or religious pedigree.

However, the point here is to focus specifically on the role Christians play as prophetic leaders and professionals who are called and equipped by God to teach and lead in both public and private life in order to bring an understanding of what is good and what is possible for human beings. Such wisdom and insight consistently fall beyond the reach of mere secular analysis of human desires and abilities. Ironically, however, such wisdom can be tested and validated by *a strictly secular study* of our world. For instance, we must deepen our study of the degree to which qualities like loving action, patience, or thankfulness contribute toward positive change in our individual and communal lives. In large measure this is what the Greater Good Science Center at the University of California, Berkeley—in collaboration with the University of California, Davis—is attempting to accomplish.[15] Funded by a $5.6 million grant from the John Templeton Foundation, the center states its goals with regard to gratitude as:

Expand the scientific database of gratitude, particularly in the key areas of human health, personal and relational well-being, and developmental science;

Promote evidence-based practices of gratitude in medical, educational, and organizational settings and in schools, workplaces, homes and communities; and in so doing . . .

Engage the public in a larger cultural conversation about the role of gratitude in civil society.

Similarly, it would be appropriate, and perhaps enlightening, for Christian leaders and professionals to address the broader public with the meaning and application of what can be learned in a comparison of the secular and Christian perspectives on, and designs for, human flourishing.

WELL-BEING IN COMMON

If life on earth is to progress ever closer to what is experienced in the presence of God in the heavens, then we must move closer in our abilities to live in harmony and peace with one another. Perhaps John 17 is a picture of the sense of community and relational wholeness or *shalom* Jesus describes, envisions, prays for, and even longs to accomplish. One of the most important aspects of Christian well-being (and flourishing) is its fundamentally *relational* or communal nature. That is, Christian flourishing is connected to our relations to other persons (beginning with God) and encompasses the people with whom we share our most intimate and abiding relations. These are our "neighbors," but modern usage has robbed this word of some of its most important meanings. The first and most primary reference is to our family members and those we are closely engaged with in living a common, collective life.

One cannot place a monetary value upon relations to the people most near to us, and these relations cannot be adequately dealt with by government action or social agencies in the ordinary sense. Such relations are loaded with factors of inspiration, creation, production, and exchange. But when these relations are ruined—especially between spouses or between parents and children—human flourishing becomes deeply impaired. "Welfare" then becomes a cloudy and confused condition that spreads like plague when people begin to search for substitutes to these indispensable human relations. There are none. This leaves the lonely individual desperately trying to fill this void by pursuing "the desires of the flesh, the desires of the eyes, and the pride of life." Flourishing for such a person devolves into a desperate search for some degree of satisfaction for these "desires." Too often this pursuit leads to addictive reliance on food, sex, drugs, money, power, relational co-dependency, fame, or something else to fill "the God-shaped vacuum" Blaise Pascal so poetically described.

The Great Commandment (Mark 12:33) by contrast directs us to first love God with every aspect of our being and to love our neighbor as we love ourselves. Finding well-being or a flourishing existence in such a condition is much less difficult than in the secular proposal. Love is not an abstraction. Christians must be continually reminded to resist making love intangible or primarily theoretical. God's kind of love must remain vital, concrete, positive, and practical. *Agape* is devoted to seeking the good of the person loved. It can and must occupy and energize our lives.

We have never known a person genuinely devoted to serving God and others from an *agape*-centered worldview to have a problem discerning the "meaning of life." To love God with divine love is to be constantly seeking to do, and be involved in, what is good, to and for God, which is also to be simultaneously committed to the good of our "neighbors." This is why each of the Ten Commandments conveys key relational dynamics that provide common benefits to the individual as well as the community. This becomes more obvious when Jesus teaches that the internalization of these laws or ways sets us free to live life at its fullest (Matt. 5–7). This comes when the ways of God are written, or imprinted, on the heart, the motivational centerpiece of human life.

Jesus reminds us that the first and most important of our "neighbors" live in our own home. The first common life we live in relationship is with our parents, and that is one reason parental honor takes primacy in the human part of God's "Top Ten" list. The command to honor our parents is also the only command directly associated with a promise of long life. Our relationship with our parents deeply determines what our life will amount to. When we marry, our closest neighbor becomes our spouse, with whom we "become one." This is a relationship that becomes even closer than with a parent.

The rest of the Ten Commandments concern not harming those with whom we share a common life and whom we may from time to time be tempted to offend. "Thou shalt not covet" is a very interesting and important case in point. We often covet what we can see, and what we can see we are in close proximity to.

Each of these relational commands is primarily concerned with protecting what C. S. Lewis called "the weight of glory" that is bestowed by God in every ordinary person.[16] This is the common blessing of the *imago Dei*, or the image of God, in every person who has ever lived. To miss the keys of these relational directives is to miss living in relationships to their upmost potential intended by God and risk enduring a deprived existence locked into a life of "quiet desperation," of which Henry David Thoreau so famously spoke.[17] The inability to relate to others slides into many forms of dysfunction and pain. To provide true well-being, much less a flourishing life, for such wounded people is often a daunting if not impossible task. In many cases healing requires an endless and expensive sequence of external goods—which nevertheless too often fail to achieve their primary objective.

With all its problems, however, desire can serve humanity well if it is governed by the presence of a larger framework containing ideas of what is good. The Christian perspective on well-being provides precisely that. Desire is controlled by the power of self-denial. The ability to resist or postpone gratification, if need be, in deference to what is good and to place desires in their order of genuine importance is an inestimable gift of Christian virtue. Desire, without some outside principle of good, will always degenerate into power contests. Desire is inherently conflictual, both within the individual and between persons and groups. There are always a number of desires in play, and a desire, merely as such, is no indicator of what is good or what is best. What is not good or right is often desired.

Secularism now has a track record in dealing with desire, and it has not succeeded in finding a way for public institutions and figures to say no to desire. The ultimate court of appeal then becomes legal or political power given over to the judiciary, the legislature, and finally political campaigns. In such contexts, winning has become the primary if not exclusive objective. Little consideration is given to finding and applying what is true, good, and right. That is the nature of the political scene today. All that is required or sought in these secular processes is to cast an idea of the good and then stand within a convincing proximity of its shadow. Advertising the desire to fall under the constraint of some vague code of morality is the façade under which too many power contests play out within popular culture.

CHRISTIAN CITIZENS IN A DEMOCRACY

Perhaps one of the most troubling and convoluting subjects in many contemporary Christian settings is the issue of the appropriate role Christians are to play in a democratic society. There are good reasons for this. One of the primary reasons stems from the tawdry way Christians have engaged public issues in the past. There have developed several "unholy unions" between political and religious groups over the lifetime of our national political conversation. The assumption of many secular members of society that Christians must be from one particular political party is testament to the degree of convolution that exists on multiple levels. This coalescing of political ends gained through religious means has repeatedly occurred in subtle and presumptive ways. Yet the results are routinely awkward and unseemly.

As a result, many local church settings now contend that dealing with economic and political issues is to tempt engagement with the "world." Therefore, it is believed that our Christian leaders should abstain from anything having to do with "the principalities . . . [and] the powers . . . of this present darkness" (Eph. 6:12, RSV). As in many misinterpretations there remains a small element of truth and wisdom in this view. By default, there is simply no means by which Christian influence can, or should, be kept "private." Our local churches are automatically in the "public square" because of the positions and platforms that have been provided to people who make up our congregations, and because of the way, as everyone knows, we are all constantly interacting with and affecting "the public." The walls of the church are exceedingly and purposefully porous. This is natural if there is something being developed inside the church that others both want and need.

If the kingdoms of this world are to be transformed into the kingdom of our Christ, qualified Christians need to be deeply involved in political, legal and economic processes. Resistance to the calling to address these social issues intelligently and with spiritual force arises within some local churches and Christian traditions from a number of unfortunate tragic misunderstandings. One misunderstanding grows from the assumption that Christian moral character can and should be developed outside of the social, secular setting. This is simply impossible, because we live in a secular society. Therefore, it is equally impossible to be people who love our neighbors and practice thoroughgoing integrity if we accept practices that harm those closest to us or fail to advance and support social and political conditions that help our communities with their vital needs.

Another misunderstanding stems from mischaracterizations of the gospel itself and the mission of Christ and his people in the world. According to some, the only thing of importance for Christians is forgiveness of sins to secure the attainment of heaven in the afterlife. Such a misconception of "salvation" forces the gospel to become primarily a private matter "just between me and God." Often tied to this common fallacy is the belief that one's "salvation" has little if anything to do with developing a Christlike character. Such a story proceeds from the belief that the world is a hopelessly lost cause and thus our major, if not solitary, concern must be to "get" as many persons as possible into heaven before "the end."[18] Some are still training ministers and missionaries to go to whatever lengths necessary to attain this singular objective. For much of the non-Christian world such myopia appears self-righteously ignorant of what is good and right in any other economic, political, or social arena.

Despite such understandings and interpretations of the gospel, Jesus offers a message that describes and manifests how we can lead an eternal kind of life *now*, in the kingdom of God, out of which life with God after physical death is a natural outcome, extension, and enhancement of the type and quality of life already experienced. Jesus calls us into discipleship—apprenticeship to himself—which will directly lead us into assuming his character. Such a transformation naturally affects our social setting in the same way yeast takes over and transforms a lump of dough (Matt. 13:33). Jesus realized that transformation of individual moral character must be addressed before any meaningful advancement can be made in rectifying conditions of life in the world at large.

CHILDREN OF LIGHT ILLUMINATING THE COMMON GOODS

We can now offer a more specific application of much of what has been discussed earlier with regard to the specifics of moral theory and the application of moral knowledge and character in our leaders involved in political and economic affairs. In any form of society, but most especially in societies where a degree of democracy is in force, Christlike spokespersons and leaders aim to help anyone who has ears to hear and eyes to see how, where, why and when collective good can and must be pursued and achieved surrounding the issues and opportunities of our social life. The primary task of Christian leaders is not to initiate political, economic, or social revolution, but *to bring understanding and truth* to our lives and the issues we face in our world. In all of this, a major service of Christian professionals, leaders, and spokespersons is to keep before the public—including governments—a true picture of what human well-being is, how it functions, and what promotes it, while also detailing what well-being is not and those activities or policies in which genuine human welfare is not promoted and well served.

Again, the first and major part of this task requires the transformation of individual Christian leaders themselves (and others who come under their influence), so that they can be present to influence, guide, and bring light to those situations where policy is set and decisions made that affect human well-being and flourishing at all levels. Straightforwardly, the Christian church has not done this first step of discipleship well, and others know it. The local church must partner with Christians in our educational institutions to prepare well-formed, spiritually transformed, mature, and informed Christians for their missional callings to the existing institutions and structures of civil and public life. Thus, the first task of the individual spokespersons and professionals is to forge their own character, both in solitude and in communal fellowship and submission, in order to model, exemplify, teach, and guide others into the advanced ways of Jesus.

Such formation and maturity will ensure Christian spokespersons never endeavor to dictate, threaten, or manipulate others with regard to government or social policy and practice. It is *demonstration*, not heavy-handed *dictation*, that is the preferred means of Christian influence. We simply must not play the political game the way others do. This is a fool's errand that denigrates the witness of the church, and as a result the world loses the ability to compare and discern the differences between the ways of God and all other alternatives. It only appears as if political manipulation and "power plays" are "winning" the day. We can be assured they are not. Our future is secure, and therefore we can and must keep our eyes and hopes fixed on doing good and exposing good in all that we do and say. There are no shortcuts.

APPLYING THE FRUIT OF
THE SPIRIT IN PUBLIC LIFE

From the foundational traits, or fruits, of godly life mentioned earlier, certain characteristics that have a more direct bearing upon the flourishing of individuals and societies will naturally arise. A detailed academic study of how the fruits of the Spirit work in our communities could and should be made by our departments of social science. Here we will only make a few comments. Once again, an *agape* form of love is goodwill in action. To love something or someone is to act or be poised to act for the good of that thing or person. Love of neighbor is a disposition to act for what is good for others. If you see harm coming to them, you act to deflect or diminish the harm. And if they need some good thing, you do what is reasonably in your power to supply it. Thus, for example, parents will seek a job, or even two, to provide what they can for their children much more out of love than out of a sense of obligation. Both may be in play, but most often the love is stronger.

Likewise, in the larger social or governmental setting, love does what it can to establish and sustain arrangements and practices that will benefit everyone or as many as possible. Love will also oppose institutions and practices that hurt or fail to help "the public." Thus love at the public level compels us to care deeply for the economic, political, social, familial, and religious circumstances within our communities, because we care for (love) the people interacting and engaging in all these aspects of human life.

For example, love (especially conjoined with joy) will most certainly promote the inspiration for and creation and production of quality goods and services. Love naturally focuses upon the production and proliferation of what is good and seeks to make it widely available. As mentioned earlier, joy is an indispensable quality to have as a prudent investor. Joy allows us to accept a degree of uncertainty that might otherwise paralyze those who are unsure about the impending good that surely follows us all the days of our life, as we rely on the Good Shepherd's provision inside the kingdom of God (Ps. 23:6).

A report published by the Templeton Foundation found that almost half of all Americans feel God's love at least once a day. The national survey found eight out of ten Americans claim to experience God's love at least once in a while. A similar percentage claims to have felt God's love in a way that quickened their compassion for others, while nearly a third felt this loving compassion building for others daily. Most significant, this experience of divine love is understood to be a consistent predictor of six forms of benevolent behavior, such as giving time or money, helping friends and family, or working to make the world a better place. This research suggests that, for many Americans, the experience of divine love is inseparable from their practical acts of benevolence to others. Researcher Matthew Lee concludes, "Millions of Americans frequently experience divine love, and for them this sense of God's love not only enhances existential well-being, but underlies a sense of personal meaning and purpose and enlivens compassion for others."[19]

Such a study only illuminates what has always been true of the human condition under God's care. All of creation, especially humanity, proceeds from a boundless act of God's *agape* character. Peace eliminates hostile relationships that hinder productivity and waste human talent and energy and enables helpfulness to dominate our intentions and interactions. Joy (in work and in sharing our lives and possessions) makes everything easier and adds an underlying strength and vitality of its own to every endeavor, no matter how difficult and unpleasant. These traits also foster proper restraints essential for protecting oneself and others from harm. The fruits of the Spirit also put one in a position to be patient in undertakings, capable of deferred gratification, not wasteful or foolishly indulgent, willing and able to say no to what one wants or, as a leader, to what a group wants. The ability to say no to unrestrained desire enables the individual and the group to distinguish between a want and a need, keeping wants in their proper (limited) place when decision and action are necessary.

This is of overwhelming importance at the level of government. When deficit spending has been adopted as the normal course of doing business, as it is today, we have seen "wants" run wild for lack of leaders who can't say no to their constituencies. This is of course nothing new. One only need look to Plato's *Republic* (Books 7–9) to find this as a continual struggle between the public desire and political thrift. Thrift, as a central practice, has been abandoned. But thrift, now an old-fashioned idea, is essential to the well-being and flourishing of any individual or family, just as it is for a state or government. Yet "thrift" and "flourishing" are now words that do not comfortably fit together in the contemporary consciousness. Thrift is thought of as related to things that are shabby, cheap, secondhand, or used (e.g., found in thrift shops). Thus thriftiness is assumed to be evidence of some significant failure to achieve or procure the best product or service available.

A *need*, as opposed to a mere *want*, is an essential lack of some kind. If a need is not properly met, serious results occur in the functioning of the system in which the need appears. Perhaps even the demise of the system in general could occur. Examples are found in the malnutrition of very young children, the lack of intellectual or artistic stimulation in early childhood, or perhaps the failure of an infant to emotionally bond with a significant adult. These are needs that, if unmet, cause serious and sometimes irreparable harm, even death. It is the foundational character traits proceeding from the establishment and maintenance of the fruits of the Spirit that can enable the individual (and by extension the group) to discern whether to accept or reject needs and wants and the degree to which either is beneficial or oppositional to a good life.

To repeat, we should put to rest once and for all the idea that these traits are "private" and that "public" flourishing is independent of them. Public well-being and prosperity essentially depend upon the fruits of the Spirit becoming properly understood and implemented in as broad a context as possible.

(AD)MINISTERING GOD'S GOOD KINGDOM FOR ALL

We have wonderful examples we can learn from, emulate, and model our efforts after. Christian leaders such as William Wilberforce, Dietrich Bonhoeffer, Martin Luther King Jr., Desmond Tutu, and Mother Teresa worked diligently toward political and economic change, a form of influence that often eludes those who misrepresent Paul's description of "principalities and powers." Christians like Wilberforce, Bonhoeffer, and King, whose work included turns in the political arena, were essentially demonstrating that their particular path of discipleship to Christ resulted in a dutiful political role for them as ambassadors for the kingdom of God. There is nothing wrong, ungodly, or "worldly" about their service to God and humanity.

The First Amendment is about something Congress (and, as interpreted by the Supreme Court and state governments) *cannot* do. It is not about what Christians *should not* do. We now live under the influence of a gigantic myth about a "wall of separation" between "church and state," a phrase that appears nowhere in the Constitution. It is a metaphor that describes one theory of the First Amendment—a theory with increasingly less influence on the Supreme Court. The phrase may have some value in its suggestion of an institutional separation of church and state, but it is positively demonic when it is interpreted to require separation between religious morality and the state. The world would have lost the influence of Wilberforce, Bonhoeffer, King, and Tutu had they been forced to separate their Christian morality from their demands on the state. The teaching and leading of Christian leaders and professionals will, and should have, social consequences, including consequences for the economy and political life. However, the crucial importance of Christlike leadership is found in the blessed lives of those citizens who provide knowledge, insight, and guidance, by God's grace and for his purposes and ends in our world.

Thus wise, well-informed, and trustworthy leaders, professionals, and spokespersons are absolutely essential to support, critique, inform, and direct the inspiration, production, distribution, management, protection, exchange, and oversight of vital goods and services. This must be achieved in such a way that a high level of well-being is accomplished for as many participants in our society as possible. Followers of Christ are indispensable to this exercise. Christians must be involved as influential leaders that bring unique and indispensable knowledge of how all people, throughout society as a whole, can live and thrive within the ethos and ethic of the kingdom of God in any government, especially a democratic one. The position taken here is that Christian leaders and spokespersons have such knowledge at their disposal and are required to bring it to bear for the blessing of both communities and nations.

CITIES BUILT ON A HILL

To summarize these points, over the centuries individuals, groups, and governments collectively and separately have evaluated their social, political, and economic systems and practices by reference to how well they contribute to, or detract from, well-being and flourishing. We then must define what human well-being and flourishing are. Thus far we have discussed two versions of well-being. First, the secularist or nonbelieving view of flourishing largely depends on the satisfaction of natural human desires, achieved within the limits of natural human abilities. In this view desire is expected to rule. The second view is the Christian perspective, which consists of two basic elements: the presence of God and the provisions by God in real life. Here we can reasonably assume sensible provisions in a life freed from greed and obsession with material goods; this is a life of contentment that results from service under God for the benefit of others. Christian well-being then is essentially, and for the most part, relational or communal, that is, a matter of relations to other persons.

Again, desire fails as a guide to well-being from a Christocentric viewpoint since human desire alone is unreliable. One cannot run government on desire or on what "the people" want. The Christian version of well-being subordinates desire to what is good, and enables us to distinguish needs from wants. It also enables us to deny desire altogether, if that is wise and best, or at least to bring desire under control toward the pursuit of what is good and right. The point of reference for such standards of goodness and justness is God's character and moral will.

As a result, the major service of humble Christian spokespersons and leaders in society is to keep before the public—including governments—a true picture of what human well-being is and is not as well as the ways in which genuine human welfare can and must be served. To do this, Christian professionals, spokespeople for Christ, and servant leaders must remain gentle and wise stalwarts in the public square, where they speak, guide, and serve. They and their constituencies are in the real world, meaning they cannot and must not escape into some vague and impotent vision of privatization or renewed visions of a form of "Christ-ocracy" (previously known as Christendom) centered in the local church. Instead, Jesus advocates the very sensible idea that "a city built on a hill cannot be hid" anywhere, and we certainly must not "after lighting a lamp" put it "under a bushel basket" (Matt. 5:14–16).

Love of God and neighbor—the sum total of the intentions and vision carried through the scriptural accounts—lead to and require of us a divine address to the crucial issues. Such issues are too important for human life to be set aside. There is much else for pastors, leaders, servants, and disciples to do, of course, and not every Christian leader will engage in the issues of political life to the same extent. Yet we as a church must resolve to reengage the public issues of our day in whatever ways are appropriate for us. For such a conspiracy to take root, Christian educators must prepare those who embrace such a mission to properly master their understanding of social issues, so they can speak with clarity and wisdom about all the concerns that touch human life. This includes, of course, the major nongovernmental segments of society: business, education, engineering, medicine, law, and so forth.

Of course strong opinions and opposition will follow these issues, and civil debate should occur in polite earnestness and civility. But the main concern here has to do with the differing versions of flourishing or well-being that frame a secular vision of human life when compared and contrasted to a Christian or biblical vision. Human flourishing and well-being have numerous possible dimensions. A vision of what it is to have well-being or to prosper is presupposed in any evaluation of political, economic, and religious ideas and their plans for implementation. However, too few of our educational disciplines and fields of inquiry help us develop a clear positive understanding of what constitutes human well-being. Such a question simply does not fall within the domain of educational institutions in general or the course syllabi of a university classroom in particular, though many of our educational experts often seem to presume it does. A Christian worldview offers significant benefits to educators engaging these social and political issues.

The task of Christian spokespersons, leaders, and professionals is to exemplify and teach the foundational traits of the good life Jesus manifests. But this must also include the more specific traits required in the public domain—industriousness, self-control, moderation, and responsibility for oneself and others. That is the responsibility and posture of love. The human drive to be self-supporting can be tied to a determination to be productive in order to bless others. Again, that is observable in human life. Paul remarks on his own practice: "We did not eat anyone's bread without paying for it; but with toil and labor we worked night and day, so that we might not burden any of you" (2 Thess. 3:8). And he calls upon his readers to follow his example. Again he says: "Thieves must give up stealing; rather let them labor and work honestly with their own hands, so as to have something to share with the needy" (Eph. 4:28).

So the work of responsible Christian leaders, spokespersons, and professionals is not complete simply after pointing out the traits essential to human well-being. Initially, this is the most important thing we must do. The existence of a way to such an abundant life is precious and vital. Yet we cannot stop there. This is precisely where Christian businesspeople become so crucial to God's design for creating value and providing the means to bless others by distributing the essential services and material goods necessary for the flourishing we seek.

ECONOMICS AND POLITICS

Discussion Questions for Chapter 10

1. Milton Friedman, a Nobel Prize winner in economics and adviser to several presidents of the United States, often stated that the sole purpose of a business is to maximize profitability. Do you agree or disagree? What is the danger of this perspective in light of Willard and Black's concept of "goods"? Give examples.

2. Many of our cities around the world consistently deal with the issues of homelessness, poverty, illiteracy, health care, elder care, foster care, crime, and unemployment. Should the church help to better deal with these universal problems in our community? Why or why not? Should local churches and their leaders find ways to collaborate with other organizations such as local businesses, nonprofits, and local government offices to address these key concerns? If not, why? If so, what actions are you taking or planning to take to solve these problems in your community?

3. Willard and Black suggest that *shalom* is marked by a life without either fear or want. History is full of examples that

demonstrate how various civilizations formed political and economic systems to achieve general welfare and common flourishing. What are some examples of failures? What are some examples of successes? How can contemporary societies seek higher levels of flourishing without creating an environment dominated by either fear or discontentment?

4. In what ways do our churches live out a theology of scarcity as opposed to a theology of abundance in the kingdom of God? List the choices people make when they live out of scarcity. List the choices people make when they live out of abundance. How can we better illustrate and teach the scriptures in ways that encourage actions that contribute value to our communities and enable others to live in and from God's abundance?

5. According to the authors, "The primary task of our leaders is not to initiate political, economic, or social revolution, but to bring understanding and truth to our lives and the issues we face in our world." Do you agree or disagree with that statement? State your reasons. Did Mother Theresa, William Wilberforce, Desmond Tutu, or Martin Luther King Jr., initiate a revolution or bring more understanding and truth? State your reasons for your opinion.

6. *Exercise:* If you were running for public office, what would be your platform? Would you run within the two-party system? If so, which one? If not, why not? What critical issues would you address if you were elected? How would you handle the "integrity" issues related to the public trust and the obvious partisanship that exists in Congress? In what ways would you differentiate yourself as a leader from a "city built on a hill"?

Chapter 11

Business

The sum of the whole matter is this,
that our civilization cannot survive materially
unless it be redeemed spiritually.
Woodrow Wilson

In addition to leaders in education, politics, and economics, it is imperative to have moral leaders in the various commercial enterprises that support and supply the material well-being of our societies, so that the marketplace will be a site where the creative forces of human ingenuity can add value to life and living. What far too few either recognize or appreciate today are the opportunities available for spreading God's goodness, grace, and provision far and wide through the systems and distribution networks that exist as a direct result of industrial and commercial organizations and their professionals. Therefore the "business world" is a critical aspect that cannot be overlooked and must be fully appreciated as vital in God's plan to overcome evil with good. It is simply foolhardy to assume our business endeavors are exempt from the reach of God's vision and values. Nothing in the scriptures gives any indication of such a bifurcation. Therefore, here we will discuss some of the opportunities and challenges engaged by those who seek to use their business careers to further the kingdom of God through creating, managing, manufacturing, and/or distributing products or services that bring goodness and value to the human enterprise.

THE GOD-BATHED WORLD OF BUSINESS

As was mentioned in the chapter on leadership, the unending necessity for an appropriate division of labor in our communities is as critical today as it was for Plato in the fourth century BCE. Few can successfully juggle the tasks required to be a jack-of-all-trades. The ability to be "Renaissance man" died a slow death with the increase in specialization required to navigate contemporary life. Plato recognized that such a division of labor would quickly evolve into a wide platform for merchants and commerce. The division of labor allows those with goods and skills that are needed and beneficial to others to sell or exchange them, so that the entire community can acquire the essentials products and services necessary for life and living.

It is no mistake that we have termed these products, wares, or merchandise "goods," for that is exactly what they must be. They must be "good" for both the buyer and the provider. Therefore, we must discuss "goods" as a noun and simultaneously describe that noun with a qualifying adjective. "Goods" then are not just material possessions or manufactured products. Instead, we are using "goods" here to refer to both the things and the effect they produce. Business "goods" are constructive, advantageous, and indispensable for life and living.

Having defined "goods," we are better positioned to appreciate the true value of the business enterprise as a whole. Business is a wonderful God-given system that allows the pursuit of "the good" through the processes of creating, developing, manufacturing, and then distributing material "goods" or services. A condition of blessing is manifested both when creating and when receiving material goods or services. As businesspeople are very aware, there is often an even greater blessing in discovering how "goods" and services bless customers and clients. The transactions of business life represent the divine relationship inherent in both giving and receiving. In a business relationship of integrity and honesty, there is a mutually benefiting outcome. Both parties are blessed by being involved in the symbiotic relational bond of giver and receiver.

The fact that religious leaders often resist the idea that the entire business arena is a place of divine action is testament to the lack of a holistic perspective regarding the type and nature of "good things" (blessings) God is working in and through our lives. In such circumstances local businesspeople may be farther ahead in the ways of the kingdom than those leading a local church. Business is an amazingly effective means of delivering God's love to the world by loving, serving, and providing for one another. God loves the world (John 3:16), and because he does, he has arranged the enterprise and organization of business as a primary moving force to demonstrate this love throughout human history. Thus, the field of business and its unique knowledge fall perfectly into what can and should be understood as an essential realm of human activity that can and must come under the influence and control of God's benevolent reign.

However, such a view of the kingdom of God doesn't require those engaged in a business enterprise or the giving-and-receiving relationship to understand or even acknowledge its effects in order for God to continue to work his will and way. Nor does the kingdom of God need to wait patiently for any person or ethnic or religious group to become enlightened about the blessings available through the business world for him to proceed with dispensing the goods therein. God is using, has used, and will continue to use business as a means of loving and serving people regardless of who is in alignment with God's will. We certainly advocate for aligning with God's loving will on any matter. But the point is such agreement or awareness is not necessary, only beneficial.

THE PROFIT MOTIVE

From such an understanding of business as a powerful instrument of God's love and provision we can ask a more precise question: What is business (manufacturing, commerce) for? We shall engage this question from several angles.

The expected and perhaps most common answer to this question is the singular response, "Profit." For many in our business schools to even ask such an elemental question puts their reputation on the line. We suggest such a presumption is evidence of only one of the effects of the pervasive miseducation that has occurred and continues to pervade our contemporary society. Such malformation of students in some of our greatest universities has fostered a limited definition of success only in terms of fame, position, and material goods. Is this what business is for? To be used as a means of personal ego development and materialism?

However, such a situation reflects a quite recent view of the role business plays in our society. Today there are many "successful" businesspeople who do *not* view or define success in their professional lives as limited to the attainment of fame, position, and material wealth. Ironically, business enterprises do not overtly advertise their "goods and services" to the public solely as the means through which they intend to enrich themselves or those involved with fame or material wealth. Without exception advertisers understand they must instead focus on service, quality, trustworthiness, customer satisfaction, and so forth, all aspects focused on what is "good" for the customer or client. Perhaps it would be refreshing to hear a company advertisement that simply comes out and says, "Buy our stuff, because we want to be rich!" or, "We don't offer this service because we want to serve you. We want you to serve us!" Such honesty might even bring in a new round of customers.

In fact, businesses rarely confess or articulate a single-minded desire for profit. Instead, corporations are very aware that the goal of gaining customers and clients requires the ability to effectively communicate how much care, concern, and benefit (value) the client will receive as a result of engaging in a business relationship. Such a claim has an embedded request for trust and reliability. Interwoven into this claim of trustworthiness is often a claim of expertise, longevity, tradition, and strength of reputation. One only need pay attention to the commercials or print advertisements of financial institutions coming out of the economic disasters of 2008 to see exactly what they state, at least publicly, as their main intent. There is an overt proclamation to provide great care, protection, and concern for their clients. Claims of trustworthiness and honor are routinely touted as being so deeply rooted in the corporate culture as to repel any temptations from competing interests. Words like "honesty," "integrity," and "trust," flood contemporary advertising campaigns. Sometimes these claims are made all at once.[1]

Advertisers are perfectly aware of what customers and clients instinctively need to believe about their business partners. We need to know that the people we intend to do business with are "good people," who are "good" at what they do and will do what is "right" by us. Even though perhaps some business leaders continue to structure their organizations for the single-minded aim of greater profit, such a confession is never overtly stated to customers or clients as the primary reason for the existence of the business.

These examples and the questions that arise about them demonstrate the great potential and opportunity for business and the astounding responsibility and accountability of business leaders. This fact brings a very obvious conflict to light when considering what often is a primary or even elementary lesson in the world's finest business schools. This major conflict is found in the assumption that the primary motive for any business endeavor is to maximize profit. Such an assumption is not the primary concern for a business endeavor from God's point of view. Of course, how could it be? If the only drive or motive in business is to make as much profit as "legally and ethically" possible, then we have reduced the public good to nothing more than making money. And we all instinctively know, at least when we become reasoning adults, that money cannot buy goodness or the good life. Yet where are these questions being asked? Should they be asked? Would we be better off if such questions were honestly probed in our leading business schools? Are there more ways to serve the community than only to make more and more profit? Are there tradeoffs? The profit motive is certainly a clarifying motive. Yet profit for whom and at what cost must be overarching considerations in what has only loosely been defined and applied as business ethics.

MONEY AND PROMISES

Additionally, we must consider the moral realities related to our global monetary systems. Money and our concept of money have evolved in an unprecedented fashion over the past century. Money is literally not what it used to be. We think we have money in the bank, but we don't. Very little of the coinage or currency we typically think of as "our" money is literally held in a bank vault somewhere. Instead, our financial system relies on a developed means of credit and debits that are represented by symbols on computer screens, which "sit" in an "account" under your specific numbers or codes. Of course this has made exchange incredibly efficient. We can now transfer these credits and debits across the globe, several times a day, in less than seconds into someone's "account" with the push of a button.

This is much more sophisticated and ethereal than what we think of when we imagine the colored paper we carry in our wallets. Such a transition is even more revolutionary in scope and effect than the first transition from the barter system to coinage. At least pigs and pennies we can see and touch. Despite these sophistications, many of the basic features of our monetary system are the same as those that Jesus encountered in the first century. Our system of exchange, our credits and debits, widely rests on promises. Our financial system is not as complicated as it may appear. It is the strength of our word, our honest appraisal, our commitments, our promises—to pay or repay—that drive our financial system. For promises to be effective, a level of confidence is required. Otherwise statements such as "the full faith and credit of the United States government" mean nothing.

Trust, confidence, and belief in the promises made in agreements between human beings of goodwill and moral character form the only basis upon which our monetary systems and commercial enterprises can operate. When such promises are not maintained and honored, when borrowers lie on loan applications, when bankers accept fraudulent loan documents, when appraisers bloat home prices, when salespeople are interested only in generating commissions, when investors only look at returns and not the veracity of underlying securities, when firms falsify earnings reports, when government officials are interested only in placating the public and not in the greater good, the entire economic system teeters on the brink of collapse, because such a system is not based on reality. Knowledge of, and confidence in, the actual state of affairs—the facts—is not a luxury of human existence, but an undeniable necessity enabling living creatures to successfully navigate their world. This is especially true in our business affairs, a fact we are now more painfully aware of than perhaps in decades past. Time will tell if we have truly learned our lesson.

GOD-BATHED COMMERCE

The major focal point to reflect on here is that business, despite all its various and sundry faults and failures, and there are many, remains a glorious and essential aspect of life that cannot and should not be ignored. We must change many of the deeply ingrained assumptions and biases—some of which are maintained by teachers and pastors in Christian schools and churches—that a business profession is somehow a lesser calling than a "vocational ministry." Our communities of faith are simply left bereft of many of the good and great things offered by those disciples of Christ called into business careers, if cynicism or classism and bias are allowed to exist within our Christian congregations. There should be no doubt that God is as fully at work in the "business world" as he is in any other "world," including the "church world." In general, with some notable exceptions, such as pornography, gambling, or parts of the so-called entertainment industry, God is willing and able to bring about good in and through a business enterprise as easily, and in some cases perhaps more easily, than any religious or nonprofit organization.

Consider just one of the many wonderful aspects of the business realm. Business networks and distribution systems tend to have an intrinsically reliable and almost effortless ability to convey the benefits of their product or service through multiple channels, reaching people through social or relational networks (what we call a "word-of-mouth" phenomenon), which can even attain global dispersion (going viral) in very short periods of time. Business entrepreneurs also tend to have a wonderful sense of both what people need and want and how to supply it. These are skills the local church has struggled to both develop and maintain throughout its long and illustrious history. Perhaps the clergy must acquire these aptitudes and skills from those within the various business-related fields willing and able to share such valuable knowledge and experience.

Therefore, when we come to the subject of business, we must ask ourselves this question: What could God be doing and what would be best for all concerned within the business situations and circumstances of our contemporary lives? What would a Christ-like perspective be on issues such as profit motives, consumer faith or confidence, regulation versus deregulation, promises, and material goods in relation to overall human flourishing? Such questions may cause us to begin reading the business sections of our digital newspapers as documents giving insight into the workings and movements of God. Could we possibly begin to consider starting our daily "quiet time" with the *Wall Street Journal* next to or in concert with our Bible as we enjoy our morning cup of coffee? If God is in our business endeavors, if God is working with and through our businesspeople, professionals, and leaders as they direct our economic, financial, and political lives, what justifiable resistance could there be to such a proposal? How else are we to conform the kingdoms of this world to the kingdom of our God?

For example, if we start to ask these kinds of questions of our contemporary world, we could begin to consider the creation and development of Facebook. Very little public knowledge existed about Facebook before it became an international powerhouse. What Facebook provided caught the public's attention and began spreading like wildfire. Without disparaging the competency or ingenuity of Facebook's management, the company was running at a level far beyond the initial conscious motives of those who originated it. Such superhuman, supernatural realities are exactly the kind of wonderful divine work God is able and willing to produce with humanity in the development of "goods" for the benefit and enjoyment of his beloved world. This can and often does happen with or without the principal agents involved being aware of or instrumental in God's grace. Although Facebook may be an extreme example of the "wildfire" phenomenon, such elemental experiences lie at the very core or essence of business activity. Can you imagine how people felt when the wheel was invented?

We must come to the place where we engage the commercial endeavors and leaders of our world and ask questions such as: What is God doing in the fields of technology, medicine, or law? Business is a primary moving force that acts as a blanketing system for providing and demonstrating the love of God for the people of the world. The question is not whether business is good. The bigger question is whether the people in their respective businesses are good? Or perhaps we could even stay with the Facebook case study and ask if "going public" was actually the "best" thing for Facebook and its customers as a whole. We could ask if the need to turn Facebook into a huge profitable success (à la Microsoft) is the primary objective it should pursue. Was Facebook's IPO in the public's best interest? Was that even a consideration for Facebook's owners and officers? Should it have been, or were profit and the pursuit of profit the only meaningful considerations? Again the issue is not whether IPOs are good or bad or whether profit is good or not. The question is when and why such actions should be implemented or avoided and what role profit should play in a business where there is an overarching concern and commitment to the benefit of all concerned? Which in the case of Facebook would involve untold millions if not billions of very "concerned" and affected patrons.

CASE STUDY: MALDEN MILLS

The key issues in such decisions deal directly with ethics and virtues. A wonderful case study now being reviewed in university textbooks on business ethics is found in the circumstances surrounding the Malden Mills textile factory fire.[2] The fire injured twenty-five workers, leveled the Lawrence, Massachusetts, plant, and put almost fourteen hundred employees out of work only weeks before Christmas in 1995. Resisting the opportunity to close the factory or perhaps move to an international location with substantially lower labor costs, CEO Aaron Feuerstein elected to rebuild. Furthermore, he elected not to have his employees resort to unemployment insurance or their personal savings and instead continued to pay employee salaries while the mill was reconstructed.

Shortly after reopening the mill, product sales and employee productivity rose significantly. Yet the debt increase caused by higher reconstruction and retooling costs for a new state-of-the-art facility created fiscal shortfalls. Additionally, the volatile textile industry, warmer than usual winters, and Feuerstein's decision to remain in the United States with its higher labor costs combined to cause Malden Mills to declare bankruptcy in November 2001. As a result Feuerstein lost his company and his position as CEO. However, the company was able to regain financial solvency due to the flexibility of its creditors and restructured again in 2007 when its assets were repurchased. The company is now doing business under the name Polartec, LLC.

What is often overlooked is that Malden Mills was a privately held company. It was Feuerstein's decision alone to not take the nearly $300 million fire-insurance settlement and begin a lucrative retirement. The question often asked of this scenario is whether Feuerstein's idealism caused his company to fail. Should he have been more interested in profit than personnel? According to his employees and the community leaders of Lawrence, Massachusetts, Feuerstein is considered a hero, a rare CEO/owner who put his people above profit and personal interest. For a time this strategy of doing the right thing appeared to also translate into more sales and increased employee productivity. But in the end did Feuerstein's idealism blind him to the realities of his business?

Some may argue such idealism has no place in the hard-nosed practical realities and the dog-eat-dog vision of corporate competition depicted in Donald Trump's reality show *The Apprentice*. Are these our only options, or is the truth of these situations found neither in blind idealism nor ruthless pragmatism? It is true that—as the sole owner of his private company—Feuerstein did not have shareholders to whom he was responsible. He alone held the authority to manage his company as he pleased. That is the point. What pleased him was to apply the ethics of the Jewish Torah to his contemporary situation. "You are not permitted to oppress the working man, because he's poor and he's needy, amongst your brethren and amongst the non-Jew in your community," said Feuerstein.[3] From this understanding of what was good and right, he invested his $300 million and borrowed $100 million more to build a new plant that was both environmentally and worker friendly. This mill is still active today and remains the largest employer in the community. Thus, Feuerstein considered his own interests, the interests of his employees, and the interests of the community and made the "business" decision he believed was ultimately the best for all involved.

Those who might argue that market forces demand never paying wages that are not "owed or earned"—need to consider the "soft" cost involved in such decisions. There are several successful and profitable companies in various businesses that pay higher wages than their competitors and engage in what we could call "soft" or progressive management practices. Companies such as Costco, Trader Joe's, Southwest Airlines, In-N-Out Burger, and Chick-fil-A are but a few that have discovered the benefits of employee retention, satisfaction, and productivity.[4] The increased effort and productivity these companies enjoy are directly attributed to what are called employee "wellness" strategies.[5] In the often unpredictable industries of air travel, food service, and grocery outlets, the difference between financial success and failure can hinge on maintaining very thin profit margins. Securing a fulfilled and loyal workforce with demonstrable values and ethics can be the edge required to achieve not only survival, but profit as well.

Nothing can protect a business from the evolution of certain products and services beyond their life cycle. Seeking common goods is not a guarantee a company will last forever. Many uncontrollable and evolving factors remain in play. Despite his ethics and values, the textile market shifted and brought Feuerstein's personal career to a halt. Yet Feuerstein's story does testify to the fact that good treatment of employees added to the business and contributed to his bottom line. Well-treated employees tend to show up and are more loyal and committed to the overall success of their company. Customers who are treated honestly and fairly—as we would like to be treated if we were in their shoes—tend to be repeat customers who refer others. These are basic principles that nearly every small-business owner knows instinctively. They seem so obvious that one could honestly wonder why legislating such ethical standards would be difficult or even necessary.

How does Feuerstein want to be remembered? What epitaph does he want on his tombstone? "Hopefully it'll be, 'He done his damnedest,'" says Feuerstein. "You know . . . that I didn't give up, and I tried to do the right thing." It is in just these kinds of situations where a beachhead of the kingdom of God emerges. Malden Mills is an example of the type of business that literally crawled out of the ashes of ruin, in a completely upside-down manner. This is an example of the kingdom at work, confounding the wise, foolishness to some, yet beautifully compelling to others (1 Cor. 1:23).

SACRED VERSUS SECULAR

If we begin to consider the business arena in an appropriate light, thinking about the workaday world as in no way a "second-class" choice that settles for the secular rather than the sacred, but rather as a ministry field of the gospel of Jesus, who seeks to revolutionize the world for good and therefore requires ministers in every commercial endeavor, we will begin to recognize the full weight of the vocation, or calling, of every disciple of Christ. The work, whatever it is, of businesspeople under the guidance and obedience of God becomes a sacred calling. There is no need for some additional leadership position in a local church organization from which to engage in "ministry" or to validate one's giftedness and skill. Such a realization must be the first of many required for bridging the gap that currently separates the classifications of secular and sacred offices.

Every disciple of Jesus is called to be a minister of the gospel in his or her workplace. Wherever we are engaged in the efforts of his kingdom, we are acting as ministers administrating God's goodwill on earth as it is in heaven. The intent of a disciple is to participate in any operation intended by God to create the means through which human beings can love one another and cause the glory of God to shine. Jesus taught, "Let your light shine before others, so that they may see your good works say, 'Isn't God wonderful!'" (Matt. 5:16, paraphrased). Many ministers seem to assume this passage is specifically denoting "church work" as it has come to be understood today. Although this does not exclude work or ministry done in a local church setting, this is not an exclusive distinction. Our light is our life, our entire life. What we are stating here is that disciples of Jesus should not presume that priority is given to the activities of a local church organization over the activities of ministering in any arena of life, including a business vocation or profession, for the furtherance of the kingdom of God.

The barriers between sacred and secular or between work, home, and church must come down if a holistic understanding of the kingdom of God for all of life is to proceed. We will cover this in greater detail when discussing the role of the priests and pastors, but briefly stated here, the local church is to serve businesspeople by empowering and equipping them to achieve and implement the kinds of decisions and responsibilities John Ruskin describes that were highlighted in our earlier chapter "Moral Leadership." Those already positioned in critical leadership roles spread throughout local and global business enterprises must be equipped and prepared to carry out these essential duties with moral courage and wisdom. The pastor's role as a shepherd of a local gathering of believers is to develop, encourage, and minister to the needs of these key leaders as they conduct these responsibilities within their respective vocational roles. This would include but not be limited to regularly following their careers, perhaps weekly, praying through difficult decisions, offering insight, counsel, and advice where necessary and appropriate, and celebrating milestones and victories. To do this, ministers need to be seen as credible sources of wisdom and advice, aptly displaying equal measures of character, competency, and courage. What business leaders and professionals must understand and be willing to admit is the depth of moral character required to engage their daily tasks. Honestly engaging this fact will require a level of personal transparency that all Christian servant leaders, in any profession, including ministers, must become willing to accept and engage.

GOD'S BUSINESS

So again we return to a key question: What is business for? There has always been a degree of ambiguity or at least less clarity about the roles of merchants and manufacturers than the roles of the older professions of clergy, doctors, and lawyers. Nevertheless, merchants' special position and power in a community are understood to bring with them unique and unavoidable moral responsibilities and opportunities. Here again we reflect back on Ruskin's insights. Ruskin clearly grasped the indistinctness of purpose that hovers around the various positions and unique responsibilities related to businesspeople. He understood the travails of multiple divided objectives and interests, which can create weighty dilemmas around the issues of profit, generosity, labor, management, customers, debt, natural resources, community benefits, and so on. He was sure few understood this unique role in his day and, as a result, merchants "never have had clearly explained to them the true functions of a merchant with respect to other people."[6] In an attempt to clarify the merchant's role and function and the goods that they supply to the people in the community, Ruskin landed on the idea of *provider*. He proposed that merchants and manufacturers can never pluck from the community the resources and means that serve only their own self-aggrandizement. Instead, Ruskin argued:

> It is no more his function, to get profit for himself out of that provision than it is a clergyman's function to get his stipend. The stipend is a due and necessary adjunct, but not the object of his life, if he be a true clergyman, any more than his fee (or honorarium) is the object of life to a true physician. Neither is his fee the object of life to a true merchant. All three, if true men, have a work to be done irrespective of fee. . . . That is to say, he has to understand to their very root the qualities of the thing he deals in, and the means of obtaining or producing it; and he has to apply all his sagacity and energy to the producing or obtaining it in perfect state, and distributing it at the cheapest possible price where it is most needed.[7]

Ruskin proceeded to emphasize that the other primary responsibility of merchants is to care for the well-being and success of those in their employ. Merchants have direct governance over their employees. Therefore, "it becomes [the merchant's] duty not only to be always considering how to produce what he sells in the purest and cheapest forms, but how to make the various employments involved in the production or transference of it most beneficial to the men employed." Hence the function of business requires, "the highest intelligence, as well as patience, kindness, and tact, . . . all his energy . . . and to give up, if need be, his life in such a way as it may be demanded of him." As the captain of a ship is duty-bound to be the last to leave the ship in disaster, "so the manufacturer, in any commercial crisis or distress, is bound to take the suffering of it with his men, and even to take more of it for himself than he allows his men to feel; as a father would in a famine, shipwreck, or battle, sacrifice himself for his son."[8]

That Ruskin may not be left to stand alone in a minefield of critique, we also cite the words of Louis Brandeis, a brilliant legal mind and Supreme Court justice. In his commencement-day address to Brown University in October 1912, titled "Business: A Profession," Brandeis remarked:

> The recognized professions . . . definitely reject the size of financial return as the measure of success. They select as their test, excellence of performance in the broadest sense, and include, among other things, advance in a particular occupation and service to the community. These are the bases of all worthy reputations in the recognized professions. In them a large income is the ordinary incident of success; but he who exaggerates the value of the incident is apt to fail of real success. . . . In the field of modern business, so rich in opportunity for the exercise of man's finest and most varied mental faculties and moral qualities, mere money-making cannot be regarded as the legitimate end.[9]

Brandeis devotes most of his lecture to illustrating how real success in business must be determined. In this analysis, such success must be "comparable with the scientist's, the inventor's, and the statesman's." He, like Ruskin, emphasizes the nobility of the merchant's function.

If we consider these models as a guide and if existing leaders and our top educational institutions were willing and able to follow the type of example set by Aaron Feuerstein, surely the term "big business" would quickly lose much if not all its sinister connotations and would instead take on a fresh and beneficial meaning. "Big business" would subsequently refer to business carried out in a grand manner, great in service and important in function, not done in a heavy-handed fashion indicative of raw power set on profits alone.

Unfortunately, Ruskin and Brandeis are not popular references in our schools of business, economics, management, and sociology today.[10] To quote another voice from the Ruskin-Brandeis era, these schools, for all their good, tend instead toward paying far too much attention to "the excuses which selfishness makes for itself in the mouths of cultivated men."[11] Clearly, unequivocally, in business one must seek to attain a profit in order to simply survive, much less continue as a going concern. We are not at all advocating for all businesses to move into a nonprofit arrangement, because simply eliminating the profit motive does not assure an honorable end. Our governmental and religious organizations have provided ample proofs of this lamentable fact. However, profit simply must not be gained at the expense of the public good and the well-being of individuals whose lives depend on the goods and services they procure. Profit becomes a vice, not a virtue, if, for example, one must sell tainted food or shoddy furniture or faulty electronic devices just to stay afloat, much less to make money. Very plainly, profit cannot remain the solitary objective of those involved in any business enterprise.

It is a convenient and often lofty-sounding justification to argue that "the market" will drive you out if you don't follow "commonsense" business practices. Christian businesspeople must recognize higher powers—"stronger hands," shall we say, than Smith's invisible hand—at work in the world.[12] "Living and dying by the market" and the idea of "market forces," when combined with an unrestrained devotion to individual consumerism and a lack of moral leadership, can create minefields of injustice that often prevent the kinds of holistic flourishing and economic prosperity we seek.

We must be clear in stating capitalism and free-market economies are not bad or evil in and of themselves. In fact, the opposite is the case. Free-market economies—when organized, driven, and overseen by moral servant leaders with a devotion to common goods—have provided fertile soil in which the means necessary to build the flourishing societies we so desperately seek can be developed and acquired. What must be resisted is the temptation to assume whatever the "market" does or does not do is always "good" and therefore necessitates justification as such. The "market," as with all human endeavors, social realities, inventions, and institutions, must be engaged and directed by moral persons in order for it to consistently produce the kinds of "goods" we require.

The concept of the "invisible hand" can become problematic if it is allowed to overwhelm activation of the moral calling and moral character required of our leaders who are tasked to pursue, preserve, and protect the general welfare. If an "invisible hand" is allowed to justify an unfettered drive to fulfill every consumerist desire in our culture, we have created an idol, not an economic tool. Thus, in any economic policy or platform, including our free-market economies that utilize a form of capitalism, the markets cannot be left alone. They must be properly and effectively stewarded toward an honorable end by honorable people.

There is no legitimating support for the notion that young college graduates should make the drive for material wealth, fame, or power the primary basis of their pursuit of a professional or business career. Rather, we must restore in both our educational institutions and their graduates a convincing framework of *calling and character*, if professional life is to be directed in a manner that—surely everyone knows "deep-down"—is best suited to the greatest functions of business. There is no reasonable alternative to Ruskin's charge if we wish to provide for and protect both the common welfare and well-being of individuals throughout our neighborhoods and beyond. The greatest challenge to an officially post-Christian world is to provide a more robust framework than the endless search to satisfy the unquenchable desire for more material goods that results in mountains of consumer debt. To this point we must admit the need to do much better at casting a vision of God's kingdom life, which may first require a long, steady journey down the path of personal and institutional transformation toward Christlikeness.

Surely the best course is to take up one's own business vocation as a divine appointment from God through intelligent discipleship to Jesus Christ. This provides a time-tested and experiential foundation for professional life that yields the nobility seen by Ruskin, Brandeis, and many others. We must come to the point where all Christian businesspeople understand the opportunity and necessity of embodying the life of Christ in their cubicle, at their desk, in their boardroom, at their counter, and on their shift. This is the kind of life Francis Havergal had in mind when he penned this well-known hymn:

Take my life, and let it be
Consecrated, Lord, to Thee;
Take my moments and my days,
Let them flow in ceaseless praise,
Let them flow in ceaseless praise.

Take my hands, and let them move,
at the impulse of Thy love;
Take my feet and let them be
Swift and beautiful for Thee,
Swift and beautiful for Thee.

Take my voice, and let me sing
Always, only, for my King;
Take my lips, and let them be
Filled with messages from Thee,
Filled with messages from Thee.

Take my silver and my gold;
Not a mite would I withhold;
Take my intellect, and use
Every power as Thou shalt choose,
Every power as Thou shalt choose.

Take my will, and make it Thine;
It shall be no longer mine.
Take my heart; it is Thine own;
It shall be Thy royal throne,
It shall be Thy royal throne.

Take my love; my Lord, I pour
At Thy feet its treasure-store.
Take myself, and I will be
Ever, only, all for Thee,
Ever, only, all for Thee.[13]

When we begin to seriously endeavor to "ordain and establish" Havergal's vision of an incarnational life, we will individually and collectively orchestrate God's will and way in and through our daily responsibilities, in our businesses, serving others, creating goods, adding value, providing livelihoods, and sustaining, if not actually saving, lives. Such a reality will enable and provide for the kind of lasting peace earlier generations had in mind when attempting to create a means to achieve "prosperity for ourselves and our posterity."

Thus far we have considered the institutions and leadership roles of education, economics, politics, and business. Now we must turn our attention to the specific professions of medicine, law, and ministry, for it is in these indispensable professions where a significant degree of our flourishing hangs in the balance. Therefore the need for Christlike leaders and shepherds devoted to the accomplishment of God's will in these areas of expertise is essential to the common flourishing we seek.

BUSINESS

Discussion Questions for Chapter 11

1. Some believe that when the kingdom of God is fully realized, there will be no reason for commercial enterprise. In other words, the business world will not exist. But what if commercial enterprises will exist in eternity? What would they be like? How would the leaders serve in their role? How would it be different from our current system? How would it be "good" for customers, owners, and workers?

2. Do a little Internet research. Take a glance at two or three Fortune 100 company websites and find their mission or vision statements. Do you find any indication in these statements about whether the organization exists only for self-proliferation or for the good of others? What values and ethics are recognizable in these mission statements? In what ways do these organizations intentionally declare their pursuit of the common good? Are there any differences in mission statements between public and private companies?

3. The authors mention a few well-known companies with "soft" or progressive management practices, such as Southwest Airlines and Chick-fil-A. In what ways (if any) do the mission or vision statements of these companies differ from those researched in the Fortune 100?

4. As mentioned earlier, Milton Friedman was clear about his belief that the sole purpose of a business is to maximize profit. However, what is the primary concern of God? How could some of the mission statements studied above be reshaped to reflect the purposes of God to bless and cause humanity to prosper? What potential impact could be achieved in the

communities they serve by adapting the vision and values of our commercial enterprises toward the overarching objectives conveyed in the fruit of the Spirit? Is such change possible? Why or why not?

5. How might a Christlike perspective affect one's view of issues such as profit motives, consumer confidence, regulation, downsizing, budgets, and personnel? Should Christians maintain a unique outlook on these matters different from that of non-Christian or non-religious businesspeople? If so, in what ways? If not, why?

6. *Exercise:* All disciples of Christ are called to be ministers of the gospel wherever they go and in whatever they do. When is the last time businesspeople were invited to share their challenges and triumphs from the ministry field of their industry? When was the last time you witnessed a church gathering specifically called to pray for or commission a local businessperson? How might church leaders reconsider ways of reintegrating the entire congregation into their gatherings? Consider finding ways to encourage and support ministers in the professional fields, businesses, and workplaces of our communities within your local congregational context.

CHAPTER ·12

Professionals

I am not influenced by the expectation of
promotion or pecuniary reward. I wish to be useful,
and every kind of service necessary for the public
good becomes honorable by being necessary.

CAPTAIN NATHAN HALE, 1776

T HERE IS ARGUABLY no area riper for both blessing and abuse than the professional fields. There has perhaps rarely been a time in recent history when devotion to excellence in one's profession and the integrity required to fulfill its ethical responsibilities were more in demand than today. Each of the professional fields has come under increasing degrees of scrutiny, even direct attack in some quarters, from several sectors within our society. Teachers, ministers, physicians, lawyers, accountants, merchants, politicians, soldiers, and many others find themselves in the once unthinkable and surprisingly perilous position of defending their existence.

Although the details are many and varied, the essence of the outcry seems to surround the abuses or perceived abuses of power, prestige, and economic privilege combined with a rising level of ineffectiveness in accomplishing the goals and objectives for which the profession exists in the first place. This is not to assume that such complaints are accurate, only that the public's perceptions and the din of its grumblings have risen to the level of "moral" condemnation. The accompanying resentment and frustration within the public now hovers slightly below fever pitch, ready to strike at any perceived infraction.

This rising frustration gnaws at the very foundations of any social structure and universally erodes both the possibility and, more menacingly, the hope of social and individual well-being. No free society that values the egalitarian virtues that form our liberal democracy practiced in the United States can abide the demise of ethical practices applied within the professions. Professionals must take all necessary and appropriate measures to assure their high moral conduct so that the public can trust its leaders to carry out their sacred calling of cultivating, then conveying the services and expertise required for human flourishing.

For God's good will to thoroughly revolutionize our world, righteously upright and proficient professionals must lead the way. One can see this is an ongoing theme throughout this work. In general we assert that the health of a society depends primarily on the health and quality of those overseeing its institutions and organizations, and this is mainly where our professional fields are engaged. If our professionals are effective and respected, our societies will not only be sound, but also will roundly flourish. If our professionals are incompetent and disparaged, then there will be confusion, turmoil, and suffering.

Therefore, we must first begin to consider why it is essential to deploy trusted and trained men and women devoted to the cause of Christ into these indispensable fields, for it is in the professions that the presence—or lack—of knowledge, expertise, and character is accentuated. As we will learn, the professions have a degree of autonomy different from the other leadership positions within our societies. Second, we will treat the subject of the heroic and valorous characteristics of professionals, which must return to the fore if we are to attract dedicated young men and women to the purpose-filled existence offered them in professional life. We will then briefly engage three key traditional professions—medicine, law, and ministry—and their unique callings.

It is important to note that our purpose is not to offer direction as insiders. This would invalidate our claim of the internal accountability required of each profession. Rather, we offer suggestions as curious outsiders, hoping to instigate thoughtful discussion and probe new paths for each profession to consider as it sees fit. We hope to illuminate issues that can be broadly discerned and discussed across all professional fields. Still, in order for the kingdoms of our world to be conformed to the kingdom of Christ, the role and responsibility of each profession overseeing its duties in ways that pursue the common good cannot be overstated. How this is to be done in the many layers of minutiae specific to each discipline is beyond our purview here. Thus we will address only some of the larger, perhaps more notable concerns present within the awareness of the general public.

A HISTORY

Although we want to avoid being too reductionist in these matters, it is important to at least provide a general understanding of what a professional is. The root of the word "professional" is of course "profess." According to sociologist Everett Hughes's etymology, the word "profess" is related to vows taken in connection with a religious order.[1] Yet by the late seventeenth century the word had become more secularized to include not only a religious vow, but also the oath or "profession" by one duly qualified in something. The Hippocratic oath is perhaps the oldest of the well-known professional vows. Hughes writes, "The word 'profession' originally meant the act or fact of professing. It has come to mean: 'The occupation which one professes to be skilled in and to follow. A vocation in which professed knowledge of some branch of learning is used in its application to the affairs of others.'"[2]

In summary, Hughes rightly concludes that professionals are those who profess to know best the nature of certain matters and, further, to know better than those who depend upon their knowledge of what is good for them and their affairs. Therefore, the first key to understanding the nature of professionals is to grasp the claim that underlies their existence. Professionals "profess" the right, authority, or license to use their specialized knowledge and expertise for the benefit of others. As the origin of the word suggests, such a position carries the weight of a sacred duty, one accepted and held dear, as precious as any marital or religious vow.

Even today many professions use the term "engagement" in their contracts and agreements with clients. One "engages" the services of an accountant or an attorney. Again, this language elicits and describes a level of intimacy or private relationship in which the depth of information shared is likened to that in relationships consummated with vows. Such responsibility requires professionals to abstain from violating their fiduciary responsibility to establish and maintain a certain objective distance that prevents them from ever being "bought" or controlled because of this unique commitment. Professionals are required to know best, and their special dignity derives from their devotion to objectives that transcend the limits of both their own self-interest and the interests of their profession.

In large measure the promise of upward mobility is precisely the reason behind the unchecked growth of professionalization in the United States over the past century and a half. The power and prestige of a professional life is quixotic in a democratic culture, which prizes as an ultimate virtue a sociopolitical structure in which all persons can hope to attain their individual potential (for life, liberty, and happiness). Such potential remains a key component in the elusive pursuit of the American dream. Historically, immigrants have flooded America precisely because of the assumption that many of the barriers to achieving one's potential have been either theoretically or legislatively breached. Not to mention the countless success stories of people having "found the brass ring" of success as a result of the benefits of American opportunism. From the mid-1980s through the turn of the millennium, the call sign of this success was to be considered a yuppie (young urban professional).

THE PROFESSIONAL VOCATION

Now that we have provided some basic history for how the professions came to be established, we can discuss three basic criteria for professional practice. Historian Nathan Hatch has presented a very simple yet holistic understanding of what a profession must maintain in order to best serve the public in achieving the good it seeks.[3] First, a professional arena encompasses a specific body of knowledge that is structured, definable, and conveyed through training toward the goal of mastery. Second, a profession carries a moral imperative to support and defend the greater good of the public it serves. This moral obligation far exceeds, but does not preclude, the effects of market forces or profit motives. Third, because of the often esoteric, complicated, or special information and training required in a profession, there is an inescapable degree of autonomy and privilege attached to professional authority. This creates a level of advantage that too often initiates the downfall of many a professional career. This privileged status must be self-regulated and overseen by the profession's own guild or association. Doctors watch over and hold accountable other doctors, lawyers do the same for other lawyers, ministers for ministers, and so on. This is due again to the unique knowledge and training characteristic of the professions themselves, which limits the number of persons qualified to properly supervise and adjudicate professional conduct. This is often experienced in the court system, where medical doctors are the only experts who can properly testify against their colleagues in matters particular to their specialty.

This unequal, preferred status creates a situation wherein members of a profession are unequivocally obligated to continually assess, oversee, and regulate their own in order to protect the common welfare of the society they serve. A professional body must safeguard its public trust and respect by providing continual evidence it is imparting expertise in a manner that benefits the public at large. The services the professions offer societies are owed, because without public permission, trust, and empowerment, a profession could not exist. The professional life, the very act of professing, is directly tied to the request for trust and thereby demands certification of trustworthiness in both expertise and intent. If a professional or a profession becomes motivated solely by self-interest, trust is lost, no matter how qualified or experienced those practicing may be. In the final analysis, professionals must do what is in the interest of the public or their client, and never just what is in their own self-interest.

These three marks of a profession then form the basis for professionals in "good" standing to attain both status and dignity. A true professional then is essentially a person with authority and honor in society. Historically this is where the phrase "a gentleman and a scholar" became associated with the professional role in society.[4] To maintain this honor and authority as a person above reproach, professionals can never be "for hire" in the ordinary sense and instead must steer clear of what we regularly term "conflicts of interest."

Again, when we bring in the discussion of "the common goods," "public interest," or "the general welfare," we mean those goods that *all* members of society would reasonably benefit from or have access to either directly or indirectly. Examples of areas of public interest might be commerce, legal institutions and processes, public safety, medical care, education, housing, transportation, and news. Given the importance and necessity of such areas of common interest and concern, the public benefits by having the activities that take place in them monitored or governed by qualified, competent, and conscientious individuals dedicated and held accountable to their high calling. More plainly stated, this calling is to both maintain the interests and seek the benefit of *all* individual citizens as well as the whole of society.

The benefit to a society of well-functioning professions can be seen as we envision the range of professional interactions with the public at large. In order for the common good to be best served, these activities must be properly and expertly executed. This mandates extraordinary dedication, training, accountability, and moral character. It logically follows that because of these special talents, knowledge, and abilities, such accountability must largely be provided by peers of the same high qualifications, expertise, and moral courage. Such special dedication, training, knowledge, and regulation, when institutionalized in the appropriate respects, necessarily form *a profession as a social entity.*[5]

Although there are divergent opinions as to which vocations qualify as professions, most scholars tend to agree that law, medicine, and ministry constitute what could be called the original "big three."[6] In the eighteenth and nineteenth centuries, emerging claims for new professions were defined by using their "family resemblances" to these three "classic" professions as models. It is interesting to note how those who were tasked with the pursuit and maintenance of justice, health, and faith were esteemed enough to be used as the standards for determining the qualifications for any new profession. It is sobering to consider the public's view of the "big three" today and whether or to what degree these professions could continue to be used as a standard measurement for quality and integrity in professional life.

Today, it may seem odd to consider these three areas as the ones that began the entire discussion on professionalism. Yet since the Middle Ages, Western societies traditionally and routinely recognized these three facets of life as maintaining essential bodies of knowledge that could not be engaged properly or effectively by untrained or inexperienced novices. Therefore, by law, these prototypical professions were accorded a level of dignity, accountability, and honor. This reverence was not accorded because of the particular persons who bore the responsibilities, but because of the awesome power for good or ill that these individuals wielded as a natural consequence of their knowledge and position. Great gravitas was connected with the life-altering circumstances and decisions these professionals were tasked with. This has not changed.

However, in our contemporary context, the "big three" as we have labeled them have fallen on hard times. They each have not only lost much of their illustrious glory in the public eye; they are routinely used as the butt of jokes that tend to suggest the direct opposite of honor and reverence. Ironically some of the most distasteful of these jokes are created and shared by professionals themselves. This is but one sign of the significant dilemma the professions are in. Financial, political, legal, social, ethical, and scientific concerns, working in concert, have left many in these fields feeling powerless and frustrated. Some of our most intelligent and gifted individuals who serve diligently in the pursuits of justice, health, and religion are finding their calling almost futile, increasingly degraded, and sometimes altogether ineffective.

The circumstances that have created these results are multifaceted and ever evolving. Yet the professions themselves hold the responsibility to create and manage self-governing agencies to address these concerns, due solely to the fact that the knowledge and expertise the professions possess are specialized and esoteric. Therefore, only the possessors of such knowledge can rightly adjudicate their peers and guide future action. This creates what some have termed "hidden hierarchies" within the realms of economic, religious, legal, and political power.[7] Such power and influence, if not focused on attaining the common goods for the society they exist to serve, can begin to erode the sense of a profession's necessity to defend, equip, and protect others. It is now routinely assumed that some professions have devolved into primarily a means for pursuing self-interest and eluding public accountability through unduly influencing our economic, legislative, and political processes.

Diverse economic philosophies come to the fore in such discussions. Some advocate unrestrained deregulation of the professions in order to allow free competition to sort out and settle who is and who is not "good" at the profession. Still others argue that such unrequited trust is a recipe for public disaster. Instead, those favoring increased regulation tend to advocate more oversight provided by nonprofessional governmental systems in hopes of ensuring public protection and welfare. This unresolved tension between experts and society in our democratic form of government is an ongoing negotiation that ebbs and flows largely on the tide of perceived or realized successes or failures of any given profession in the moment.[8] Perhaps this is never truer or more crucial to the life and effect of any profession than for the three professions we will focus on here.

PROFESSIONAL ETHICS

Being a professional is both a status and an identity in society at large. With this identity come proper recognition, social power, and financial opportunities. Such a preferred status can prevent professionals from being judged or held to account by the public they are tasked to serve. Regrettably, it is now becoming increasingly evident—perhaps more now than at any other time in history—that the professions have too often succumbed to overt tendencies that diminish their potential for effecting public good. When allowed to operate unhindered, professionals can become inclined to maximize—and abuse self-centered rewards and financial advantages—the power derived from their privileged positions. As a result there exists something of a love-hate relationship between the public and some professions.

Despite this on-again, off-again relationship between the public and its professionals, the professions afford sweeping opportunities for upward mobility. At the same time, such opportunities often result in larger barriers between the professional and nonprofessional vocations. In this vein, one significant concern arising in the wake of the global financial crisis and economic recession brought on by the mortgage crisis is whether the demand for virtuous character and moral courage has kept stride with the massive expansion of economic and social prosperity afforded to some professionals. The abuses of experts and "insiders" who use their privileged positions for personal gain has created a disdain that smolders just under the surface of the public consciousness.

The data gathered on public perception of those in our professional fields is illuminating. The general public appears to be more aware now than in eras past of the opportunity for professionals to abuse their power and position. Gallup has kept a running yearly poll measuring the public perception of the honesty and ethical standards of twenty-two vocations.[9] At the top of the list in 2012 were nurses, pharmacists, and medical doctors. Eighty-five percent of the public believes nurses have very high or high standards of honesty and ethical behavior. At the other end of the spectrum were advertisers (11 percent), members of Congress (10 percent), and auto salespeople (8 percent). Of significant note was the drop in confidence in the clergy. In 2009 the clergy hit a thirty-two-year low. Only 50 percent of those polled considered the clergy to represent honest and ethical standards of conduct.[10] In the following years the clergy as a class inched up slightly (to 52 percent) while remaining eighth in comparison to the other twenty-two professions polled. Lawyers ranked fifteenth; only 19 percent of those polled believe legal professionals have high or very high ethical standards and display honest behavior. Business executives and bankers fared slightly better but only maintained 28 percent and 21 percent of the public's confidence, respectively. HMO managers ranked in the bottom five vocations (12 percent).

Although Gallup did not offer any details on precisely why each vocation scored as it did, we suggest confidence and trust are present in professional life when power and knowledge are used in ways that benefit the common good. When power and knowledge are abused, integrity is lost and confidence falls. It is likely that if the Gallup research organization were to probe into the reasons for the responses it received, two types of professional abuse might tend to affect the rankings.

The first is some form of individual obsession with personal advancement (status and rewards) that is allowed to grow within a professional framework. The malfeasance of the many professionals involved in the Enron scandal is perhaps a good example. In these cases professionals appear to have focused upon financial rewards or advancement to the detriment of the standards of ethics and excellence required to perform their duties. The result was catastrophic, not only to them personally, but to all those relying on their proclaimed and expected professionalism.

The second type of abuse is often manifested in the development of prized qualities, objectives, and accomplishments *within* a particular profession that are not conducive to the public good. This is often a highly debated matter when it occurs. An excellent example of this is found in the area of what is now thought of as investigative journalism. Investigative reporters play an invaluable role in a free society in checking and holding public leaders accountable. However, if uncovering successive sensational, muckraking events of the kind that tend to end in a "gate" suffix (e.g., Nannygate) becomes an obsession and the measure of journalistic excellence, then much of the public good that *could* come from such investigations is lost. Citizens need the critical financial, educational, political, and cultural information that journalists provide, but when either the motivation for or the facts of the stories are suspect, it results in more harm than good. The same critique, albeit in different terms, can be levied against the professions of medicine, ministry, law, and education. What professionals recognize and reward within their own ranks as "good work" and "success" may in fact conflict with the public welfare, which they exist to advance and protect.

PROFESSIONAL VALOR

What is key here is that both these opportunities for abuse occur when professionals ignore their task of serving an adjudicating role in society. Professionals provide more than technical expertise in the competitive marketplace. The older, perhaps more traditional, definition of the professional calling assumed and provided *a foundational social and moral framework* that was more obvious and defensible before the days of megasocieties that promote urban anonymity. It was once expected that the individual merchants, doctors, lawyers, pastors, and so on more or less "governed," settled disputes that came to them in the course of their activities and served on committees and councils with and for those living within the close-knit community. The respect given them was, in earlier days, an appropriate response to the special and potentially self-sacrificing good that they made available to those gathered around them, in pursuit of the health of the commonwealth in all areas, political, economic, legal, physical, moral, educational, and religious.

However, although the descriptions of morality listed in our chapter on moral theory undoubtedly apply to each of the professions, the problem of morality for professionals is much more expansive than simply applying moral standards. The demands of ethical conduct in the professions far exceeds following rules. The spectrum of moral action in professional life encompasses personal motives and character of individuals engaged in the professional realms as well as general practices and customs. Many professionals may resist such a claim as an unwarranted intrusion into their and their clients' "private" lives. Nevertheless, we must face the fact that society has a vested interest, a very deep interest, in the quality of the professionals they employ.

From a very pragmatic point of view, much of professional expertise and effectiveness depend on the ability to persuade. Professionals routinely seek to convincingly influence clients, constituencies, and fellow professionals, whether competitors or allies, toward a certain means of action. Because of this aspect of persuasiveness in the professional office, it is vital to appreciate, as Aristotle astutely recognized, how the public tends to believe and trust those they believe are good "more fully and more readily than others: this is true generally whatever the question is, and absolutely true where exact certainty is impossible and opinions are divided."[11] This may not be the ideal we long to achieve, yet Aristotle's perception of the nature of human relations is true nonetheless. As a result personal "goodness" remains a significant factor in assessing the intention and means of both the professional advice and direction we require and those individuals providing these services.

Here again it is important to restate that professionals are much more than experts at a task or masters of a field of esoteric knowledge. They must also be interested in more than self-advancement, financial gain, or even their own expertise. Professionals do not have the same effect on society as others who are also significantly devoted, even to the point of self-sacrifice, simply due to the professionals' duty to administrate crucial public goods. Though a person may have expertise and function within a defined profession, unless there is a willingness to subordinate the self and hold others to a similar standard of service and sacrifice, there is no basis for justifying a professional classification. Returning to Ruskin's proposal may help clarify and define the heroic potential of the professional calling. He believed professionals are under a specific obligation, in certain circumstances, to die if necessary to fulfill their function as a professional in their area of responsibility. Such a weighty and solemn perspective is sorely needed in contemporary applications of professional life.

A case in point is found in the tragic yet heroic story of the four soldiers assigned to Navy Seal Team 10, three of whom succumbed to their wounds during the ill-fated Operation Redwing, deep in the rugged mountains surrounding the Afghanistan–Pakistan border.[12] Marcus Luttrell was the sole member of his team who survived to tell their harrowing tale of heroism, self-sacrifice, and moral courage. Seal Team 10 stands in a long line of countless other military personnel over the centuries who clearly demonstrated their willingness to die in order to fulfill their sacred duties as professional soldiers in battle. Yet some in the media tended to portray their deaths as complete losses that carried no intrinsic meaning or significance. Some even wondered if these deaths were senseless.[13] Yet as professional soldiers, Luttrell and his comrades understood the honor of their oaths and carried out their duties with full knowledge of the high costs and consequences attached to their responsibilities. Did Luttrell and his colleagues, did we as a society, not gain something invaluable in witnessing the totality of their devotion to their professional oaths both to each other and to their country?

If attorneys, pastors and priests, or business executives were to give themselves to their professions in the ways Seal Team 10 demonstrated, which is a perfect model of the nature of the commitment Ruskin describes, is it not reasonable to assume the public's respect for the status of these professions as honest and ethical pursuits in the Gallup polls would improve? Could this not become true of all vocations?

ETHICAL MARKS OF A PROFESSION

As discussed earlier in our investigation of political leadership, democratic action lies in a vast nexus between voting and representation. How long can a democracy exist when only 11 percent of the public has confidence in the moral character of members of Congress? Therefore, the problems of a contemporary democratic form of government can only be solved by a pervasive public commitment to highly developed moral practice and conscientiousness in our leaders. This is especially crucial for those leaders who are professionals possessing the specialization, authority, and knowledge required for societies to flourish.

The Gallup poll demonstrates precisely why "professional ethics" and moral knowledge are so crucially linked and why it is paramount for contemporary society to reestablish them in order to pursue common flourishing. We often hear the term "ethics" at the worst possible time, usually after some significant abuse has occurred. Yet bringing public attention to an abuse after the fact is tantamount to crying over already spilled milk with no plan for preventing future spills or replacing the milk that was lost. Therefore, we suggest three general ethical requirements are necessary through which we as a society can address the crucial problems of professional life.

However, three preliminary observations are required. First, the pursuit of "professional ethics" as now publicly invoked is an attempt on the part of either the government or watch-dog agencies to control professional *behavior*. Nearly always these oversight organizations, whether public or private, strive to apply rules and standards that deal specifically with (a) how the professions go about the task of making money, (b) how and where money is used, and (c) regulation of engagements regarding influence and power, especially in matters of favors or privilege given to positions of various kinds. In addition to these oversight organizations, the professions themselves regularly, although not uniformly, create and promote some sort of code of ethics to which the appropriate public agency may then, supposedly, hold the profession and its members accountable.[14]

The second observation is to realize that neither the oversight agencies nor the self-mandated codes of ethics rarely if ever state anything about the practice of the profession being *a means through which moral self-realization can be both pursued and achieved.* The point here is that for a code of ethics to be robust, it must expect that the very profession it governs must also provide a means through which a people can become good, admirable, or moral persons *while engaging their work or performing their duties.*

This is crucial for future generations of professionals. The students graduating from universities and colleges today come out of those institutions with a high degree of idealism and willingness to sacrifice and serve for the greater good. Many of these young adults desire to spend their lives promoting the general welfare through their pursuit of professions such as law, engineering, medicine, or government service. Yet this idealism is routinely crushed on the rocks of the very codes that govern their work. It is an all too frequent experience within the hallways of professional institutions to encounter "wide-eyed" new professionals who have come to the realization that their position, as it is taught and practiced in "the real world," has begun to smother their original inspiration to positively affect the world through their chosen field.

What "rookies" soon learn is that the codes of conduct and ethics that can and should set the ideal standards of moral virtue are in practice primarily devoted to keeping one out of trouble with clients, the law, and competitors. What is rarely if ever spoken of, but what every professional soon comes to understand with time and experience, is that one could stay out of such trouble and still be a pretty rotten person. There is a wide difference between staying out of trouble and being the type of morally competent individual who is capable of successfully navigating the legal, ethical, and moral dilemmas that are routinely encountered in the normal course of fulfilling professional duties.

The third observation is that behavior commonly judged either ethical or unethical makes its impact and has its effects regardless of whether such behavior is properly acknowledged, classified, or held to account. Good behaviors have an effect, as do bad behaviors. These effects occur regardless of what we call them or whether they are recognized properly or even mentioned. Following bad behavior, one seldom "gets away scot-free." For example, think what a vast difference in the course of life good behaviors such as telling the truth, being generous, abstaining from stealing, and acting for individuals' welfare, as opposed to intentionally doing harm (malice), would make in any workplace environment. Consider what an incalculable transformation such actions would have on human life if routinely applied in a family. Or imagine a society in which all professionals were chiefly and intelligently committed to their specific role in society above self-advancement or financial rewards. The difference in such cases would be staggering, irrespective of whether we acknowledge or apply any qualifications such as morally "wrong" or "right" to these activities.

We—all of us—do in fact reap what we sow in our own behaviors, thoughts, and actions (Gal. 6:7). Reaping occurs whether we want it to occur, whether we realize we are reaping, or whether we accurately acknowledge the consequences of our actions. This is why determining what is moral and ethical behavior is so crucial to the professional arena. There is always fruit produced as a result of our motivations and decisions.

Finally, if professional ethics are to accomplish something beyond or in addition to ethics generally (recall John Maxwell's Golden Rule ethics here), then it seems at least three requirements must be included in such attempts. Professional ethics must endeavor to:

Explain why people of professional standing may or ought to do things that, if done by others, would be morally wrong. For instance, a surgeon has the authority to use a scalpel to open someone's chest. A nonsurgeon would likely be charged with a crime for such behavior.

Explain what special moral obligations those in each of the professions have (i.e., the specific ethical requirements of a lawyer, those of a physician, etc.). These differences should be described, defended, and publicized in order for the profession to be held to account for its moral standards.

Explain how the professional field serves as an arena of moral realization. There must be a clear description of how being, for example, an attorney, an accountant, or a pastor promotes and encourages the means of becoming and remaining a good person working toward the common good.

APPLYING MORAL KNOWLEDGE IN PROFESSIONAL LIFE

We have argued previously the key mark of a professional is the presence of extensive knowledge in an essential arena of life. Furthermore we have stated that a basic human need is to find the knowledge adequate to sustain and prosper in life. This includes knowledge of right and wrong. A profession requires such knowledge as well, in order to promote the good that the profession aims to achieve. To be effective in their fields, professionals must first endeavor to attain the appropriate knowledge of these areas. So the proper question then is: When can we discern one has attained this knowledge? Again we state one knows something when one is able to represent it *as it is on an appropriate basis of thought and experience.* Also, truth and suitable evidence are essential for acquiring moral knowledge.

In an attempt to draw the importance of moral character and moral knowledge together, let us consider for a moment the profession of accounting. The American Institute of Certified Public Accounting has a professional code of conduct.[15] In the preamble of this document are two articles:

1. Membership in the American Institute of Certified Public Accountants is voluntary. By accepting membership, a certified public accountant assumes an obligation of self-discipline above and beyond the requirements of laws and regulations.

2. These Principles of the Code of Professional Conduct of the American Institute of Certified Public Accountants express the profession's recognition of its responsibilities to the public, to clients, and to colleagues. They guide members in the performance of their professional responsibilities and express the basic tenets of ethical and professional conduct. The Principles call for an unswerving commitment to honorable behavior, even at the sacrifice of personal advantage.

Articles 1 and 2 of the code of conduct itself speak specifically to the responsibilities of accountants to their profession and to their clients:

Article 1. As professionals, certified public accountants perform an essential role in society. Consistent with that role, members of the American Institute of Certified Public Accountants have responsibilities to all those who use their professional services. Members also have a continuing responsibility to cooperate with each other to improve the art of accounting, maintain the public's confidence, and carry out the profession's special responsibilities for self-governance. The collective efforts of all members are required to maintain and enhance the traditions of the profession.

Article 2, Section 1. A distinguishing mark of a profession is acceptance of its responsibility to the public. The accounting profession's public consists of clients, credit grantors, governments, employers, investors, the business and financial community, and others who rely on the objectivity and integrity of certified public accountants to maintain the orderly functioning of commerce. This reliance imposes a public interest responsibility on certified public accountants. The public interest is defined as the collective well-being of the community of people and institutions the profession serves.

Think about what might have been prevented if the accountants involved in the Enron scandal had courageously followed these simple yet powerful rules, which they swore to uphold. Accountants are in a perfect position to discover the overarching financial health and condition of a company. Yet to accomplish this there must be an understanding (knowledge) of what a loss, a debt, a liability, or a risk actually is. Any attempt to hide, "redefine," manipulate, ignore, or obfuscate these elements and not report them to the public (as certified public accountants are tasked and sworn to do) is to demonstrate a lack of either integrity, knowledge, or perhaps both. When these professional responsibilities are not carried out, then the potential for a crisis of confidence is created in the public marketplace and dire consequences such as those witnessed in the Enron debacle are allowed to ensue.

There is plenty of guilt to go around on the Enron matter. The point here is that the calamitous nature of the crisis could not have reached the levels it did if those sworn to uphold the truth and report the underlying facts actually followed through with their moral and professional responsibilities. This is the obvious and essential nature of moral knowledge and a tragic example of its absence in everyday matters of great importance. In fact, there was a right and wrong way to classify, count, represent, and report corporate assets and liabilities. In the Enron affair, those tasked with this professional responsibility did not use their knowledge of their profession to protect and serve the public.

Generally speaking the possession of knowledge gives one the right—and even the responsibility in certain circumstances—to act, direct action, form or implement policies, and teach and guide others into the knowledge attained. This is why knowledge claims are both very powerful and potentially dangerous. If and when the features and attributes of moral knowledge are reinstated into the professions, then there is no reason why professional life shouldn't once again be a primary means through which goodness, justice, blessing, and flourishing will prevail in our communities.

PROFESSIONALS AND THEIR MONEY

We have discussed the reasons behind why professionals have both an obligation and an opportunity to demonstrate their moral goodness in ways that allow those who heed their persuasive arguments to pursue both individual and common flourishing. We have also argued that professional status offers rights and privileges not available to nonprofessionals. Now we must engage the issues of compensation for our professionals. Matters related to the compensation of our professional ranks are as essential as those related to the profit motive in business. It should therefore come as no shock that the ways in which professionals both earn and demonstrate the product of their livelihoods are yet another public witness to and expression of the values and virtues that the professions require.

First, the professions have a duty to lead our society in setting an appropriate, beneficial, and applicable standard of fair compensation. This is crucial for helping everyone within the economic universe to understand proper rewards and incentives for labor that can withstand moral critique. What professionals are up against today is a significant amount of misunderstanding as to the nature of their work and a major assumption within our society regarding what can be called the inalienable right to self-aggrandizement. In Western consumer-driven socioeconomic climates, there is a growing tendency to believe that one has the right to make as much money as possible, provided such money is attained legally. Today athletes, musicians, inventors, prospectors, investors, traders, and landowners are all conceded that right. In such a system there is no reason to assume that professionals cannot be afforded the same right as well, if they are otherwise fulfilling their obligations to clients and society at large. If professionals are accused of lowering the standards for their services or increasing their own self-interest over those they serve, this is another matter altogether. This is precisely why professionals should never let the call of money itself detract from the proper delivery of their expertise and advice, a matter we will pick up again shortly. What is more critical for our professionals to consider is the degree to which this idea of an individual right to unlimited self-aggrandizement is itself good, right, and therefore worthy of pursuit throughout our society.

This is not an argument against capitalism or free-market economies. Rather, this is a general investigation into some specific effects of wealth on individuals and societies that are seeking common goods and general welfare. Money itself is not moral or immoral. The same can be said for those with or without money. The important point here is that the presence of money or the promise of wealth does have power over human beings, not only in the sense that money is used in various ways to persuade people to perform certain behaviors, but also in that those with money, simply by virtue of being who they are, often have influence over the course of events whether or not they actively exercise such influence. Therefore, money is a certain type of power, though certainly not the only or the most dominating force in our world. Still, we could say that some of the most wealthy maintain and even spread their influence without directly using their wealth at all. Often the mere presence of massive accumulations of either money or possessions tends to affect those of modest means who come in contact with or move in orbits around the wealthy. Therefore, since money is a type of power, the prospect of an unlimited right to ever increasing degrees of wealth would logically lead to the unlimited right to increasing degrees of power and influence over others. Is this what we seek? Should there not be at least some means of holding such power to account? We do hold all other powers to account—political power, judicial power, military power, creative power, and so on. Is there not a connection to be sought in holding the power of wealth to account? If so, who is to do such accounting, if not those in our professional arenas?

The power required to hold the influential to account is necessarily demanding and must be reserved for only those who can be impeccably trusted to wield it well. Fortunately, with some very notable exceptions, our society and the world greatly benefit from untold numbers of materially prosperous individuals who have not misapplied their monetary influence and instead routinely use their substantial resources in support of the common welfare. In such cases, these individuals are in fact not falling prey to the principle of unlimited self-aggrandizement, but are instead endeavoring to use their resources in ways that supremely promote the general welfare. What we have to consider is what will happen as this sense of moral obligation and opportunity is lost or overwhelmed by competing interests.

It is therefore the responsibility of our professional leaders and spokespersons to demonstrate the high calling of professional life and the responsibilities that accompany such great privilege. Fortunately, some of the wealthiest individuals in the world are currently doing just this. The work that the Bill and Melinda Gates Foundation and Warren Buffet have done together is but one example of professionals understanding their responsibility to use their influence well. However, it is easy to assume only the wealthiest carry such a burden. Instead, we suggest every professional is charged with determining how to manage the privileges and material rewards of professional life in ways that focus on the common welfare and not the building of individual financial empires. Philanthropy, the love of humanity, must return to its rightful place in our social consciousness, and the professions must lead the way.

THE PROFESSIONS AS INSTRUMENTS OF RIGHTEOUSNESS

We propose that leaders who are concerned, dedicated, and capable of pursuing and achieving the common good for all those dependent upon their services and expertise are a natural and necessary component within the structure of any human society that diligently seeks to achieve a good and flourishing life for its citizens. Though its precise form will vary from culture to culture, depending on the primary values that govern it and the history of its institutionalized development, professionalism is a natural progression of specialization that is conducive to the well-being of the whole of which it is a part—in this case, of the populace—and thereby of the individuals that make up our societies.

Again, returning to our understandings of the divisions of labor (and the apostle Paul's understanding of the parts of the body of Christ as mutually dependent on each other to serve the whole, 1 Cor. 12:12–31), we must realize and acknowledge that maintaining different roles in society does not mean that any are underappreciated or treated unequally. Professionals have a degree of responsibility and importance for conducting life in complex societies, and failures in carrying out these responsibilities often have more serious consequences than with nonprofessionals. However, a good and flourishing society is not made up of only professionals. Such is hardly the case or the objective.

The goal is that all who are served by our professional ranks are blessed by them, through their expertise and experience, to accomplish what they could not accomplish on their own. As necessary and beneficial as each role is to our communities, the major public goods in society upon which our well-being depends are in the hands of professional people. These individuals and the power they wield to effect good or ill is wide sweeping in ways and effects that are plainly unique. We must begin the process of acknowledging this social reality.

CHAPTER 13

Physicians, Lawyers, and Pastors or Priests

T O RECAP, WE are not attempting a comprehensive or detailed investigation into any of these professions here. Further, we realize it is a difficult task for professionals to remain consciously aware of all the ethical and moral considerations pertinent to their actions and of the proper weighting each action should have in relation to a specific situation or client. What further complicates matters is the ongoing and rapid rate of change, especially in highly technical fields. Hence, we are not attempting to cast any disparaging light on any of the professions.

Instead, as outsiders using the disciplines of philosophy and theology, both of which pursue and investigate the effect and objective of ethics, we hope to cast something of a new or at least an unaccustomed light upon the ethical assumptions and pursuits of these three key professions. The desire is to briefly consider how experts in a few fields might see their way through the fog of our contemporary society to focus more clearly on how the overarching effect of their professions can better benefit society as a whole. This will require first understanding the traditional purposes of each of these professions and critiquing either competing interests or self-interests that may threaten to derail the essential service each of these professions must provide and protect.

PHYSICIANS

*A physician is obligated to consider more
than a diseased organ, more even than the whole
man—he must view the man in his world.*

Harvey Cushing (1869–1939),
FOUNDER OF NEUROSURGERY

We can start the discussion of the medical field by looking more closely at the Hippocratic oath. Maybe then some degree of the seriousness of the medical calling can begin to renew our expectations for all the healing pursuits. This version of the Hippocratic oath was quoted in a work published in 1987:

I will look upon him who shall have taught me this Art even as one of my parents. I will share my substance with him, and I will supply his necessities, if he be in need. I will regard his offspring even as my own brethren, and I will teach them this Art, if they would learn it, without fee or covenant. I will impart this Art by precept, by lecture, and by every mode of teaching, not only to my own sons but to the sons of him who has taught me, and to disciples bound by covenant and oath, according to the Law of Medicine.

The regimen I adopt shall be for the benefit of my patients according to my ability and judgment, and not for their hurt or for any wrong. I will give no deadly drug to any, though it be asked of me, nor will I counsel such, and especially I will not aid a woman to procure abortion. Whatsoever house I enter, there will I go for the benefit of the sick, refraining from all wrongdoing or corruption, and especially from any act of seduction, of male or female, of bond or free. Whatsoever things I see or hear concerning the life of men, in my attendance on the sick or even apart there from, which ought not to be noised abroad, I will keep silence thereon, counting such things to be as sacred secrets.[1]

No doubt the special mention of abstaining from abortion procedures is something that will quickly draw the attention of many readers. For our concerns here, we will focus on the words "covenant," "disciples," and "sacred." These words convey a religious context or conviction to the oath. In fact, that is exactly what this oath demonstrates.

What is now routinely left out of the Hippocratic oath quoted above is a short preamble that lists the divine beings to whom the oath was offered. The "swearing" of the oath was traditionally made to several ancient Greek gods, namely, Apollo, his son Asclepius, and Asclepius's two daughters, Hygeia and Panacea. Ancient Greeks believed that these specific gods and goddesses were the key divine figures who governed health and well-being.[2] Among other things this fact highlights how early physicians understood the necessity of divine intervention in the fulfillment of their duties. The practice of medicine was then, as now, a delicate and dangerous endeavor. The profession demands inordinate amounts of time, effort, and experience to develop the knowledge and skills of diagnosis and treatment. Symptoms are elusive, if not invisible. A patient's prognosis can be both the most valuable and at the same time the least desirable information ever received. A physician's success in previous diagnostics can lead to a deadly sense of overconfidence. Misdiagnosis is a double-edged sword. Offering a negative prognosis followed by a positive outcome may injure the soul as deeply as a negative outcome from a positive prognosis could injure the body.

To whom does the physician call for aid in such quandaries? In ancient Greece such prayers flowed to the gods. Apollo was a very logical choice for the physician's prayer,[3] because he was the god of healing, reason, and prophecy, all skills needed to discern the nature of and foretell the progress of disease. Greek mythology suggested Apollo maintained a significant fondness for human beings, having fallen in love with the princess Coronis. Asclepius was their star-crossed love child. Thus, for the physician, personal and corporate obligation, moral duty, religious faith, and scientific reason have long been intertwined in an extended, conflicted, yet memorialized legacy.

Bioethics professor Ronald Numbers notes this conflict has ebbed and flowed over the past century. The voice of the medical professional has not always been as marginalized as it is today. Numbers quotes American Medical Association president Nathaniel Chapman, lamenting the trajectory of his profession:

> The profession to which we belong, once venerated on account of its antiquity—its varied and profound science—its elegant literature—its polite accomplishments—its virtues—has become corrupt and degenerate, to the forfeiture of its social position, and with it, of the homage it formerly received spontaneously and universally.[4]

Ironically, Chapman's words were part of his address to those gathered at the inaugural meeting of the AMA—in 1848. What is it in Chapman's appraisal that appears to be if not identical, at least distinctly similar, to what many both inside and outside the medical field sense is amiss today?

Prior to the mid-nineteenth century the medical profession in America was composed mostly of well-educated elites. Some outlaw healers ran about, but most had earned medical degrees and professional status. By the time Chapman presided over the AMA, the medical profession had degenerated into something akin to a trade; doctors were similar to butchers or barbers. This was part of the dark side of an enterprising new American opportunism. In a new land marked by individual freedom, it was possible to try your hand at even the most sophisticated and delicate disciplines without training or license, even where life and death literally hung perilously in the balance.[5] Thankfully, the medical profession reorganized and in less than a century, Numbers argues, developed into an even stronger, more robust, and more prominent profession. Laws were developed, standards set, and credentials protected; knowledge increased. A century after Chapman's ominous appraisal, the medical professional had regained much if not all of its previous respect and admiration.[6]

However, since World War II significant shifts have effected prominent changes, many of which have detrimentally impacted both the profession and the public it serves.[7] Sociologist Paul Starr and others suggest the most significant change resulted from the partnership between the medical profession as a whole and federal and state governments.[8] The consequences were many and varied. Yet the most significant outcome was the creation of an enduring conflict of interest when the promise of public funds for medical universities and research was tied to the acceptance of Medicare and Medicaid insurance payments by individual physicians and hospitals. At the time few physicians were willing to submit the autonomy of their medical practice to a federal bureaucracy. But eventually the entrance of the government as a third party came down to a standoff between funding medical research in the academy and intrusion of the government into the previously sacred doctor-patient relationship at the local practitioner level. Most of us are now intimately aware of which side prevailed. Today approximately 90 percent of office-based physicians accept Medicare patients.[9]

The medical research and technology side of the equation has exploded in post–World War II America with much added value and benefit to the public. Astounding advances are made almost daily, but increasing costs have created a crisis of overspending on both federal budgets and corporate ledgers. The advances in technology have simultaneously raised patient expectations to an unreasonable level, often fueling the belief that everything, eventually, will be treatable. Personal health has now become assumed as a right, not a blessing. Any medical result that is not acceptable to the patient or the patient's family creates the threat of legal action. Physicians are not gods, but they are regularly expected to produce an unreasonable standard of godlike success.

Conflicts or lack of cooperation in government-funded health research and private pharmaceutical research have also created significant social and ethical questions. Who decides, and how do they decide, what is really in the best interest of common flourishing with regard to which diseases and ailments will gain top priority in our medical research laboratories? How should these decisions and the courses of action involved in directing the limited resources available for disease research be pursued? If it is true there are only so many public funds available for medical research, is it reasonable to assume there should be a means of determining our collective priorities and health needs? Setting priorities is, in part, what the national budget process is designed to do. Where is the evidence of sustained cooperation between our medical professionals who lead government-funded health research and our publicly or privately owned pharmaceutical companies in determining where and how to direct medical research in order to pursue the greatest public benefit and overall wellness? Which diseases should receive top billing and why?

Here we return to the issue of fiduciary responsibility. Who determines what is in the best interest of the patient? Should this be the primary responsibility of the medical professional? Does it lie with the official representing the interests of the private insurance company and its shareholders or with the government health-care administrator, or does this responsibility belong in the hands of the patient? Until recently the for-profit insurance industry had largely stepped into this gap. Although many of these businesses do a very fine job in difficult situations, we can and should honestly evaluate the ways other countries have endeavored to answer these questions and to what effect. We can at least ask how the way we have structured relationships between the government and for-profit and nonprofit organizations affects the level and scope of care provided in our country.

The apparent shift in duties from medical professionals to insurance companies and government agencies has created the opportunity for a confusion of priorities. Medical professionals—including not only the health-care providers, but also the insurance companies offering coverage and other professionals involved—ought to determine how much profit and how much prioritization of profits is best in the medical industry. Perhaps regulation of profit margins is not the answer to the concerns of one's health and quality of life. Many for-profit medical facilities provide wonderful care. Again, profit in itself is not the issue. The question is: Does a focus on profit currently get in the way of the mission of the medical profession, which is to provide care—and if so why, how, and what ought to be done about it?

By now it should be obvious how these questions require more robust engagement than has occurred thus far in the public domain. Limiting the debate to only public-policy issues—such as whether we should have more government subsidies versus a freer market—is inadequate. These debates are important and pivotal. But is it our political or judicial system that is best prepared and equipped to oversee these dilemmas? Does the law or do our legal professionals or elected officials possess the expertise to negotiate these issues best?

This brings us again to why moral leadership in the professions is so crucial. We argue that a concert of ethical voices offering reason and wisdom must proceed from the medical profession itself. Political activists on both sides of the aisle claim to speak for the medical profession. We must hear more from the medical profession as a profession itself. Its expertise is paramount and should be given primary consideration on these crucial matters.

One must also ask how much of the runaway costs involved in our current health-care system can be directly attributed to physicians ordering testing procedures simply in an attempt to, as we say, "cover their backside." This has become an area insurers have highlighted to good effect. Still, the problem tends to arise from an overly litigious political climate led by some legal professionals who are both willing and able to create doubt or assign blame where none is to be found simply in the hopes of garnering a large settlement. Is it best for all concerned that our medical professionals are concerned first and foremost with managing their risk of a lawsuit, and our health insurance companies or government agencies are discerning what treatments are necessary or "covered"? Perhaps it is. How would we best come to a rational decision about these matters on an appropriate basis of both thought and experience? Currently, physicians are often forced to begin even routine diagnostic exams on the defensive in order to protect valuable careers in the event they are called upon to defend themselves against not only the unforeseeable but also the indefensible. Is this the best means of providing oversight to our medical professionals?

Finally, we can think about how the consumer mentality has progressively invaded the medical profession. Are consumers/patients always "right" when it comes to health concerns? How do consumers/patients determine what is in their best interests for their own health needs? Is perfect health a reasonable expectation for all persons? Is it beneficial for patients to continue developing unrealistic expectations that a pill or procedure be made readily available to them in order to solve every ailment and cure every disease? Is the presence or absence of pain or the procurement of a final cure the primary means of determining whether physicians or medical professionals have done their duty properly? If consumers alone are left to determine and gauge the effectiveness of their treatment based on the widely subjective measurement of "consumer satisfaction," what are we to do with the concept of convalescent and terminal care? In these situations, what is a reasonable expectation for quality of care, and who should set these standards, consumers/patients or medical professionals?

Many of these issues came up for public debate and consideration during the effort to forge new health-care legislation. Unfortunately, instead of engaging in open and intelligent debate, much of the country found itself caught in an ongoing deadlock between competing lobbying groups, most of which appeared more concerned with power, money, and self-interest than pursuing the common welfare of all concerned. Where does all this stand today? Very few can accurately explain and even fewer have effectively communicated what program or system of health care is currently holding sway. There have been lawsuits, blockages, filibusters, state programs, federal programs, local programs, private programs, and multiple combinations of all the above. Meanwhile ordinary citizens, many of whom are advanced in years, find themselves wading through a deluge of paper and choices that are crucial to their well-being yet are nearly indiscernibly complicated. Exactly who can the public trust on these issues?

Fortunately, there are untold thousands of physicians and health-care workers who, despite their circumstances, political climates, and working conditions, remain faithful to their calling to love and care for the people they serve whether in an office, in a hospital, on an operating table, or in a laboratory. The key phrase here is "despite their circumstances." What the medical profession must consider is how to improve not only its services, but what services, products, and goods it must pursue, accomplish, and avoid.

These difficult issues, set on a massive scale, require equally complicated decisions, which cannot be addressed appropriately here. That is the point. Medical professionals must work together in tackling these matters precisely because they have the knowledge and expertise to properly address them. It is not in the boardroom, on the congressional floor, in the voting booth, or in the jury box that these matters should be ultimately pursued and solved. Certainly each of these arenas of expertise can and must offer their particular assistance as appropriate. Even still, the medical profession, by definition, is not one that can or should be engaged by barbers or butchers any more than it should be led by government agents, politicians, lawyers, or business executives.

This is a fact so obvious as to seem ridiculous. As in all professions, only those with the requisite knowledge of the field can bring to bear the full spectrum of issues and opportunities the public faces every day.

Herein lies the very nature of what it means to be a steward or shepherd of people in a fiduciary relationship. A large number of health-care professionals go about their calling with great honor and skill. The hope and encouragement here is for these men and women to take up the charge of the crucial work of reform. Physicians must uniformly develop a strategy to reclaim their professional interests for the good of the whole. However, in doing so, they must also keep at the forefront the key attribute of professional conduct, self-governance. Those within the medical fields have historically been reticent to clean their own houses of incompetence, malpractice, and fraud. Undoubtedly careful, reasonable, and legally prudent steps need to be taken in making these judgments with justice and due process. This is part of the issue. The medical profession alone must determine how to dedicate itself to wholesale elimination of fraud, cover-ups, overbilling, and substandard care within its ranks and thus form efficient means to accomplish the necessary ends. Until this oversight is established, there is little reason for the public or the government to feel secure in reallocating its full faith and trust to the profession.

We face countless wide-ranging and complicated medical issues today with global consequences. Of course very few issues have been discussed here; there are many more issues related to medical ethics that would require much more sophisticated investigation. We have only scratched the surface. The major point is that the medical profession must recapture what is essential to its creation and purposes: to, with all hast and vigor, heal and guide toward wellness those within our society who are desperate for their care and knowledge. This is the great call of mercy and comfort, which has been a central tenet for so many Christian orders down through the ages. It is to the care of the body (hospitals), care of the soul (churches), and education of the mind (schools) that both Catholic and Protestant traditions alike have dedicated the bulk of their resources and devotion over the centuries.

Healing, comfort, care, restoration, and well-being are components that together form *shalom*. The medical profession is precisely the instrument to achieve just such a high calling. Perhaps the time has come to reach back to a much earlier era when an oath was made to a higher power for the courage, faith, and wisdom to "benefit . . . patients according to ability and judgment, and not for their hurt or for any wrong." Surely a good and loving God such as Jesus describes would hear such a cry for blessing and honor and give abundantly more than we could even ask or imagine in reply.

LAWYERS

There is a vague popular belief that lawyers are necessarily dishonest. I say vague, because when we consider to what extent confidence and honors are reposed in and conferred upon lawyers by the people, it appears improbable that their impression of dishonesty is very distinct and vivid. Yet the impression is common, almost universal. Let no young man choosing the law for a calling for a moment yield to the popular belief—resolve to be honest at all events; and if in your own judgment you cannot be an honest lawyer, resolve to be honest without being a lawyer. Choose some other occupation, rather than one in the choosing of which you do, in advance, consent to be a knave.

Discourage litigation. Persuade your neighbors to compromise whenever you can. Point out to them how the nominal winner is often a real loser—in fees, expenses, and waste of time. As a peacemaker the lawyer has a superior opportunity of being a good man. There will still be business enough.

ABRAHAM LINCOLN

In pursuing God's invitation to revolutionize the world so that his justice and righteousness are both known and experienced throughout all creation, the profession of law is of paramount importance in both achieving and maintaining flourishing for our societies. In continuing our focus on professional oaths that seek to assure excellence and integrity in these pursuits, we note several such proclamations that cover the legal profession. There is one for every state. Just for the sake of reference we will list here the oath for admission to the State Bar of Arizona:

> I, (state your name), do solemnly swear that I will support the Constitution of the United States and the Constitution of the State of Arizona;
>
> I will maintain the respect due to courts of justice and judicial officers;
>
> I will not counsel or maintain any suit or proceeding that shall appear to me to be without merit or to be unjust; I will not assert any defense except such as I honestly believe to be debatable under the law of the land;
>
> I will employ for the purpose of maintaining the causes confided to me such means only as are consistent with truth and honor; I will never seek to mislead the judge or jury by any misstatement or false statement of fact or law;
>
> I will maintain the confidence and preserve inviolate the secrets of my client; I will accept no compensation in connection with my client's business except from my client or with my client's knowledge and approval;
>
> I will abstain from all offensive conduct; I will not advance any fact prejudicial to the honor or reputation of a party or witness, unless required by the justice of the cause with which I am charged;
>
> I will never reject, from any consideration personal to myself, the cause of the defenseless or oppressed, nor will I delay any person's cause for greed or malice;

I will at all times faithfully and diligently adhere to the rules of professional responsibility and a lawyer's creed of professionalism of the State Bar of Arizona.[10]

It is interesting to consider the number of television shows, movies, and bestselling vacation novels that would never see the light of day if these simple and straightforward statements were actually followed by lawyers. Perhaps the only dramas that attract our attention are those that highlight the various ways in which legal professionals find ways around these oaths.

In addition to oaths, statements of moral character are also required for practicing law at the highest levels. There is an application and approval process for those who wish to argue a case before the Supreme Court of the United States of America.[11] Of specific interest is the "Statement of Sponsor." What this section requires is a list of existing members of the Bar of the Supreme Court of the United States who are not related to, but are personally acquainted with, the new applicant. Such sponsors must be willing to validate "that the applicant possesses all the qualifications required for admission to the Bar of the Supreme Court of the United States, and that [they] have examined the applicant's personal statement and believe it to be correct, and [they] affirm that the applicant's moral and professional character and standing are good."[12]

There it is, right out in the open for all to see, the unabashed expectation of good moral and professional character as a requirement for those engaging in the legal profession. Again and again we see the crucial issue of expert knowledge matched with impeccable moral character. Here we must ask again, how is one to determine the standards for defining moral character? Obviously the application to practice law before the Supreme Court assumes this is possible. There must be a relationship—personal knowledge and experience—that allows the discernment of the moral character and professional standing of one person by another. Of course it is assumed such a "sponsor" must also be a person of high moral character. The members of the Bar of the Supreme Court assume that "it takes one (a moral person) to know one (a moral person)." Again, what a revolutionary, if not somewhat old-fashioned, idea.

What we stated earlier regarding the necessity of moral self-realization in the practice of a profession is key to remember on this point. How is the prerequisite of good and valiant moral character to be discerned for a legal professional who desires to be admitted to the Bar of the Supreme Court of the United States? Who is to judge the degree of such morality whether present or absent? Not to be too cute about this, but it seems such a judgment, if not made in one's favor, is just the sort of slight where one might claim damages and sue for slander or defamation of character. Undoubtedly, suits like this do happen—not necessarily because such character is actually judged incorrectly—but because there is no agreed-upon standard by which to compare instances of moral character. Therefore, a judge must decide. But how is such a judgment to be adjudicated? This is but one example of the problem moral and ethical subjectivism has created in our society as it relates to our legal system.

It is for these reasons that, when comparing the three professions discussed here, the field of law must require a higher standard of character in its practitioners. The legal profession is arguably more susceptible to political temptations and attempts to avoid public accountability than any other professional arena. Many of those in governmental positions (elected officials, staffers, appointees, etc.) or connected with governmental functions (e.g., private lobbying firms) are legal professionals themselves. This is certainly not a new phenomenon. Of the fifty-five delegates who attended the original Constitutional Convention in 1787, nearly 60 percent had received legal training, were practicing lawyers, or had been judges at one time in their careers.[13] Of course it is appropriate and good to have individuals who are capable of discerning legal qualities and requirements when preparing documents as far-reaching and important as the Declaration of Independence and the Constitution. Declaring independence from Great Britain and founding a country are no small matters. Even still, the point stands that such legal expertise can, in the wrong hands, lead to abuse. For example, the choice to not outlaw slavery in the originating documents of our new nation is evidence, for some, of a lack of moral character and a misuse (nonuse) of the legal power these professionals wielded.[14]

For purposes of clarity, let us focus more specifically on a single issue. Ask yourself the question: Today do we, as the American public, generally act as if we believe that those in the legal profession are "moral" people, demonstrating moral character, who can be trusted to write on our behalf documents as important and consequential as the Declaration of Independence? Perhaps one way to measure this kind of inquiry is to consider the general public reaction to the proposed changes in the health-care system. Public opinion polls, such as they are, seem to point away from what one might call "exceeding confidence" in our legal professions and their discernment about to what is just, legal, and beneficial in the enacting of health-care legislation.[15] We must start to probe the underlying sources of this void of confidence.

We can begin by considering why the oaths and applications mentioned above ask questions about moral character in the first place. Simply stated, moral character is a prerequisite for understanding, pursuing, and protecting justice and righteousness in public life. Such virtues have traditionally been at the very foundation of what the rule of law endeavors to seek and apply in legal documents as general as the Declaration of Independence or as specific as health-care legislation. We now have to ask ourselves the question: Do we, in general, believe that personal and professional morality is a primary objective for those practicing in the legal profession today? Is justice the overarching objective of our legal system and those who operate in it? In negotiating and applying the laws that govern our lands, are these groups pursuing that which is good, right, true, just, and best for the general well-being of all concerned?

Again, we can return to the single issue mentioned earlier regarding health care. Are the laws that have been enacted regarding public health in the best interest of the common good? How would we know, or what would the public use as a reference or measurement, to determine what was best? How much of our cost and confusion in the health-care arena is attributed specifically to frivolous litigation that does not meet the standards of maintaining "any suit or proceeding that shall appear . . . to be without merit or to be unjust"? How many legal proceedings require a defense that cannot honestly be believed "to be debatable under the law of the land"?

Rarely is this the end of the matter. Such suits create an opportunity for substantial financial benefit to legal professionals and their clients in the form of an out-of-court settlement. In practice, because the legal profession can levy such hefty fees, a settlement is often less injurious than the cost of seeking justice. In such cases, determining the ethical differences between a "negotiated settlement" and extortion is often impossible, although under the law one is permissible and the other isn't. Furthermore, how can we allow something to be morally and ethically indefensible yet legally acceptable? How could such a reality be tolerated in the contemporary consciousness? That something could be legal (just) and at the same time highly immoral (unjust) on the basis of some legalese directly contradicts the moral gravity the law must maintain in order to command any respect or authority to govern human behavior. Juxtaposing concepts such as "innocent" and "not guilty" is another example of the ethical high-wire act that very few in the legal profession can perform without serious dishonoring consequences. Legal professionals must remain first and foremost dedicated to truth over and above what can be proven in the processes of our court systems, which are overseen by those holding sway over both the legislative and judicial branches of our government. The fact that these two priorities can at times be mutually exclusive has had catastrophic effects on our judicial system, especially for those who are required to put their lives in the balance of the "blind scales of justice."

The Justice System

Additionally, we need to discuss those professionals who are tasked with law enforcement, applying justice in our court systems as officials representing the people. These are our attorney generals, judges, district attorneys, city attorneys, state prosecutors, and officers of the Department of Justice. Multitudes of legal professionals in the criminal justice system face the daunting task of weeding through the crimes and punishments of a broken society. Often these are heart-wrenching circumstances with devastating results. As officers of the court they are regularly put in the position of attempting the Solomonic task of bringing some resolution, truth, and justice to bear on realities that are sometimes too evil and awful for the general public to imagine. Still these servants of justice devote endless hours to investigation and study in order to bring some degree of *shalom* to horrible and devastating realities. Fortunately, there are countless selfless individuals who protect and serve the greater welfare of our communities with great honor and distinction.

Part of what puts the integrity of these faithful servants of law and justice at great risk is the perilous connection of these positions with public office and the political temptations that develop from it. This is a common occurrence in public life. For instance, legal officials who have larger political aspirations, say to run for mayor or governor of the state, may be tempted to use a particular case or crisis to attract notoriety and implant their name and reputation in the minds of the public. Losing such a case—what for all intents and purposes can become the single key to their future fame and "success"—becomes unthinkable. A "win at all costs" attitude ensues. Ambition can cause mistakes, cut corners, tarnished integrity, and injustice. This is precisely the kind of tragedy that happens in political life and has been documented by journalists time and again.

For example, we have all witnessed the incredible progress being made in the DNA sciences. Now one of the great benefits is that DNA can be used to determine innocence or guilt in criminal cases where biological evidence is available and relevant. Yet every time a conviction is overturned by new DNA evidence, an unmistakable crisis of confidence shakes the very foundations of our criminal justice system. When terrible injustices are meted out to innocent individuals, a deadly blow is suffered throughout our entire society. In many of these cases, but certainly not all, citizens discover how overzealous prosecutors pursued personal victory by manipulating juries or directing investigations in ways that went against their sworn duty to consider all the facts of evidence.

Where is the internal oversight within the legal and criminal justice professions in these situations? Are those in the judicial system fearful of correcting and punishing their own peers? Furthermore, where is the accountability and what role does assessment for reaccreditation play in our schools of law tasked with producing ethical standards in their graduates? Why are we unwilling as educators to teach and then produce men and women who are able to pledge their lives, with integrity of character, to upholding the kinds of ethical oaths they are called to swear upon? Our society desperately needs those within the legal profession, in all its many facets, whether in legislatures or in civil or criminal litigation, to develop the vision, intention, and means to simply and easily follow the expectations of their oaths. Such men and women will "employ for the purpose of maintaining the causes confided to [them] such means only as are consistent with truth and honor; and to never seek to mislead the judge or jury by any misstatement or false statement of fact or law." And society will flourish as a result.

PRIESTS OR PASTORS

Why do you want a letter from me? Why don't you take the trouble to find out for yourselves what Christianity is? You take time to learn technical terms about electricity. Why don't you do as much for theology? Why do you never read the great writings on the subject, but take your information from the secular "experts" who have picked it up as inaccurately as you? Why don't you learn the facts in this field as honestly as your own field? Why do you accept mildewed old heresies as the language of the church, when any handbook on church history will tell you where they came from? Why do you balk at the doctrine of the Trinity—God the three in One—yet meekly acquiesce when Einstein tells you $E=mc^2$? What makes you suppose that the expression "God ordains" is narrow and bigoted, while your own expression, "Science demands" is taken as an objective statement of fact? You would be ashamed to know as little about internal combustion as you know about Christian beliefs. I admit, you can practice Christianity without knowing much theology, just as you can drive a car without knowing much about internal combustion. But when something breaks down in the car, you go humbly to the man who understands the works; whereas if something goes wrong with religion, you merely throw the works away and tell the theologian he is a liar. Why do you want a letter from me telling you about God? You will never bother to check on it or find out whether I'm giving you personal opinions or Christian doctrines. Don't bother. Go away and do some work and let me get on with mine.

DOROTHY L. SAYERS

The third profession we must briefly investigate if we are to revolutionize our world through the good will of God and his kingdom is the profession of ministry. Perhaps no other profession has fallen as far and as quickly during the past two centuries from the heights it once enjoyed. Medical and legal professionals have retained, and in some cases improved upon, their social status. This does not appear to be the case for the clergy. So, unlike with physicians and attorneys, it is necessary to begin with a discussion of how the role of the "divines" (as John Adams called them) defines itself as a valid profession and adds value to the common welfare.

What are the common goods promoted by the ministerial profession? What is its special knowledge and skill? Is it more than the crude description of officiating at the ceremonies involved in "hatching, matching, and dispatching" human beings in their progression through life? Even some of our more devoted Christians who regularly attend and volunteer their time and energies to their local church may seriously and honestly be unclear about their answers to such questions. We believe the ministerial profession is needed now more than ever. But we find ourselves in a cultural climate where proving this need is necessary. So we must be clear on these points.

One scholar states, "The professions taken most seriously and regarded as most honorable are those with some evident connection to matters of ultimate concern." He also argues, "Respected professions are also those which deal with what the culture considers important and dignified subjects."[16] It is for these reasons that during the Middle Ages (the fifth through the fifteenth centuries) the clergy was *the* profession. Upon the development of other professions, even through the seventeenth century, the clergy remained the most honored and respected of professions.

The Function of Ministry

At the founding of the American colonies during the mid-eighteenth century the role of the clergy in American history changed largely due to the ever increasing autonomy of the individual in religion, government, and social ethics. This has led to the progressive "disestablishment" of the clergy or professional ministers.[17] Why this is the case is a long and involved story, so there are only a few issues that we can discuss here. But the primary reason for the disestablishment of the clergy today stems from a lack of understanding and appreciation of religion and therefore increasing resistance to religious worldviews. Ironically, as it turns out, very frequently highly religious people offer some of the most stalwart resistance to the clergy as a professional class. So we must start from a different place than we did with the other professions, because religion no longer enjoys a widely appreciated, understood, and accepted role within contemporary secular societies.

The clergy in society serve two interrelated and necessary functions in human existence. First, ministers maintain knowledge pertinent to transcendental realities, or "ultimate concerns." Among others, these ultimate concerns are related to God, human destiny, the meaning and purposes of life, love, suffering, evil, death, and eternity. Ministers are required to offer wisdom and perspective on these crucial existential issues. Second, ministers engage and supervise the management of the moral concerns of their community based on their knowledge of the divine attributes of God.

Together these two functions of professional ministry, enabled by ministers' transcendent knowledge of God and his character, can require, when appropriate and necessary, that ministers stand in judgment of the political and social situations they engage. The knowledge of the divine nature gives them an authority that is not subject to social manipulation or subsumed by traditions, trends, and interpretations of their cultural climate. Again, Dietrich Bonhoeffer, Martin Luther King Jr., Mother Teresa, and Desmond Tutu are excellent examples in contemporary history. What made these ministers credible was both their claim of transcendent revelations of the truth about what was good and right and the manifestation of these realities in their lives, which at the time rose above, and therefore opposed, the sociopolitical currents of their culture.

The Role of the Divines

Unlike with the other professions engaged previously, as ministers, and teachers of ministers, we do maintain some expertise and experience regarding the profession of ministry. Therefore, as colleagues and insiders we feel more at liberty to offer pointed suggestions and insights. So let us be clear about the exact goods professional Christian ministers of the gospel of Jesus offer their societies. First, Christian ministers mediate the Christian religion's understandings of God's good will and loving power to human beings by manifesting the reality of God's heavenly kingdom. This is accomplished by administering the sacraments, teaching, preaching, and sacrificial service that demonstrates God's love both in and through the local assembly of believers to the world. Second, the minister is responsible to see—or oversee—that good is understood and practiced in the main areas of human life, especially for those living under their care. Third, and perhaps the greatest good professional ministers offer, both historically and in contemporary life, is the guidance they provide to people who look to their religious faith to be trained and equipped to discern the good and then accomplish it in their particular areas of responsibility.

This ability to both know and be able to do the right thing is summarized in the Greek New Testament by the term *dikaiosune* mentioned earlier. *Dikaiosune* is often translated in the New Testament as "righteousness." Like those in no other profession, ministers are specifically tasked to teach, demonstrate, and advocate for *dikaiosune,* first in themselves and then in and through others. This is the specific service of the clergy toward the overarching general welfare. If the clergy fail in this responsibility and opportunity, then what follows is a significant collapse in all the accompanying structures of public and private life.

We have no desire to elevate pastors or priests above any other profession. All professional roles are interdependent, and all Christian professionals must live and work in relationship. Yet it is the pastors or priests who are tasked with disseminating the invaluable information about the nature of God, the ways of the kingdom, and the intention toward goodness that must be present in the activities and priorities of their specific communities, all while bearing testimony of the power of *agape* to transform every aspect of human life and history. Once again, an *agape* form of love is an overall condition of the embodied, social self, poised to promote the goods of human life that are within its range of influence. When *agape* is present there is a disposition or character of goodwill (benevolence) displayed in a readiness to act in pursuit of the highest and best good. *Agape* is not an action or a feeling or emotion, nor is it contained in an intention as we commonly understand "intentions" today. However, *agape* will "spur on" good intentions and actions of a certain type and is associated with some "feelings" while remaining resistant to others. *Agape* is the form of divine love God has for humanity and is marked primarily by an overarching disposition to seek and achieve the good for oneself and others.[18]

Quite simply, there is no other social institution, no other arena of public life that remains exclusively devoted to the definition and proliferation of *agape*, truth, goodness, general welfare, and holistic flourishing than the church of Jesus Christ. If local churches and the professional ministers charged with their care are not focused and resolutely devoted to the promotion of these qualities and the character of individual leaders who embody them in the world, no other group, charity, agency, or institution is prepared and equipped to carry such a task to completion. Clearly, as Jesus rightly understood, the foundational knowledge of Christ and his reign as the Son of the living God builds up the body of Christ, his church, which provides an eternal life from the heavens against which the gates of hell haven't a chance of succeeding.

The Twofold Focus of Christian Ministry

Jesus can be trusted to build his church. Those tasked to lead and care for the local church are therefore undershepherds, coworkers, students, and friends, but not the chief or head Shepherd. That position has been filled once and for all. Therefore, professional Christian ministers must focus on two primary areas of special knowledge essential to the common good and therefore areas to be properly mastered and held accountable for by their peers. It stands to reason these two areas are the most important aspects of human life. The first is connected to the life and function of the *mind,* and the second, to the nature of *spirit.*

These two priorities may appear odd to some. In fact, they may appear so counterintuitive as to offend. Let us be clear. We are not arguing for some Gnostic focus on "head knowledge" or an increased fascination with the mystical. In fact, quite the contrary. Understanding the essential function of the mind and spirit in both human life and kingdom living is foundational for ministers of the gospel. Faithfulness (the established quality of placing confidence in something) and righteousness (*dikaiosune*) are two key determiners of both the outcome of our lives and eternal destinies.

Life in the Mind: Where we put our thoughts—what we think of, what we choose to dwell on—is one of the most important and fundamental aspects of human existence. Therefore the realm of thought is the primary, but not the exclusive, battleground of the gospel in human life. The mind is crucial, because the gospel is initially, and for a time remains predominantly, a collection of ideas that must be considered and understood before the truth of the gospel can take hold of the will.[19] Total mastery of all the ideas connected with the gospel is not required, but there must be a degree of understanding and a sense of settled awareness of what the ideas amount to before action can begin. And the greatest and most pressing of all possible sets of ideas is the one that centers on what one thinks or understands about the nature of God. It is priests or pastors who are assigned the great privilege and service to represent, teach, and guide others to the knowledge of God in our world. This will directly affect how people and societies think about God, their own existence, and the purpose of individual vocational callings and professional responsibilities.

Such an idea is one that has increasingly fallen on hard times, both inside and outside of churches. Yet Romans 1 paints a picture of much of the evil in human life that comes from turning one's mind and thoughts away from divine realities to focus on things of human origin.

We live in a world of fear and uncertainty where the uppermost obsession in our minds is likely to be ourselves. That is why many New Testament teachings center upon the death of self, giving up one's life to save it, picking up one's cross, and denying the desires of the flesh (Luke 9:23–24; Rom. 13:14). Such teachings directly confront most, if not all, of the motivations underlying human activity. When we are endlessly settled on saving ourselves and caught in the progressively inward spiral of self-preservation, exactly the opposite result is achieved. Life is lost, not saved.

Such obsession with self is also a result of many devastating wounds inflicted at the hands of others. Wounds require attention. When we hurt, as we all do in one manner or another, we can become conscious of ourselves to the extent that we become imprisoned by our own self-attention. Run-of-the-mill admonitions to "stop thinking about ourselves" rarely make a dent in the long-established habits of the self-centered mind. Such is the power of habitual thought alone. Even still, becoming locked in a fruitless focus on self prevents us from engaging God with our minds. Finally, anger and desperation routinely lead to attack and withdrawal in our relationships in both subtle and overt ways. Such relational discord stems from the hopeless futility in thinking anything or anyone but God can deliver us from our myopic self-interest.

The question that lingers in the air within our communities and world at large is: How is one to know about God? This is why the proclamation of the gospel as the knowledge of God is absolutely fundamental, essential, and unequivocally necessary for the common well-being. The preaching and teaching of the Logos of God is to reveal the nature of God and his ways. Very simply, this is what the gospel consists of. The gospel is the good, true, and real news about God. In order for us to understand the entire gospel, we must also understand it in the fullness of God. Therefore reducing the gospel to certain doctrines pertaining to things like salvation, justification, atonement, or social/political activism, as important as these are, risks overlooking that these *are subsidiary to the fullness of the nature and essence of God's person.* If we merely think of the gospel as the work of Jesus during a few moments on a cross during his earthly existence, we will miss the grand entirety of his mission on earth. Most crucially, we will miss the essence of God as he is in himself, including his trinitarian relationality, and the ways in which he provides for all of those who are created by him. This is what Paul is attempting to bring across in Ephesians 4:17–24:

> Now this I affirm and insist on in the Lord: you must no longer live as the Gentiles live, in the futility of their minds. They are darkened in their understanding, alienated from the life of God because of their ignorance and hardness of heart. They have lost all sensitivity and have abandoned themselves to licentiousness, greedy to practice every kind of impurity. That is not the way you learned Christ! For surely you have heard about him and were taught in him, as truth is in Jesus. You were taught to put away your former way of life, your old self, corrupt and deluded by its

lusts, and to be renewed in the spirit of your minds, and to clothe yourselves with the new self, created according to the likeness of God in true righteousness and holiness.

Paul is painting a picture of the world apart from God. We must notice the words Paul uses here. "Futility of their minds," "darkened in their understanding," "ignorance," "learned," "taught," "truth"—all are terms that apply to actions of the mind. Why is the mind dark? Because it is alienated from the light of God. Who has this light? Jesus states Christian disciples have this light. We are to be the light to the world, and the local church is the intended location where this light is lit and then sent out into the world to become a shining city on a hill for the world to see (Matt. 5:14).

Finally, one more crucial point about the mind. It is through the mind that we make primary contact with reality. There is nothing mysterious here. We make contact with all the sources of power in the universe through our minds. Even the most primitive individuals living in the farthest reaches of our planet, who make bows and arrows to survive, are engaging items such as shafts of wood, points of stone, and strings through their minds. It is in the mind where we learn of electricity, or steam, or solar power. Because we develop this knowledge, we can use it. The mind can follow the action, and as a result we can move fairly effortlessly from idea to idea, place to place, listen to someone's voice across a wire from a distant land, and understand the intricacies of what is occurring in time and space. The mind, and what we turn our mind to, is the key to our lives. God made us this way.

If we do not use our ability to turn our minds and thoughts toward God, we do not have contact with God. Undoubtedly God could move into the human realm and invade the mind. If God did act in such a way, what are the chances the receiver would properly interpret such an encounter, if there is no knowledge of God at all? Therefore, what human beings can and must do is progress to the point where we consciously, intentionally focus our minds on God. The minister of the gospel is tasked with the very special and essential calling of directing and illuminating our minds toward the reality of God and his ways.

The primary failure of the profession of Christian ministry is the proliferation of legions of self-professed Christians who demonstrate that there is little knowledge of God dwelling in their minds. When turning their minds toward God or contemplating God's attributes, many of these lifelong "believers" routinely experience a sense of sheer emptiness. When asked to reveal what is in their minds, very little of anything significant or substantial comes forth regarding God and his character or kingdom. Much of this emptiness of thought can be traced back to the increasing levels of biblical illiteracy. The subject of God tends to remains a foreboding, unexplainable mystery, too huge to even fathom. This leaves little on which we can live, much less thrive.

Before professional ministers fall into the depths of despair, we must realize these conditions are not new. Recall that Nicodemus was tied in knots by Jesus's simple questions (John 3:1–10). He didn't know he had to be born from the realm above, the spiritual realm. He didn't know he had to have a life in him that was other than the natural life he received through his body. He didn't know about God's spiritual nature. And Jesus purposefully chided him because he was claiming to be a teacher of Israel. In fact, Nicodemus could have known these things, because the history of Israel is full of the reality and essence of God's character. Yet in fact, these truths simply didn't *mean* anything to Nicodemus. He didn't know what he was talking about.

The frightful question today is how many of our ministers, like Nicodemus, have no sense of what it is to know the nature of God. Such misinformed professionals, when faced with simple issues such as prayer or the kind of living Paul describes as reigning through righteousness leading to eternal life through Jesus Christ, are found hopelessly deficient. In fact, for all practical purposes, for too many, God, as he actually is, remains unknown. We must, through our minds, bring the knowledge of God into our lives so that we can then act on that knowledge. Eternal life is to know God and his Son (John 17:3). We must start there, and our ministers must carry this knowledge forward.

Life in the Spirit: The second most significant task of ministers is to understand and explicate to others the nature of spirit. This is due to the fact that the first and chief attribute of God's existential nature is his spiritual essence. God *is* spirit (John 4:24). This is largely what Nicodemus had so much trouble with. God's invisible, disembodied, personal power is what undergirds all life and reality. Human beings' ability or inability to engage successfully with the spiritual realities of our world, how they think about spirit, will by and large influence the degree of flourishing they can experience. The fact that this often presents itself as some great mystery that eludes Christians is yet more evidence for a significant lack of proper teaching and preaching from professional ministers.

The first chapter of Romans argues that humanity's entire responsibility before God is to know God. One passage describes how the human condition is based upon the failure to deal with God *as he is.* This is a stunning claim that can and should redirect all human pursuits of the divine in general and in religious endeavors in particular. In that passage Paul argues:

> For what can be known about God is plain to them, because God has shown it to them. Ever since the creation of the world his eternal power and divine nature, invisible though they are, have been understood and seen through the things he has made. So they are without excuse; for though they knew God, they did not honor him as God or give thanks to him, but they became futile in their thinking, and their senseless minds were darkened. (1:19–21)

Even today in an increasingly secularized world, the percentage of people in the United States who declare belief in God hovers just over 90 percent of the population.[20] According to *The World Factbook* approximately 2 percent of the world's population is atheistic and less than 10 percent is nonreligious.[21] Therefore, with the exception of societies where, for instance, there has been a long and established intent to teach an ideology that specifically resists belief in God (such as Marxism), what we find still in the world today is the natural tendency of human beings to engage the world around them with a belief in a divine power of some sort.

What or who this God is that the majority of the world claims belief in varies from religion to religion, but a survey of the many different religions yields some common characteristics. "World theology," if we can use that term lightly here, nearly always involves an ultimate invisible power. This invisible, spiritual power is, in one degree or another, personal or what we will describe as "personlike." Some animistic religions have less of a personal emphasis, but in most nonanimistic religions God is treated as someone who interacts with individual human beings.

In the previous scripture passage Paul is describing something that remains true today—God has revealed or shown himself to the world through creation. We then can ask the question: How big would one expect God to be, considering the world that proceeded from God's acts of creation? One can quickly begin to grasp the immensity, omnipotence, and omniscience of God simply by engaging in the wonder of the "works of his hands" (Ps. 8:3–6). The worlds were made by the Logos of God in a manner that enables human beings to understand that the *visible*, namely, the physical world, was created by the power of God's *invisible*, *spiritual* reality (Heb. 11:3). Here we have only scratched the surface, but it is a most profound surface for humans to engage. Theologian Adam Clark gives us a fairly dense definition of God that is very useful:

The eternal, independent and self-existent Being; the Being whose purposes and actions spring from himself, without foreign motive or influence; he who is absolute in dominion; the most pure, the most simple, the most spiritual of all essences; infinitely perfect; and eternally self-sufficient, needing nothing that he has made; illimitable in his immensity, inconceivable in his mode of existence, and indescribable in his essence; known fully only to himself, because an infinite mind can only be fully comprehended by itself. In a word, a being who from his infinite wisdom, cannot err or be deceived and who from his infinite goodness can do nothing but what is eternally just and right and kind.[22]

The kind of God Clark describes is an invisible being who has great power and dominion over every thing that is created, for God created all things in the world. It is often argued that God created the universe out of nothing. However, this is not a biblical concept. Instead, out of the energy and will that is inclusive of the person of God he acted and created matter. God is personal power or energy, and he used that energy to create matter. One of the great discoveries of the modern sciences is that what we call matter is full of energy. Something as tiny and as seemingly insignificant as a single uranium atom we now realize contains immense amounts of power. So much that, when released, the very foundations of the earth will shake. What this demonstrates is that energy, not matter, is the basic reality of our world.

What we need to then move to is an understanding that God is personal nonmaterial power. God thinks. God wills. God has values and choices. And in like manner, human beings have energy, personality, thought, will, values, and choices, all of which are invisible, or spiritual, realities. There is no physical matter in God, but there is power, massive amounts of power and energy. Power is the ability to do work. While in the desert, what was Jesus's reply to Satan's first temptation to turn stones into bread? "One does not live by bread alone, but by every word that comes from the mouth of God" (Matt. 4:4; Deut. 8:3).

What Jesus understood about the difference between bread and the words of God was the difference between matter and energy. Matter is not self-sufficient. Everything around us, every physical thing, every piece of matter came from something else and is going to become something else. All matter is contingent. That is why Paul recognizes that everything that is created, the entire physical realm, is perishing, falling apart, in need of being maintained, dependent, and therefore nonsufficient (1 Cor. 15:54).

The material universe points to a being who logically must be totally and ultimately self-sufficient and so unfathomably power-filled that it is easier for him to exist than to not exist, who out of his mere nature pours out matter in infinite quantities. Such a being would necessarily be so utterly indefatigable and everlasting as to never cease and never be exhausted of power and potential. Such is the basic essence of God's spiritual nature.

This is also why God commonly represents or manifests himself in the scriptures as something akin to fire. Fire is energy being let loose, and the scriptures talk of God as a consuming fire (Heb. 12:29). John the Baptist realized that Jesus was going to come and do much more than baptize with water. Jesus's disciples would become totally enveloped in the consuming reality of God's personal, invisible power and energy (fire) in the depths of their very being (Luke 3:16).

Jesus's miraculous works demonstrated his complete confidence in and total comprehension of God's invisible spiritual power. These supernatural actions were the result of a total competency that proceeded from an intimate, recondite knowledge of the nature of God's overwhelming sufficiency to meet every human need. This is what life lived in and through the Spirit of God makes real.

Undoubtedly, human beings do not have enough energy to create even an infinitesimal piece of matter such as a single uranium atom. Such a task would require untold amounts of energy—much more than we can be trusted with. However, human beings

PHYSICIANS, LAWYERS, AND PASTORS OR PRIESTS   283

do have the power to create. We can make, for instance, a very nice salad or condominium, each of which originates from our will and thoughts. Yet we need to start these projects in the garden or the forest. In both instances our thoughts are in these creations before they become realities. Human beings can rearrange matter (seeds into vegetables, then into salads, or trees into lumber, which is used to build homes), but we cannot create matter simply because we do not have the energy to do so.

We have been given dominion over the matter God has created for us as stewards. We even have dominion over our own bodies, and one of the most wonderful creative acts of human existence is in the use of our bodies to create other persons, in concert with God. In combining our minds, bodies, and relationships, the power of human life is reflective of the image of God as our wills are brought to bear on our world to significant effect. What is left to be determined is how we will use this power and to what end. This is where our earlier discussion of morality and ethics becomes central.

Fortunately God's moral acuity is able to handle his omnipotence. Both are unlimited. It is for this same reason Jesus could be trusted to take five loaves and two fishes or several barrels of water and produce matter from the energy that was at his command. The goal of learning from Jesus how to live our lives is indelibly tied to the training necessary to be empowered to do God's will, in just the same manner that Jesus wielded his power. The awesome effects that can result are only mirrored by the responsibility such power demands. Power cannot be entrusted to individuals unable to direct and control its use for good ends. This is the single purpose behind discipleship and the sole objective of the church.

An impotency gap is created if a disciple of Jesus does not appreciate the nature of God as spirit or have the proper understandings of God in the mind. The cost is the total collapse of the character required to empower change in human life. If people remain unaware of who and what they are—unceasing spiritual beings with an amazingly beautiful destiny with God and others in the universe he designed specifically for our benefit and enjoyment—they have little opportunity to make the kinds of movements toward God that can effectively revolutionize their life, their personal relationships, and their communities at large.

Coming to know who God is and then coming to know who we are as both spiritual and physical beings, created in and representative of God's image, will lead directly into the means by which we can be transformed into what disciples of Jesus must become in order to fulfill God's destiny for creation. Such a transformation is what the scriptures term the baptism of the Spirit and fire. These two objectives bracket the overarching objectives of professional ministers.

Knowing God, knowing the self, and navigating the difference or overcoming the gap by God's grace to accomplish his purposes through his power is the foundation of all Christian ministry. These were the simple and straightforward objectives of Jesus's earthly ministry. They have not changed. Jesus put humanity into a position where we can make contact with God and allow his power to flow through us to accomplish abundantly more than any could hope or imagine (Eph. 3:20). God is the source of absolute sufficiency. Only when these fundamental concepts are mastered by ministers and then communicated and manifested throughout our congregations can the leaders and professionals in the other fields begin to step into their respective arenas of expertise fully empowered to successfully navigate their vocations in concert with the ethos, ethics, and power of the kingdom of God.

SUMMARY

We have considered here the nature of three key professions, the moral knowledge and expertise they maintain, and the essential roles they play both individually and in concert toward the transformation of the kingdoms of this world into the kingdom of Christ. Jesus comes into the world to offer a rock-solid foundation upon which we can live and thrive in the freedom that only comes from authentic engagement with things as they really are; there is nothing on the earth that remotely resembles the moral foundation he established for our professionals to build their lives and communities upon. Our professional ranks can and should continue to test his statements through study, reason, and critical reflection. If there is something better, let us all find and apply it with great haste. Until then, we must resist being swept away by fads, feelings, or political movements. What Jesus said is true and moral. If professionals and leaders in every area of life will abide—live in—his words and let his words live in them, we will all truly know and experience the grace, power, freedom, and flourishing we cherish for ourselves and those we love dearly. What we suggest here is that there now exists a body of moral knowledge derived from the life and teachings of Jesus Christ that can form an appropriate basis for nonrepressive human flourishing that professionals and leaders can access for the greater good of all.

What we must now engage are some practical means our local congregations can pursue in their attempts to transform the kingdoms of this world into the kingdom of God and of his Christ. In our concluding chapter we will investigate the primary means through which God has manifested this reality among us. God's kingdom is an all-encompassing, universal phenomenon that includes all of human life—the economic, political, social, and religious arenas—and is governed and directed under a rule of a benevolent and omnipotent sovereign. What is left to consider now is how our leaders can better form and shape our local congregations in ways that will bring common wellness, peace, and flourishing into our world. Primary to our focus will be the ways Christian leaders and professionals can work together to manifest the kind of flourishing and prosperity representative of the wisdom inherent in the kingdom of God. Such a life would absolutely include both the individual and our public institutions. What does such a life look like? It is to this *shalom* type of life, lived in the light and sufficiency of God among his people, that we now must bring before our minds and hearts.

PROFESSIONALS; PHYSICIANS, LAWYERS, AND PASTORS OR PRIESTS

Discussion Questions for Chapters 12 and 13

According to Nathan Hatch's definition, a professional must maintain the following in order to serve the public in achieving the good it seeks: (1) expertise and training within a specific body of knowledge; (2) a moral imperative to support and defend the public's greater good; (3) both self- and peer regulation to oversee the power, autonomy, and privilege that accompany the public trust. Historically, medicine, law, and the ministry are considered the classic professions.

1. In a Gallup poll, there was a significant drop in public confidence in many of the professions, including attorneys and clergy. Out of twenty-two professions studied, the clergy ranked eighth. Slightly more than half of the American people were reportedly willing to offer a minister their trust. In your opinion, what are the reasons for such low ratings? Do these low ratings have anything to do with the violation of or lack of higher standards advocated by Hatch's threefold marks of the professional?

2. Who holds you accountable in your profession? Most professions require annual continuing education so that practitioners maintain their skills and knowledge. What standards does your profession have? What classes, seminars, or workshops

have you taken in the past twelve months to further your knowledge and expertise?

3. What is the single most important thing you do as a professional? What do you focus on most during the course of your day? Consider your job description. If you could alter it, how might you better state the intention to be an "instrument of righteousness" in your field?

4. In what way has the healing profession changed in your lifetime? If you are a medical professional, what has been the impact of government and private insurance participation in your practice? Who provides the best care and guidance to a patient and why? How has the rising cost of medical care impacted your professional abilities? What recommendations would you offer to better align the medical industry with the goal of common flourishing?

5. Studies reveal that much of the public maintains a low opinion of the legal profession and those who hold public office (a high percentage of elected officials have legal training). Is this opinion justified? If not, why not? If so, why? In what ways can the legal profession increase the public trust? What if anything could a pastor or priest offer those in the legal profession with regard to the challenges of trust and public confidence?

6. The numbers of those involved in Christian denominations are declining in concert with those attending seminaries. We have more pastors leading our churches with less religious education than ever before. If accountants, physicians, attorneys, counselors, and teachers are required to attain certain academic credentials and industry certifications, is a standard ministerial credential also warranted? Is the rise in noncre-

dentialed ministers due to a decrease in the perceived value of the ministerial profession in general? In what ways are character and competencies connected to being an effective and trusted minister of the gospel?

7. *Exercise:* Conduct a private inventory. Ask yourself the questions: Am I a true professional? Do I hold inviolate the fiduciary relationship with my clients and constituents? Have I done all I can do, and should do, to master my field? Who are my peers, and how am I actively engaging their oversight and accountability? In the next six months, what course, seminar, or class can I enroll in to develop my intellectual, professional, and spiritual qualifications for my profession?

CHAPTER 14

The Kingdom of Our God

Eagerly, musician,
Sweep your string,
So we may sing,
Elated, optative,
Our several voices
Interblending,
Playfully contending,
Not interfering
But co-inhering,
For all within
The cincture of the sound
Is holy ground,
Where all are Brothers,
None faceless Others.
Let mortals beware
Of words, for
With words we lie,
Can say peace
When we mean war,
Foul thought speak fair
And promise falsely,
But song is true:
Let music for peace
Be the paradigm,
For peace means to change

At the right time,
As the World-Clock
Goes Tick and Tock.
So may the story
Of our human city
Presently move
Like music, when
Begotten notes
New notes beget,
Making the flowing
Of time a growing,
Till what it could be,
At last it is,
Where even sadness
Is a form of gladness,
Where Fate is Freedom,
Grace and Surprise.

W. H. AUDEN

Occasionally in life there are those moments of
unutterable fulfillment which cannot be completely explained
by those symbols called words. Their meanings can only be
articulated by the inaudible language of the heart.

MARTIN LUTHER KING JR.

O NE FINE DAY the people of God will live in perfect communion with the persons of the Trinity and one another
under the sovereign and complete rule of Jesus Christ. He is the
one who sits on the throne, and all authority over heaven and
earth has been given to him. The kingdom of God is a reality
now, and it is coming to pass in ever increasing fullness like an
avalanche of goodness overwhelming and engulfing the entire
cosmos. This is what the apostle John believed he was seeing a

glimpse of in his vision of the coming new creation. The construction is under way and has been for some time now. Such a vision needs to do more than seep into our hearts and minds. We need to regularly allow this beatific vision to sweep us off our feet, onto our knees, and with raised voices extol the wonder and majesty of our Messianic Lamb and Lord.

The heavenly reign of new creation will necessarily include every realm of human interaction and existence. All of the innumerable personal kingdoms that comprise our hearts and minds will be enfolded and maintained under the sovereign benevolence of God's *agape* foundation. It may be difficult to imagine what a reality such as this would provide for the world collectively and for each citizen individually. But we must take the time to contemplate the accessibility and undeniable eventuality of this heavenly reality that is coming at us with such force and grandeur as to wipe away evil and darkness like the eternally impotent nuisance it is.

This is precisely what Christian leaders and professionals who manage our world and its systems and institutions must understand, come face-to-face with, develop experience in, and increase their confidence about in order to accomplish God's divine conspiracy to overcome the evil with good. The chapters that have preceded this have attempted to build a basis and provide but a few examples of what such a social structure will require from Christ-following leaders. We will know we are coming ever closer to our goals when life both exemplifies and produces the features and benefits of the Psalm 23 kind of existence. Such is a life that stems from the settled understanding that Yahweh, the LORD, is our shepherd.

If contemporary priests and pastors (shepherds) are to accomplish their professional calling, they too must understand the primacy of pointing to the nature of God. This is the work of ministry leaders, spokespersons, and teachers: to understand and describe the nature and "reasonings" (*logia*) of God (*theo*) as a loving, attentive, present, protective, and providing Shepherd. It is the nature of a good shepherd to lead his sheep along good paths, where what is good can be seen, demonstrated, and duplicated. These are the right ways that produce righteousness (*dikaiosune*). Such goodness, provision, protection, soul care, restoration, righteousness, and flourishing allow one to face shadowy dangers and uncertainties that threaten life and living without fear. Living without fear is the same as living a life without want. This is the product of Jesus's flock, of his church, and we must remember to hold ourselves to account for measuring the fruit of abiding in Christ as the vine and nothing, or no one, else.

Jesus describes this exact type of life in John 17:3: "And this is eternal life, that they know you, the only true God, and Jesus Christ whom you have sent." To truly know the Shepherd is to have life that never ends, life that is limitless in time and quality.

The God that Jesus knew was perhaps very different from the God often described in our contemporary world. The God Jesus knew perfectly and testified to is a self-sustaining, self-sufficing, all-encompassing being who is also immaterial, intelligent and free, personal and perfectly good, wise and powerful, who created the universe and continues to sustain and govern it by his providence. The moral attributes of God as loving, beneficent, and generous flow out of the plentitude of his being. There is nothing to fear. We are in fact more than conquerors when we are called and obediently follow in God's purposes and plan (Rom. 8:28).

We have argued that the crucial task for our professionals and leaders today is to know—read that again—to *know* God. This must precede our endeavors to build a city on a hill that has the potential to bless or illumine our world. As we have discussed, this is the primary role of professional ministers. Their responsibility is not to build grand worship centers, raise money, or devise programs that will attract consumers of religious products and services. As good as all these things can be, the primary and essential task of ministers is to teach, preach, and manifest in their own lives and ministry the power and truth available for all of life and living within the knowledge of God.

But in no way are they alone. Ministers are but one instrument in a complete orchestra of gifted, talented, and called leaders, spokespersons, and professionals who can and must engage the power that lies beyond themselves to achieve what cannot be accomplished by any other means. Hence the answer to our problems today can be directly tied to our leaders, key insiders, and persons of influence who suffer from a lack of understanding about the nature of God. All of the troubling questions about our families, marriages, social structures, and governments can be traced back to a holistic ignorance, a famine as Amos described, of the knowledge of God and his character. Green pastures, calm waters, restoration, safety, security, and provision—this is the life we long for and seek after. Jesus came to correct all the gaps in our vision for life and to fill the voids of our understanding of God's provision for life to the full.

INSTRUMENTS OF RIGHTEOUSNESS

God's design for his church is very simple, which is not the same as saying it is easy. The great metaphor Paul uses is the human body, whose members all work together to accomplish the ends that Christ, who is the head, desires. And until this happens routinely, easily, and naturally, the whole earth groans. Pastors or priests need not worry specifically about being the primary agents for meting out social justice, or healing, or employment, or clean water in their communities. When our professional ministers focus their efforts on faithfully and appropriately illuminating the minds of those in their care about the nature of God and the nature of human life when connected to the power and beauty of God's kingdom, God will bring forth a bountiful harvest of righteous healers, justices, merchants, community servant leaders, public officials, teachers, and parents. Such congregations will be overflowing with disciples who walk with God in our world as ambassadors who both seek and achieve for themselves and their neighbors the full benefits and blessings of God's love, wisdom, care, and grace on every human level. This is one of the key pillars required for building a bridge over the traditional sacred-secular divide in the professions.

In fact, this is what Paul had in mind in his Letter to the Ephesians. The ministers he describes (apostles, prophets, evangelists, pastors, and teachers) are not to *do* the work of the ministry as much as they are to *equip* those in their care for the work of the ministry in building up the entire body of Christ (4:12). There is great confusion and guilt over this misapplication of purpose in professional circles of the clergy. In short, our communities will remain helplessly deadlocked in futility until the leaders of our local congregations become involved in and dedicated to what the local church is and should be: a glorious beachhead of the kingdom of God where disciples of Jesus the Christ are trained to receive divine empowerment, responsibility, and blessing. There is one place and one place only that provides the incubator of loving sufficiency by which such a task can be accomplished. This is the church, the body of Christ, the hope of the world.

Human persons were created to live and work in a domain of the mind and spirit from which we learn that out of all the aspects of reality God is the most primary. To miss this fact is to miss the most elemental building block of human existence. Sadly, such basic education is widely missing in our society today. Again, we will state the objective here perhaps more clearly: the principle responsibility of ministers is to faithfully and accurately represent to others the nature of God and his ways so that people who are willing and able to listen (those with ears to hear and eyes to see) can begin to think about and imagine who God is, who they are, and how the world is designed to work effectively in harmony with God's good will.

BUILDING A BRIDGE BETWEEN
THE SACRED AND THE SECULAR

If the ministers of God do not take the lead in these matters, it will not happen. There is no other office, arena, discipline, or institution within our society today where the buck stops. As ministers tasked with teaching other ministers in a professional manner, we must say that on the whole the degradation of our society is not primarily the results of evil that has breached the walls of the local church and marginalized the gospel. Surely evil is at work. Yet evil cannot overcome good. It simply does not have the power to do so. The only thing that allows evil to gain the upper hand is when good is missing. Therefore the role of the local church is to manifest goodwill in abundance by training individuals to be ambassadors of good and light in every area, every corner, and every aspect of our shadowy world. When this happens, evil must flee as surely as darkness flees in the presence of even the smallest of lights.

To accomplish this task, like other professions, the ministry requires a long and dedicated course of study. This includes character development and skills training in order to properly form a heart and mind in ways that can expertly administer the gospel Jesus revealed in our time. Some may argue that Jesus's first disciples are an exception to this rule. We disagree. Their three years of intense study, reflection, and debate, character transformation, and skills training were exactly what seminary training has, in its better incarnations, sought to instill in subsequent generations of disciples. The current trend for ministers to abstain from formal training, when other professions are moving in the exact opposite direction, is a troubling but perhaps telling indictment of the current state of the profession of ministry and the lack of self-respect and appreciation it is afforded.

The marginalization of the local church and the lack of professional respect for our ministers within contemporary society can be reversed just as quickly as they began. This requires pastors, priests, and ministry leaders in our local churches to fully appreciate and then seriously undertake to reassert their rightful and essential roles within our societies. When this is so, the church and its members will be seen and experienced in our culture today as the blessing God intended them to be. This is not a new phenomenon, but rather has been a frequent role the church has routinely assumed over the centuries.

To seriously engage God's mission of revolutionizing our world and our lives now and into eternity, pastors or priests must realize that the Gallup trends mentioned earlier represent a striking call to reevaluate their current status and professional role. One of the factors that may need reconsideration is the amount of time and energy pastors should expend on the skills necessary to manage, develop, and advertise their church's specific brand of "goods and services" in order to compete in the spiritual marketplace of Sunday worship attendance. Again, we have stated that the purpose of the church is to make disciples, so that pastors should be devoted to that primary task above all others. Religious consumerism and the pitfalls of this in our Western individualist context make entertainment and worship difficult to distinguish. Yet they are very different indeed. Worship is placing the mind rightly on God and allowing that reality to spill over into the entirety of the soul. Entertainment is focused on the self in order to pass time and to create a sense of contrived drama that can be used as a substitute for actual meaning and purpose in our lives. The church, above all, must know and distinguish the differences.

If pastors and priests are willing to reassert their calling to teach, train, and equip disciples and resist the temptation to succumb to the demands of religious consumerism, a second suggestion would be to investigate the phenomenon of executive coaching and its increasing popularity across many areas of our society.[1] According to a *Harvard Business Review* survey, a majority of executive coaches are hired to engage three common areas with their clients.[2] Forty-eight percent of the time coaches are hired to develop potential and/or navigate transitions; 26 percent of clients use their coach as a sounding board; and 12 percent engage a coach to address their own derailing behaviors.

Surprisingly, when coaching clients were asked what they looked for in a coach, respondents were split on whether certification was necessary. Further, 45 percent versus 13 percent of respondents stated psychological training was not necessary. Unlike counselors and therapists, coaches tend to: (a) focus on the future, not the past, (b) foster individual performance in the business context, and (c) help clients discover their own path.[3] Most telling was the description of how the coach-client relationship shifts over time. Companies who hire executive coaches may intend for their time and money to be spent on professional issues. Yet 94 percent of the coaches interviewed indicated that inevitably their coaching conversations migrated "to bigger issues such as life purpose, work-life balance, and becoming a better leader."[4]

The areas listed above are those where pastors can and must offer their services, in both personal wisdom and professional expertise, to the workforce, especially industry leaders, as coaches of righteousness and light. We suggest that much of what executive coaching entails today is identical to what in previous eras was classified as pastoral care and discipleship. Leaders of any stripe will find the skills they need to do the task required of them. The question is where these individual leaders will find help, and from whom. Pastors and priests, as leaders and possessors of the knowledge of God and his ways in our world, should recognize their duty to be qualified contributors who offer their skills as coaches, guides, sounding boards, and encouragers to the professionals within their congregations. The objective is not to offer specific legal, accounting, medical, or business advice. The objective is to forge character and wisdom in Christian leaders, so that through them and their decisions every area of our society can benefit and flourish. This is exactly the kind of "coaching" Jesus demonstrated and pastors must consider reengaging today.

To accomplish this task, priests and pastors must earn the right to be heard. They must acquire the formal education required to wield their skills and knowledge well. Therefore seminaries and schools of theology must provide competent and experienced instructors to train ministers well. This is crucial and something seminaries and graduate schools must continue improving upon. But lest we think seminary-trained pastors are unqualified to engage in the business world, consider the results of the *Harvard Business Review* study. Qualifications and certifications were found to be less important to clients than a demonstrated track record and the character of the individual coach. And in light of the Gallup poll data on professional ethics, many professions could stand to learn what ministers of the gospel might understand about right and wrong.

Thus far we have mentioned the opportunities. Yet if such a mutually beneficial relationship between pastors and lay leaders is to thrive, a few key difficulties must be addressed as well. There is a fairly well known and not so hidden bias that business leaders and professionals who minister outside the local church have against the clergy as a group. As is the case in all professions, the clergy have some in their ranks who cannot and do not represent the profession well. This is verifiable despite claims of divine calling. One of the few detriments of the decrease in denominationalism is a reduction of the number of clergy supervised by their peers and the resultant lack of oversight and accountability. Members of the clergy must work at finding ways to hold themselves accountable, especially given the significant increase in nondenominational, independent local churches. Just as was noted with the medical profession, increased accountability, formal continuing education programs, and peer training would go a long way in reestablishing the reputation of the clergy as an esteemed profession by nonministry professionals.

However, the local church is not a business, despite those who might treat it as such or wish it so. Various efficiency and effectiveness standards simply do not apply in many ministry situations. The soul is not like the body in its ability to heal. And the relational and sociological dynamics of the local church do not work the same as those of a corporation, a factory, or a government agency. Although there is much wisdom in the ways businesses and nonprofit organizations work that the local church can and should learn from, applying identical expectations and standards is inappropriate in many situations and circumstances. Nevertheless, good quality work that benefits others and adds value can and should be expected of our ministers and the organizations they lead. Elders, deacons, and denominational leaders must see to it that our pastors and priests are afforded the education and training they require. Then ministers must be held to account for their job responsibilities. However, just as with medical and legal professionals, professional ministerial duties must be overseen by peer review. And ministers must take the lead on this. Admittedly, this has been a hit-and-miss proposition over the past several decades.

However, the Gallup poll suggests that many professionals struggle with a public relations perception that goes to the heart of their ability to do their jobs well. Some significantly so. Therefore business persons and leaders outside the church can and should consider how their local minister can help them navigate or coach them through the many and various ethical and moral dilemmas they face as a normal result of "being in business." Can we imagine a time when a car dealer engages the services of a local parish priest, and not an advertising or PR firm, to seek ways in which their company can improve the public perception regarding dishonest and unethical behavior? For this to happen, we will need to develop mutually respecting and honest relationships. Leaders outside the clergy, especially Protestant leaders, have tended to be exceedingly hesitant about being transparent regarding the struggles and temptations they face, given the true nature of their personal and professional lives. Excuses that pastors "just wouldn't understand" the intricacies of their professional duties is often an attempt to avoid admitting the truth and revealing their true character in these matters. Therefore an outsider (coach, consultant, or counselor) tends to be a more appealing confessor.

Lest we put the entire onus on business leaders, the clergy as a group has at times been rightly perceived as having no interest in the daily grind of professional life, or as the saying goes, "being so heavenly minded as to be of no earthly good." Seminary education is often blamed for this impractical mind-set. There is no excuse for ministers to focus exclusively on the esoteric. The sheep are in the pasture, not in the library. This was Jesus's focus. His teaching was brilliant and the product of much study and contemplation. Yet the hard work of study is to make the complicated understandable, accessible, and practical. Pastors must take their sermons and teaching opportunities as sacred occasions to challenge the minds and spirits of their congregants with the insights and wisdom required to change their lives and empower their vocational callings. Getting to the heart of the matters crucial to everyday life, not tickling ears or "dumbing it down," is the great challenge of Christian teachers. Our congregations should be full of people who leave the church thinking deeply and conversing with others about the nature of their lives and activities as a result of the sermon they heard.

Another hurdle lies in the fact some ministers have developed and maintained a reputation for condemning the "perks," or material benefits, often associated with nonministerial professional life. What can result is a sense that the gospel of Jesus has nothing but bad news to offer the "up and in" and is only good news for the "down and out." Often, not always, such inaccurate, overt criticism, usually offered from the safety and distance of the pulpit, is cloaked in a godly warning against the love of mammon. However, this motivation can more often be found to spring from jealousy or covetousness of another's goods or good fortune. Further, lay leaders are all too aware that ministers rarely hesitate to initiate personal contact and offer thanksgiving for material wealth when the church organization faces a financial need of some kind. The irony is not subtle, nor is it lost, that the very wealth condemned in one setting is welcomed in another. These kinds of inconsistencies, stigmas, and stereotypes tend to create barriers that prevent the unity we need. Instead, pastors and priests might consider approaching lay professionals and leaders in their congregations more benevolently, altruistically, and offer themselves, their time, attention, and wisdom as a gift instead of engaging in relationship as a means of seeking a gift.

Finally, research on the biblical descriptions of the roles of a shepherd, prophet, and king offers helpful insights into this situation. In historically biblical terms, each role is intended to function as a complement and correcting force to the others. A recent study funded by the Kern Family Foundation found that the leadership traits of shepherds, prophets, and kings transcend the limits of presumed professional duties or vocational roles.[5] The research suggests that in relation to the individual personality characteristics of those persons filling these roles, there is no clear distinction, or necessary reason to distinguish, between clergy and laity. This kind of cross-pollination of leadership roles and skills throughout all of our social institutions is a great blessing and demonstrates the inadvisability of creating leadership patterns that constrain people in certain categories because of their vocational choice. Such biases only demean and limit the diversity that God has purposely and wonderfully created in human beings for the greater good.

Other issues also prevent the crossing of the secular-sacred divide. However, if ministers of the gospel in both clerical and nonclerical roles decide to own their internal conflicts on these matters and intentionally develop relationships of mutual trust, admiration, support, and respect, the kingdom of God will once again act in the unity of the body of Christ. This will take time, effort, forgiveness, and humility, all of which are formative traits required of the types of leaders we so desperately need. We hope to start the conversation through which courageous professional Christian leaders of all fields can find and develop effective ways of bridging the gaps that currently separate them. If our Christian leaders and pastors can better work together as co-laborers in God's ripening vineyard that is waiting for harvesters, we would be able to demonstrate Paul's vision for the church to the world at large:

> The gifts he gave were that some would be apostles, some prophets, some evangelists, some pastors and teachers, to equip the saints for the work of ministry, for building up the body of Christ, until all of us come to the unity of the faith and of the knowledge of the Son of God, to maturity, to the measure of the full stature of Christ. We must no longer be children, tossed to and fro and blown about by every wind of doctrine, by people's trickery, by their craftiness in deceitful scheming. But speaking the truth in love, we must grow up in every way into him who is the head, into Christ, from whom the whole body, joined and knit together by every ligament with which it is equipped, as each part is working properly, promotes the body's growth in building itself up in love. (Eph. 4:11–16)

For leaders like apostles, evangelists, pastors, teachers, and prophets to work effectively together, to even get all those egos in the same room, much less on the same page, Paul also knew, from experience, there was only one way to foster unity. Thus his encouragement in Philippians:

> If then there is any encouragement in Christ, any consolation from love, any sharing in the Spirit, any compassion and sympathy, make my joy complete: be of the same mind, having the same love, being in full accord and of one mind. Do nothing from selfish ambition or conceit, but in humility regard others as better than yourselves. Let each of you look not to your own interests, but to the interests of others. (Phil. 2:1–4)

This was the task for the first-century church, and it is still our task today. We must be willing to serve one another, thinking more highly of others' roles, gifts, talents, and leadership skills than our own when it comes to benefiting the kingdom of God. When we do, the world will take notice. How we love and serve one another is a foolproof way of testifying to whom we serve, how we lead, and what demands our ultimate allegiance.

TO THE GLORY OF GOD

If we are to positively affect our world, our societies, our neighborhoods, and our own lives, through and for Christ, we must take into our minds that God is a certain kind of being who existed before the creation of the earth, in all of his plentitude. God is not now sitting off somewhere in the cosmos like a neglected senior citizen waiting and hoping for someone to sing a song to him. Nothing could be farther from the truth of the matter. Instead, he is currently surrounded by innumerable glorious beings and angelic hosts, whom he has made, and they worship him rightly, ascribing worth and proper glory to the King of the universe. He is in the constant communion of the loving sufficiency shared between the great persons of the Trinity. Think of the most wonderful, the most attractive, the most magnanimous, the most thrilling, the most vibrant personal company you could imagine, and then multiply that by a factor of infinity, and you have only begun to get a glimpse of what God is doing, where he is, what he was before the foundations of the earth were a glimmer in his mind's eye, and what he will be doing forever.

Nehemiah 9:6 reinforces this glimpse. When the people are gathering around to offer a blessing to Yahweh, Ezra starts by saying:

> You are the Lord, you alone; you have made heaven, the heaven of heavens, with all their host, the earth and all that is on it, the

seas and all that is in them. To all of them you give life, and the host of heaven worships you.

Job also describes this heavenly activity:

> Then the Lord answered Job out of the whirlwind: "Who is this that darkens counsel by words without knowledge? Gird up your loins like a man, I will question you, and you shall declare to me. Where were you when I laid the foundation of the earth? Tell me, if you have understanding. Who determined its measurements— surely you know! Or who stretched the line upon it? On what were its bases sunk, or who laid its cornerstone when the morning stars sang together and all the heavenly beings shouted for joy?" (38:1–7)

The most amazing thing we can imagine in human existence is the unending fellowship of endlessly loving people. We yearn to love and to be loved, to know and be known, to enjoy and be enjoyed in creative adventurous discovery. What these passages indicate is that this kind of wonderful existence was created and is watched over, maintained, and led by the King of Kings in his kingdom. This kind of wondrous, awe-filling reality has existed and flourished from all eternity and in all eternity. God is reigning over an everlasting festival that he has invited us to participate in, contribute to, share in, and reap the blessings from.

God has an awesome project working here on earth. But his complexity and sovereignty extends far beyond us. In fact, the nature of this earthly project doesn't seem to make much sense to the angels. God is creating something unique, mysterious, and precious on the earth. But this is not his only iron in the fire. His glory and potentiality extends far beyond this little blue ball hovering in just the right place for us to dwell and move and have our human experience.

This is the foundation of Jesus's theology. To live and lead like Jesus we need to think like Jesus. He knew who he was speaking of. He knew to whom he was introducing others. He knew Elohim's capabilities, purposes, and priorities. Jesus knew and acted on the fact that Yahweh is limitless, boundless, and unrestrained in power, grace, mercy, peace, joy, hope, and love. All things are possible. All things. Jesus knew his Father's name, and he knew when to evoke it to do his will, creatively, adventurously, and joyfully, for himself, for the well-being of others, and ultimately for the entire world.

As disciples of Jesus, following in his footsteps, this is what we must know and do as well. This is the great divine conspiracy: To have this humble, peaceful, wise, and loving festival of goodwill overwhelm every competing agenda, fearful scheme, or desperate plan to build our lives on the shifting sands of arrogance or ignorance. Such lonely acts of despair are forged only by those whose ears are deaf to the music and eyes blind to the beauty of the symphonic plentitude on which God has set all creation. Such a God comes to the weary and burdened to whisper hope in our ear. "Little children, let us love, not in word or speech, but in truth and action. And by this we will know that we are from the truth and will reassure our hearts before him whenever our hearts condemn us; for God is greater than our hearts, and he knows everything" (1 John 3:18–20). No greater meaning can be found to human existence than what God has appointed to those who know and love him and his ways with their entire being. This is the church's greatest opportunity—to model, demonstrate, and manifest the fruits of such a life as both a witness and a beneficiary of God's overflowing goodness and *agape* love.

Insofar as there is a solution to the problem of providing the goods of a decent social existence through professional activity and Christlike moral courage and character, it must lie primarily in leadership by individuals who, by their intelligence and devotion to *agape* love, see to it that such provision is realized—that the leaders operate in such a way as to meet the needs of those they serve out of God's abundance and grace.

There are groups, some of which are powerful and well-funded, that continue to search for a system, an idea, a belief, a plan, a system of law, a tax, or program that will solve most or all of the problems we encounter today. Of course some systems or ways of organizing the social and political order are better than others. But no system can accomplish what is needed apart from the character of the people in the system; and the individual initiatives and acts that such people undertake in their social roles can make good systems fail or even (moderately) bad ones succeed, if there is enough character present within the human beings involved. *If we want to change our world and our lives for the good, we must choose to.* In *Man's Search for Meaning,* Victor Frankl, considering the horrors of Nazi concentration camps, states:

> Man is ultimately self-determining. What he becomes—within the limits of endowment and environment—he has made out of himself. In the concentration camps, for example, in this living laboratory and on this testing ground, we watched and witnessed some of our comrades behave like swine while others behaved like saints. Man has both potentialities within himself; which one is actualized depends on decisions but not on conditions.[6]

Frankl argues that ultimately, despite our conditions, travails, professed beliefs and stated objectives, we live the life we choose and therefore we have the life we want. Which life do you want? What do you seek? (John 1:38, NASB).

GOD'S DIVINE CONSPIRACY

The sense of futility is one of the greatest evils of the day. . . . People say, "What can one person do? What is the sense of our small effort?" They cannot see that we can only lay one brick at a time, take one step at a time; we can be responsible only for the one action of the present moment. But we can beg for an increase of love in our hearts that will vitalize and transform all our individual actions, and know that God will take them and multiply them, as Jesus multiplied the loaves and fishes.

DOROTHY DAY[7]

In concluding this work, let us briefly recap the main points we have covered one final time. The great "divine conspiracy" of God is to overcome the human kingdoms of this world—at both the individual and the corporate or governmental level—with love, justice, and knowledge of truth. "The kingdom of the world has become the kingdom of our Lord and of his Messiah, and he will reign forever and forever" (Rev. 11:15). This is an eternal reality. The question we have pursued time and again is: How can we best participate in this reality as soon as possible?

Our suggestion has been that leaders, spokespersons, and professionals who are well experienced and knowledgeable in God's truth and wisdom must work together as the body of Christ, through God's empowering grace, to responsibly and explicitly address the public issues, proposals, and processes of society and usher in the kingdom ways of God by modeling and manifesting the reality of the benevolent love of Christ. This is the way we lead others as co-shepherds with Christ. We are to follow Christ under the imperative of God's character, to love our neighbors as ourselves. Our responsibility is to pursue with all diligence what honors God and what is good for the public in the economic, political, professional, and social issues that impact life and living. As such we become a city on a hill, salt and light, and messengers of grace and peace.

How this is done is as unique and creative as the number of those choosing to live as followers of Christ. We should assume a chemist, for example, who is a disciple of Jesus and is in constant conversation with Christ should be, all things being equal, a better chemist than she would otherwise be if she were not a disciple of Jesus. Such an idea is thought extremely radical today, even perhaps bigoted or prejudicial. This need not be the case, but may be in some instances, only if such persons abuse or misuse their potential to ill effect, which of course disciples of Jesus would not want to do. Yet it is not the moral dimensions of Christianity alone that we are referring to here. There is much more to truly "Christian" chemists than the manner in which they may go about their job. There is also a very practical ability for the Christ follower to tap into the knowledge of reality, which includes chemistry, that we believe Jesus actually can and does give access to. This is true not just in chemistry, of course, but in every profession, even every task. We should expect miracles, and there are miracle discoveries in chemistry and other disciplines, often because God has divulged or led people to such discoveries, much of which he doesn't get credit for. But if chemists or any other leaders who are disciples of Jesus count on God to assist them in their work, God would and does give great assistance, all of which is understood as an act of grace.

We must say, very explicitly, that one need not be Christian at all to have received great insights and miraculous epiphanies of inspired wisdom and knowledge from God. This happens quite often to those who claim alternative religious faith or no faith at all. God is not stingy or biased. He loves all people and is willing to bless by any means he sees fit. But disciples of Jesus might and perhaps should be more open and willing and therefore able to regularly benefit from tapping into the source of all wisdom and knowledge than, say, atheists. Such individuals should, for all intents and purposes, have something of an unfair competitive advantage against those who are not willing to either seek or attain divine guidance. Of course disciples of Christ should and would not use such wisdom and grace as an exclusive right or abuse of the power. Instead, followers of Jesus would openly share such a gift simply due to their understanding of why and where the power originated. Without such an understanding of the tangible benefits of God in his kingdom way, Jesus's invitation to "come and see" makes no logical sense. Come and see what? Jesus argues that we can come and see that life in the kingdom is lived better, fuller, more peacefully, more meaningfully, and more wisely than that outside the kingdom. Jesus is seen to routinely compare and contrast life with God to life without God. So should we.

We finish with a section from Hebrews 12. Because of Jesus, because we are now able to understand who God is, what he is capable of, we can begin to walk in the light of peace, hope, and love without fear. We can focus on the attributes of our Shepherd, who loves us, cherishes us, provides for us, leads us, protects us, guides us, and empowers us from an endless reservoir of power and plentitude that is as unimaginable as it is inexhaustible and illimitable. From this reality we get a glimpse of what is possible in our little, but powerful lives. Perhaps no one in our contemporary age preaches this better than Eugene Peterson.

Do you see what this means—all these pioneers who blazed the way, all these veterans cheering us on? It means we'd better get on with it. Strip down, start running—and never quit! No extra spiritual fat, no parasitic sins. Keep your eyes on Jesus, who both began and finished this race we're in. Study how he did it. Because he never lost sight of where he was headed—that exhilarating finish in and with God—he could put up with anything along the way: Cross, shame, whatever. And now he's there, in the place of honor, right alongside God. When you find yourselves flagging in your faith, go over that story again, item by item, that long litany of hostility he plowed through. That will shoot adrenaline into your souls! . . .

So don't sit around on your hands! No more dragging your feet! Clear the path for long-distance runners so no one will trip and fall, so no one will step in a hole and sprain an ankle. Help each other out. And run for it!

Work at getting along with each other and with God. Otherwise you'll never get so much as a glimpse of God. Make sure no one gets left out of God's generosity. Keep a sharp eye out for weeds of bitter discontent. A thistle or two gone to seed can ruin a whole garden in no time. Watch out for the Esau syndrome: trading away God's lifelong gift in order to satisfy a short-term appetite. You well know how Esau later regretted that impulsive act and wanted God's blessing—but by then it was too late, tears or no tears. . . .

Do you see what we've got? An unshakable kingdom! And do you see how thankful we must be? Not only thankful, but brimming with worship, deeply reverent before God. For God is not an indifferent bystander. He's actively cleaning house, torching all that needs to burn, and he won't quit until it's all cleansed. God himself is Fire! (Heb. 12:1–3, 12–17, 28–29, in *The Message*)

In this New Covenant Jesus has purchased we are given entrée into the true reality of all things. Through Christ we can draw from this reality so that we may know, in all of the areas that touch our lives—work, ministry, families, societies, cultures, governments, institutions, art, play, research, and certainly religions—the goodness and provision of an all-sufficing, want-killing, fear-eradicating, peace-loving Shepherd.

We finish this chapter with a prayer first published in *The Divine Conspiracy*. Perhaps now we are in a better place to grasp more completely whom we are addressing, whose name, reputation, and character are being engaged and evoked in these words, and more precisely what we are seeking when we seek his kingdom come on earth as it is in heaven. How perfectly right and adequate it is to come to him alone with our hopes, requests, and needs for ourselves and our world. Our help comes from the maker of the Heavens. He alone will provide, for he alone is God (Ps. 121:1–2).

Dear Father always near us,
may your name be treasured and loved,
may your rule be completed in us—
may your will be done here on earth
in just the way it is done in heaven.
Give us today the things we need today,
and forgive us our sins and impositions on you

as we are forgiving all who in any way offend us.
Please don't put us through trials,
but deliver us from everything bad.
Because you are the one in charge,
and you have all the power,
and the glory too is all yours—forever—
which is just the way we want it!
Whoopee!

THE KINGDOM OF OUR GOD

Discussion Questions for Chapter 14

1. God's "divine conspiracy" is to overcome the human kingdoms of this world with love, justice, and knowledge of truth
(Rev. 11:15). The book offers several ideas about how this
could come about. Which were most inspiring to you? How
can we best participate in this reality as soon as possible?

2. The authors suggest that the primary responsibility of leaders, spokespersons, ministers, and teachers is to faithfully and
accurately represent, teach, and manifest the nature of God
and his ways. If this is accurate, what areas of your life need
some immediate attention? Have you ever considered engaging
a spiritual director as a "coach" to assist you in this journey? If
you have a spiritual director, in what ways has she or he been
helpful to you in your walk with God?

3. If you are a lay leader or professional in your congregation, what
is the one thing you would like your pastor or priest to know
and appreciate about you and your vocational calling? If you are
a clergy professional, what one thing would you like your lay
leaders and professionals within your congregation to know and
appreciate about your vocational calling? What is it that clergy

and lay leaders do not understand about the other? What is crucial that they recognize and appreciate about the other?

4. Based on what you have read in this book, how will you be a different leader? In what ways will you be a different follower of Jesus? Would you consider contacting your local minister about coaching and encouraging you in your attempts at following Christ in your vocation? Why or why not?

5. What are you motivated to do right now that will make a positive difference in the lives of those around you? What is God speaking to your heart and mind?

6. *Exercise:* Memorize John 17:3: "And this is eternal life, that they may know you, the only true God, and Jesus Christ whom you have sent." Journal at least once a week over the next month or engage in an ongoing weekly conversation with a trusted friend about how the knowledge of God has brought you life to the full and/or how the lack of the knowledge of God has brought you suffering, loss, or confusion.

7. *Exercise:* We need an accurate vision of both God and God's purposes for our lives. Often discerning God's plan for our lives can become clearer by prayerfully considering what we desire our legacy to be. What do you want others to know about you? What good do you want to do with your life? What difference do you want to make in your family and community? What do you want your impact to have been on your world? Take the time to write out your own obituary (three hundred words or less) to better clarify your vision and purpose for your life.

Acknowledgments

I am thankful to have had the great honor to work with Dallas. Nothing I have done professionally or personally warrants this honor, and I am deeply humbled and grateful for the opportunity. Continuing without him has been bittersweet. Sweet, only because of the support and love received from those who knew and loved Dallas well. I am extremely grateful to his family, Jane, John, Becky, Bill, and Larissa for sharing their husband, father, and grandfather with me. There are others such as Jan Johnson, Keith and Christa Matthews, John and Nancy Ortberg, and Gary Moon, all of whom felt Dallas's loss deeply and whose encouragement and insight have helped me to finish well. Their dedication to the kingdom of God is inspiring and enlightening.

Also thanks to my friends and coconspirators Mike Lueken and Kent Carlson, who weeded through several preceding drafts with encouragement and a smile. David Abdun-nur, MD, Barry Hamann, MD, Chris Weber, MD, and Robert F. Cochran Jr., Professor of Law and Director of the Herbert and Elinor Nootbaar Institute on Law, Religion, and Ethics at the Pepperdine University School of Law, each graciously offered exceptional insights and direction on specific aspects of their professions. A special word of appreciation is also due my trusted colleagues Barbara Hayes, Chad Bogosian, Gregg Moder, Scott Daniels, Steve Porter, Steven Wilkens, and Don Thorsen for their wisdom and friendship, and graduate student Chris Tansey for his research assistance. Tony Baron was of exceptional assistance in helping to provide key questions and insights and developing engaging discussion topics for each section of the book. Our hope is to spur robust discussion groups, as leaders seek to better serve the public throughout the various disciplines, positions, and professions within our society.

I also wish to thank three people who walked closely with me during this period. Gary Peyrot diligently prayed over this project, and John and Danice Burdett have been a steady source of encouragement.

Greg Forster, of the Kern Family Foundation, has also been a significant advocate, supporter, and benefactor for many of these ideas. Stephen Hanselman, our literary agent, was a key counselor, encourager, and guide. Ann Moru masterfully edited this manuscript. It is a much better work having been molded under her wise and skillful hands. Mickey Maudlin of HarperOne has fully captured the vision Dallas carried of the kingdom and continues to be a trusted partner and friend. Thank you for your generosity, patient gracefulness, and expertise—you are a true professional.

On a more personal note, I am thankful for my parents, Jane and Gary Sr., who have never stopped believing what could be possible for their sons as both professionals and followers of Christ. For Sandy and Morgan Davis, who have adopted me, in an endlessly loving way, as a project in pursuit of holiness. For my daughters, Taylor and Jacy, who fill me with humble pride, and for my wife, Susie, who is far more advanced in the ways of the kingdom than me and endlessly demonstrates *agape* love for me and those around her while maintaining a joy that is contagious. I'm simply in awe of the life we have made together.

Last, of all the words Dallas has ever written, perhaps his most profound and true were those describing his wife: "Jane Lakes Willard, sweet lady, good soldier, faithful companion on the way." Dallas wanted this book dedicated to you. Grace and Peace.

Gary Black Jr.
July 2013

Notes

Foreword: Remembering Dallas

1. Gary Black Jr., *The Theology of Dallas Willard: Discovering Protoevangelical Faith* (Eugene, OR: Pickwick, 2013).
2. Black, *Theology of Dallas Willard,* ix.
3. Dallas Willard, "The Failure of Evangelical Political Involvement," in Roger N. Overton, ed., *God and Governing: Reflecting on Ethics, Virtue, and Statesmanship* (Eugene, OR: Pickwick, 2009), 74–91.

Chapter 1: God's Call to Leaders

1. Srikant M. Datar, Marc J. Epstein, and Kristi Yuthas, "In Microfinance, Clients Must Come First," *Stanford Social Innovation Review* 6,1 (Winter 2008):14.
2. Julius J. Scott Jr., "Sadducees," in *Baker's Evangelical Dictionary of Biblical Theology,* ed. Walter A. Elwell (1996).

Chapter 2: Following the Good Shepherd

1. Brené Brown, "TED Talks: The Power of Vulnerability," http://www.ted.com/speakers/brene_brown.html.
2. Kenneth L. Barker, vol. 20, *Micah, Nahum, Habakkuk, Zephaniah, The New American Commentary* (Nashville: Broadman & Holman, 1999), 251.

Chapter 3: Leaders Who Follow the Shepherd

1. Talcott Parsons, "Professions," in David Sills, ed., *International Encyclopedia of the Social Sciences* (New York: Macmillan, 1968), 545.
2. Rajeev Syal, *The Guardian,* "Google Tax Whistleblower Says He Was Motivated by Christian Beliefs," June 12, 2013; http://www.theguardian.com/technology/2013/jun/12/google-tax-whistleblower-christian-beliefs.

Chapter 4: Servant Leadership

1. Rom. 1:19–20; Acts 14:17; 17:23–29; Ps. 19:1–4; 2 Cor. 4:6; John 1:18.
2. See Isa. 11:1–9; 65:17–25; Hab. 2:14; Heb. 8:10–12; Eph. 2:19–22.
3. Dallas Willard, *Knowing Christ Today: Why We Can Trust Spiritual Knowledge* (San Francisco: HarperOne, 2009).
4. Gen. 12:3; Mic. 4:1–5; Exod. 20:1–17.
5. In Hebrew the name "Israel" was first given to Jacob after he wrestled with God at the river Jabbok (Gen. 32:22–32). According to Gordon J. Wenham, "Jacob's rebaptism as Israel is equally significant, for Israel is of course the name of the nation, and in granting it, Jacob's opponent reveals the true import of the encounter, 'for you have struggled with God and with men and have overcome.' The etymology of Israel offered by the text relates 'Israel,' to the verb *sher-ay,* 'to struggle, fight.' So the word literally means 'El (God) fights.' This is not exactly the same as 'you have struggled with God,' but it should be remembered that popular etymologies in the Bible generally take the form of a play on a name rather than a precise historical etymology." See Wenham, *Genesis 16–50,* vol. 2, Word Biblical Commentary (Dallas, TX: Word, 1998), 296–97.
6. The second mention of "fullness of time" is found in Eph. 1:10. This is accompanied by an eschatological reflection that appears to describe what Jesus refers to as "the end of the age."
7. Mic. 6:6–9; Isa. 58:1–59:15; Acts 10:34–35; Rom. 2:6–11.
8. Rom. 3:20–31; 10:1–4; Gal. 2:16; Acts 15:5–11; Ps. 119:63; Eph. 4:1–6; Gal. 3:28–29.
9. Dallas Willard, *The Divine Conspiracy: Rediscovering Our Hidden Life in God* (San Francisco: HarperSanFrancisco, 1997), chap. 2.
10. See http://www.dwillard.org/articles/artview.asp?artID=138.
11. Keith Meyer, *Whole Life Transformation: Becoming the Change Your Church Needs* (Downers Grove, IL: Inter-Varsity, 2010), Foreword.
12. Plato, *The Republic,* trans. Raymond Larson (Arlington Heights, IL: AHM, 1979), 38.
13. Plato, *Republic,* 38.
14. Initially, the three classic professions were defined as the fields of religion, law, and medicine. The boundaries defining these three professions have long and elaborate justifications. Our goal is not specifically to dispute the criteria for classifying professions, nor to argue which professions might or might not qualify as such. However, these are important and worthy issues to consider.
15. Bruce Wesley, "The Arrogance and Impatience of Church Planters," *Christianity Today,* December 26, 2013; http://www.christianitytoday.com/ct/2013/december-web-only/arrogance-and-impatience-of-church-planters.html.
16. Robert K. Greenleaf, *The Power of Servant-leadership,* ed. Larry C. Spears (San Francisco: Berrett-Koehler, 1998), 4.

Chapter 5: Moral Leadership

1. John C. Maxwell, *There's No Such Thing as "Business" Ethics: There's Only One Rule for Making Decisions* (New York: Warner, 2003).

2. Maxwell, *There's No Such Thing as "Business" Ethics*, 22.

3. Daniel P. Tulley, "Report of the Committee on Compensation Practices," *Securities and Exchange Commission Report*, April 10, 1995.

4. Maxwell makes several interesting and helpful points. See "what you want," six points, 38–49; five factors that break down Golden Rule ethics, 73–87; and five rules of thumb for living by Golden Rule ethics, 112–20.

5. The dramatic television series *Downton Abbey*, *The Good Wife*, and *House of Cards* are just a few cases in point.

6. Steven T. Dennis, "Obama Signs Partial Repeal of Stock Act," accessed April 30, 2013, http://www.rollcall.com/news/obama_signs_partial _repeal_of_stock_act-224019-1.html?pos=hln.

7. Audrey Barrick, "Study Compares Christian and Non-Christian Lifestyles," *Christianity Today*, February 7, 2007; http://www.christiantoday.com/ article/american.study.reveals.indulgent.lifestyle.christians.no .different/9439.htm. Also see George Barna, "Faith Has a Limited Effect on Most People's Behavior," accessed February 18, 2013, https://www.barna .org/barna-update/article/5-barna-update/188-faith-has-a-limited-effect -on-most-peoples-behavior#.UtHpFv1CD4g; David Kinnaman, "Christians: More Like Jesus or Pharisees?" accessed May 3, 2013, https://www.barna .org/barna-update/faith-spirituality/611-christians-more-like-jesus-or -pharisees#.UtH6pv1CD4g; and George Barna, "New Marriage and Divorce Statistics Released," accessed February 18, 2013, https://www .barna.org/barna-update/article/15-familykids/42-new-marriage-and -divorce-statistics-released#.UtH5h_1CD4g. Although somewhat dated now, see also Ronald J. Sider, *The Scandal of the Evangelical Conscience: Why Are Christians Living Just Like the Rest of the World?* (Grand Rapids, MI: Baker, 2005).

8. John Maynard Keynes, *Critical Responses,* ed. Charles R. McCann (London: Routledge, 1998), 24.

9. A wonderful book that skims the surface of this subject is James Kennedy and Jerry Newcombe, *What if Jesus Had Never Been Born?* (Nashville: Nelson, 1994).

10. John Ruskin, *Unto This Last: Four Essays on the First Principles of Political Economy,* ed. Lloyd J. Hubenka (Lincoln: Univ. of Nebraska Press, 1967). These quotations come from Essay 1, entitled "The Roots of Honor."

11. Ruskin, *Unto This Last,* 148ff.

12. Jim Collins, "Level 5 Leadership: The Triumph of Humility and Fierce Resolve," *Harvard Business Review,* January, 2001. Also see Jim Collins, *Good to Great: Why Some Companies Make the Leap and Others Don't* (New

York: HarperCollins, 2001). Collins has also written a small monograph for nonprofit organizations. See Jim Collins, *Good to Great and the Social Sectors: A Monograph to Accompany Good to Great* (New York: Harper-Collins, 2005).

13. Collins, "Level 5 Leadership," 4.
14. Collins describes the other key factors: (1) getting the "right people on the bus, and the wrong people off the bus"; (2) the "Stockdale paradox"; (3) the Buildup-Breakthrough Flywheel; (4) the Hedgehog Concept; (5) Technology Accelerators; and (6) a Culture of Discipline.
15. Collins, "Level 5 Leadership," 5.
16. Collins, "Level 5 Leadership," 1.

Chapter 6: Moral Knowledge

1. Here we will simply differentiate morals from ethics very straightforwardly. Morals can be thought of as concrete norms (mores) of what is right and wrong, good or bad, regarding any given situation. Ethics refers to a theory of morals, meaning ethics are one level of abstraction above moral discussions. Ethical questions are those that ask how good and bad are defined, whereas morals represent the definitions of good and bad.
2. Francis Bacon, "What Is Truth?" in *Essays of Francis Bacon* (Middlesex, UK: Echo Library, 2009), 4–5.
3. Friedrich Wilhelm Nietzsche, *Political Writings of Friedrich Nietzsche: An Edited Anthology*, ed. Frank Cameron and Don Dombowsky (New York: Palgrave Macmillan, 2008), 268.
4. Some of these thoughts were presented in a lecture given in April 2000 at the symposium "The Nature of Nature" in Waco, TX. See http://www.dwillard.org/articles/artview.asp?artID=46.
5. "Lifeboat ethics" takes its name from an illustration presented by ecologist Garrett Hardin in which decisions must be made about which swimmers should be allowed to occupy the last ten places in a lifeboat. Although originally a metaphor for resource distribution, it has been adapted over time to uncover what means and justifications individuals would use to determine who might live in a case where only a few of a certain population could be saved in a crisis situation.

Chapter 7: The Common Goods

1. Perhaps an example of this can be seen in Gen. 1–2, where we see the Hebrew writer commenting on God's declaration that his creation was literally *tov, tov,* or "good, good." Many translations alter this to "very good." Such a condition may in some way only be accessible when creation itself was untouched or unspoiled by events and circumstances that followed. This may also be why a new creation is required for all things to be made new and the "very" good can be experienced again.

2. Thomas Aquinas, *Summa Theologiae*, 2(1).94.2, italics added.

3. Henry Sidgwick, *Methods of Ethics, Book III* (New York: Dover, 1966), 382.

4. See Dallas Willard, *Renovation of the Heart* (Colorado Springs, CO: Nav-Press, 2002), chap. 8.

5. F. H. Bradley, *Ethical Studies* (New York: Stechert, 1911), 145–92.

6. Kant's discussion of moral perfection, virtue, duty, and motivation for pursuing moral goodness is handled in John Waugh Scott, *Kant on the Moral Life: An Exposition of Kant's Grundlegung* (Dearborn, MI: A & C Black, 1924), chap. 1; and Immanuel Kant, *Religion Within the Boundaries of Mere Reason*, trans. and ed. Allen Wood and George Di Giovanni (Cambridge: Cambridge Univ. Press, 1998), bks. 1–2.

7. Naturalism has provided a great moral benefit on this point by offering us insights and wisdom regarding the harmful effects of ignorance in many superstitions and traditions that have worked against the pursuit of truth and wisdom in our cultures. We cannot appreciate the truth naturalism provides us until this reality is factored into our deliberations of its historical effects on the Western world. See Dallas Willard, "Knowledge and Naturalism," in *Naturalism: A Critical Analysis,* ed. William L. Craig and J. P. Moreland (New York: Routledge, 2000).

Chapter 8: Illuminating the Good Life

1. More specifically, we contend that the creation of scripture required two aspects, the human and divine, participating in concert. With regard to the human aspect, there is nothing in the creation of scripture to suggest that the Bible was preserved and produced by anything less than highly competent individuals who were at least as intelligent and devout as any existing people in contemporary society. The biblical authors demonstrate their capacity to both accurately interpret and present their own experiences, understandings, and testimonials in the language of their historical communities. As such, the Bible can and should be considered a reliable and authoritative representation of the knowledge and truth God willed to be revealed to humanity. For a more detailed description of this statement, see Gary Black Jr., *The Theology of Dallas Willard: Discovering Protoevangelical Faith* (Eugene, OR: Pickwick, 2013), 57–68; and Dallas Willard, *The Divine Conspiracy: Rediscovering Our Hidden Life in God* (San Francisco: HarperSanFrancisco, 1997), 141–42.

Chapter 9: Knowledge and Education

1. George Herbert Palmer, *The Field of Ethics* (Boston: Houghton Mifflin, 1929), 213.

2. These theories tend to boil down to either utilitarianism or Kantianism.

3. August Kerber, *Quotable Quotes on Education* (Detroit, MI: Wayne State University Press, 1968), 138.

4. See Dallas Willard, *Knowing Christ Today: Why We Can Trust Spiritual Knowledge* (San Francisco: HarperOne, 2009), chap. 3.

5. Christopher Hitchens, *God Is Not Great: How Religion Poisons Everything* (New York: Twelve, 2007).

6. In our view, the New Atheist movement has not adequately understood or applied Christian principles or validly compared Christianity to other religious or nonreligious worldviews. This can be done. And we should invite this dialog.

7. Dietrich Bonhoeffer, *Ethics*, ed. Eberhard Bethge (New York: Simon & Schuster, 1995).

8. Paul Ricoeur, *The Symbolism of Evil* (New York: Harper & Row, 1967).

Chapter 10: Economics and Politics

1. The scriptures use the word *oikonomos* to describe the stewardship endeavor. Two very interesting words are joined here. The first part, *oiko*, can mean "home, house, dwelling place, or habitat." The second part, *nomos*, can be translated "rules, law, or custom." The word formed from the two parts conveys one who rules over or sets the rules for a house, what we would call today a manager, overseer, or boss. Two derivatives of *oikonomos* are the words *oikonomia* and *oikologia*. These are the Greek predecessors of the English words "economics" and "ecology." The point here is to understand that the fields of economics and ecology are areas of study that pursue understanding of the rules, activities, or customs of humans, animals, and plants in their home habitat or environment. As a result the idea of stewardship in both the Hebrew Bible and the Greek New Testament is significant, especially when considering the ways of God's economy (his house, his *oikonomia*) and the responsibilities of governance (rules) for moral living by his people (stewards). Again a significant motive in God's economy is the blessing or flourishing that is available to both individuals and groups, including governments, who respect and apply his ways (*nomos* or *nomia*).

2. According to this definition, any activity that is not essential to life would not be part of the economy. As an example, housing is a significant part of the economy because shelter is a necessity of life. In contrast, the "consumables" of the entertainment and "style" industries are rarely if ever products and services essential to life, even though these businesses can involve a lot of money and draw tremendous attention. Undoubtedly, a large number of Westerners maintain an endless desire to be entertained and remain "in style." However, their demise is not imminent if these things become elusive or scarce.

3. Richard Hofstadter also writes about these conditions. He lists four preceding stages that work together to forge the social and political climate that influenced Dewey's perspective: (1) the Civil War to 1890, a period of significant industrial growth and continental expansion accompanied by political conservatism; (2) 1890–1900, marking agrarian reform and the rise of

populism; (3) 1990–1914, World War I and the genesis of the Progressive movement; and (4) 1929–1950, FDR's New Deal and the federal government's wholesale entrance into key fiscal and domestic policies and legislation (*The Age of Reform: From Bryan to F.D.R.* [New York: Knopf, 1955]).

4. Hofstadter, *Age of Reform.*

5. Thomas Hill Green, *The Works of Thomas Hill Green,* ed. R. L. Nettleship (New York: Longmans, Green, 1906), 371.

6. Franklin D. Roosevelt, "FDR's 1944 State of the Union Address," in *Bringing Human Rights Home,* ed. Cynthia Soohoo, Catherine Albisa, and Martin Davis (Westport, CT: Praeger, 2008), 167.

7. The word "franchise" is defined here as a freedom from servitude or restraint, which is a right or privilege conferred by a grant from a sovereign or government that is vested in an individual or group.

8. Thomas Hobbes, *Leviathan: Or the Matter, Forme and Power of a Commonwealth, Ecclesiasticall and Civil* (Washington, DC: Regnery, 2009), chap. 11.

9. Hobbes, *Leviathan,* chap. 11.

10. John Dewey, *The Public and Its Problems* (New York: Holt, 1927), 27.

11. Dewey, *The Public and Its Problems,* 27.

12. Dewey, *The Public and Its Problems,* 114–15, 126.

13. T. S. Eliot, "Choruses From 'the Rock' VI," in *Collected Poems, 1909-1962,* (London, UK: Faber and Faber, 1963), 177.

14. Augustine, *The Rule of St. Augustine,* trans. Raymond Canning (Garden City, NY: Image, 1984), 70.

15. See http://greatergood.berkeley.edu; and http://greatergood.berkeley.edu/expandinggratitude.

16. C. S. Lewis, *The Weight of Glory* (San Francisco: HarperSanFrancisco, 1980), 39.

17. Henry David Thoreau, *Civil Disobedience and Other Essays* (New York: Dover, 1993).

18. There are various theories, postulations, and presumptions about "the end," most of which are derived from various interpretations of the apocalyptic sections of the scriptures, none of which we will go into here. However, we do acknowledge that much of this focus on eschatology and the ideas behind the various millennial "camps" have in the past and continue to exert tremendous influence on many of the issues surrounding well-being and kingdom living addressed in this work. Unfortunately, it appears that many of these theological positions and the tremendous amount of time and money devoted to them have not been able to induce or spread the type and quality of life Jesus articulated and demonstrated as the normative experience within the kingdom of God. Perhaps focusing so much attention on "the end" may tend to draw one away from engaging what God has already begun and will continue throughout eternity.

19. Matthew T. Lee, Margaret M. Paloma, and Stephen G. Post, *The Heart of Religion: Spiritual Empowerment, Benevolence, and the Experience of God's Love* (New York: Oxford Univ. Press, 2013).

Chapter 11: Business

1. See the car dealer who seems to have all these features working together: http://www.infinitiofnaperville.com/dealership/staff.htm.
2. Manuel G. Velasquez, *Business Ethics: Concepts and Cases* (Upper Saddle River, NJ: Pearson, 2012), 119–23. Also see Rebecca Leung, "The Mensch of Malden Mills," July 3, 2003, http://www.cbsnews.com/stories/2003/07/03/60minutes/main561656.shtml.
3. Leung, "The Mensch of Malden Mills."
4. Stacy Perman, "In-N-Out Burger: Professionalizing Fast Food," *BusinessWeek*, April 8, 2009, 68–69; Sophie Quinton, "Why the Trader Joe's Model Benefits Workers and the Bottom Line," *National Journal*, March 19, 2013; Joe Brancatelli, "Southwest Airlines' Seven Secrets of Success," *Wired*, July, 8, 2008; Karen Weise, "Company News: UBS, Southwest, General Motors," *BusinessWeek*, December, 20, 2012; Brad Stone, "Costco CEO Craig Jelinek Leads the Cheapest, Happiest Company in the World," *BusinessWeek*, June 6, 2013; Cameron McWhirter, "Chick-fil-A's Long Christian Heritage," *Wall Street Journal*, July 27, 2012.
5. Kristy Hart, *HR Strategies for Employee Engagement* (Upper Saddle River, NJ: Pearson Education, 2011).
6. John Ruskin, *Unto This Last: Four Essays on the First Principles of Political Economy*, ed. Lloyd J. Hubenka (Lincoln: Univ. of Nebraska Press, 1967). These quotations come from Essay 1, entitled "The Roots of Honor."
7. Ruskin, *Unto This Last*.
8. Ruskin, *Unto This Last*.
9. Louis Brandeis, *Business: A Profession* (Boston: Small, Maynard, 1914), 4.
10. The progressive movement of the latter nineteenth and early twentieth century was, in large part, an effort to implement in the political and social life of America the kind of idealism, somewhat toned down to be sure, expressed by Ruskin, T. H. Green, and Brandeis. What happened to that movement—how it went sour through the course of events and was gutted of its genius by currents of thoughts without viable moral content—would be a highly instructive study for those devoted to understanding our current social and personal situation in America. A good place to start might be Glenda Gilmore, ed., *Who Were the Progressives?* (Boston: St. Martin's, 2002); and Michael McGerr, *A Fierce Discontent: The Rise and Fall of the Progressive Movement in America, 1870–1920* (New York: Oxford Univ. Press, 2003).
11. Thomas Hill Green and David Owen Brink, *Prolegomena to Ethics* (New York: Oxford Univ. Press, 2003), 208.

12. See Os Guinness's indispensable book *The Call* (Nashville: Word, 1998). See, as well, the many treatments of the spiritual life by Phillips Brooks (1835–93).

13. William Rawson Stevenson, *The Baptist Hymnal: A Collection of Hymns and Spiritual Songs* (London: Marlborough, 1885), 889.

Chapter 12: Professionals

1. Everett C. Hughes, "Professions," in Joan C. Callahan, ed., *Ethical Issues in Professional Life* (New York: Oxford Univ. Press, 1988), 31.

2. Hughes, "Professions."

3. Nathan O. Hatch, ed., *The Professions in American History* (Notre Dame, IN: Univ. of Notre Dame Press, 1988), 1–14.

4. See Samuel Haber, *The Quest for Authority and Honor in the American Professions 1750–1900* (Chicago: Univ. of Chicago Press, 1991), x–xi. Haber argues, "From the beginning . . . professionalization in America was linked with the 'art of rising in life,' with upward mobility" (6). Note also the historical association with the warrior class and how that was modified under the impact of Christian ideas (9–14).

5. An entity is understood as a thing that is recognized as having the properties of independent existence and unique identification. When speaking of the professions as social entities we are suggesting each profession is uniquely identifiable within our social structures and in certain ways independent from certain aspects of our social structures.

6. See Haber, *The Quest for Authority and Honor,* x. See also Hatch, *Professions in American History,* 3; and William Sullivan, *Work and Integrity: The Crisis and Promise of Professionalism in America* (New York: HarperCollins, 1995), 2.

7. Corinne Lathrop Gilb, *Hidden Hierarchies: The Professions and Government* (New York: Harper & Row, 1966), as referenced in Maxwell H. Bloomfield, "Law: The Development of a Profession," in Hatch, ed., *Professions in American History,* 33.

8. An example of this can be found in President Clinton's deregulation of the banking industry, partly on the advice of his Treasury Secretary Robert Rubin, a past partner and cochairman at Goldman Sachs. After the 2008 bailout, more regulations and oversight were touted as the only means of staving off another such crisis. This is the type of back-and-forth negotiations between political parties and economic theorists that in recent times rarely seem to end in a stable beneficial outcome for the public. See former Clinton Cabinet member, now University of California Berkeley professor Robert Reich's comments at http://blogs.berkeley.edu/2012/07/27/the-man-who-invented-too-big-to-fail-banks-finally-recants-will-obama-or-romney-follow/.

9. See http://www.gallup.com/poll/1654/honesty-ethics-professions.aspx.

10. Solange De Santis, "Americans' View of Clergy's Ethics Hit 3-Decade Low," *USA Today,* December 10, 2009.

11. Aristotle, *Rhetoric,* ed. Paul Negri and Jenny Bak (Mineola, NY: Dover, 2004), 7.

12. Marcus Luttrell, *Lone Survivor: The Eyewitness Account of Operation Redwing and the Lost Heroes of Seal Team 10* (New York: Little, Brown, 2007).

13. When Luttrell's book became a major motion picture, CNN reporter Jake Trapper interviewed Luttrell and actor Mark Wahlberg and suggested the deaths of Luttrell's comrades were senseless; see http://www.youtube.com/watch?v=BsLk9SOHOOQ.

14. See Callahan, ed., *Ethical Issues in Professional Life,* Appendix 1, 439ff.

15. See http://www.aicpa.org/Research/Standards/CodeofConduct/Down loadableDocuments/2012June1CodeOfProfessionalConduct.pdf.

Chapter 13: Physicians, Lawyers, and Pastors or Priests

1. Roger J. Bulger, *In Search of the Modern Hippocrates* (Iowa City: Univ. of Iowa Press, 1987), 9–10.

2. Steven H. Miles, *The Hippocratic Oath and the Ethics of Medicine* (New York: Oxford Univ. Press, 2004), 13.

3. Miles, *Hippocratic Oath and the Ethics of Medicine,* 19.

4. Ronald L. Numbers, "The Fall and Rise of the American Medical Profession," in Nathan O. Hatch, ed., *The Professions in American History* (Notre Dame, IN: Univ. of Notre Dame Press, 1988), 51–72.

5. Key to our conversation here will be insights gathered from various sources, but four are primary: Numbers, "The Fall and Rise of the American Medical Profession"; Samuel Haber, *The Quest for Authority and Honor in the American Professions 1750–1900* (Chicago: Univ. of Chicago Press, 1991), 45–66; and several articles in Joan C. Callahan, ed., *Ethical Issues in Professional Life* (New York: Oxford Univ. Press, 1988).

6. Another significant aspect to this transition appears to have resulted from the publishing of the Flexner Report, written by Abraham Flexner, commissioned by the Carnegie Foundation, and published in 1910. Flexner was critical of medical education and argued that medical schools should increase their standards for both admission and graduation; see Mark Haitt and Christopher Stockton, "The Impact of the Flexner Report on the Fate of Medical Schools in North America After 1909," *Journal of American Physicians and Surgeons,* vol. 8, no. 2 (2003). Thanks to Dr. Charles Weber for this insight.

7. William Sullivan, *Work and Integrity: The Crisis and Promise of Professionalism in America* (New York: HarperCollins, 1995), 56–57.

8. Paul Starr, *The Social Transformation of American Medicine* (New York: Basic Books, 1982); Kenneth M. Ludmerer, *Time to Heal: American*

Medical Education from the Turn of the Century to the Era of Managed Care (Oxford: Oxford Univ. Press, 1999).

9. Kelly Kennedy, "Report: More Doctors Accepting Medicare Patients," *USA Today,* August 22, 2013.

10. See http://www.azbar.org/membership/admissions/oathofadmission.

11. See http://www.supremecourt.gov/bar/barapplication.pdf.

12. See http://www.supremecourt.gov/bar/barapplication.pdf.

13. Frank Lambert, *The Founding Fathers and the Place of Religion in America* (Princeton, NJ: Princeton Univ. Press, 2003), 211.

14. See Robert A. Goldwin and Art Kaufman, *Slavery and Its Consequences: The Constitution, Equality, and Race* (Washington, DC: American Enterprise Institute for Public Policy Research, 1988); and John J. Patrick, Richard M. Pious, and Donald A. Ritchie, "Equality Under the Constitution," in *The Oxford Guide to the United States Government* (New York: Oxford Univ. Press, 2001), 212–16.

15. See Henry J. Kaiser Foundation, "Kaiser Health Tracking Poll: March 2013," http://kff.org/health-reform/poll-finding/march-2013-tracking -poll/; also Jeffrey M. Jones, "In U.S., Majority Now Against Gov't Healthcare Guarantee," http://www.gallup.com/poll/158966/majority -against-gov-healthcare-guarantee.aspx.

16. Hatch, ed., *The Professions in American History,* 145–46.

17. Consider the three stages of development of the profession of clergy laid out by Martin Marty in Hatch, ed., *The Professions in American History,* 75–90.

18. For a more detailed explanation of *agape,* see Dallas Willard, *Getting Love Right* (Kindle Edition, 2012), Locations 118–21.

19. For a more detailed understanding of the life of the mind and spirit, see Dallas Willard, *Renovation of the Heart: Putting on the Character of Christ* (Colorado Springs: NavPress, 2002), chaps. 6–8.

20. Jeffery Jones and Lydia Saad, *Gallup Poll Social Series* (Princeton, NJ: Gallup News Service, 2011). This is to be distinguished from the recent increase in those who do not claim any particular religious affiliation. This category has come to be commonly called the "nones" and has demonstrated significant growth over the past several decades. Still, the "nones" represent approximately 18 percent of the American adult population. See Ruth Moon, "Is Concern Over the Rise of the 'Nones' Overblown?" *Christianity Today,* April, 2013. There is no clear data as of yet that specifically separates the nonreligious from the strict atheists or agnostics.

21. Christian 33.39% (of which the largest groups are Roman Catholic 16.85%, Protestant 6.15%, Orthodox 3.96%, Anglican 1.26%), Muslim 22.74%, Hindu 13.8%, Buddhist 6.77%, Sikh 0.35%, Jewish 0.22%, Baha'i 0.11%, other religions 10.95%, non-religious 9.66%, atheists 2.01% (2010 est.). See http://www .cia.gov/library/publications/the-world-factbook/fields/2122.html#xx.

Also see Phil Zuckerman, "Atheism: Contemporary Numbers and Patterns," in Michael Martin, ed., *The Cambridge Companion to Atheism* (Cambridge: Univ. of Cambridge Press, 2007).

22. Adam Clark, "Definition of God," in John McClintock and James Strong, eds., *Cyclopedia of Biblical, Theological, and Ecclesiastical Literature* (New York: Harper, 1894), 2: 903–4.

Chapter 14: The Kingdom of Our God

1. Katherine Reynolds Lewis notes, "A survey by the International Coaching Federation found that there were 47,500 professional coaches worldwide this year, up from 30,000 just five years ago." In "Career Coaches: When Are They Worth Their Salt?" *Fortune,* November 6, 2012.

2. Diane Coutu and Carol Kauffman, "What Can Coaches Do for You?" *Harvard Business Review,* January 2009.

3. Coutu and Kauffman, "What Can Coaches Do for You?," 3.

4. Coutu and Kauffman, "What Can Coaches Do for You?," 3.

5. See www.apn.edu/announcements/21597.

6. Viktor E. Frankl, *Man's Search for Meaning: An Introduction to Logotherapy* (Boston: Beacon, 1963), 133–34.

7. Dorothy Day, *By Little and By Little: Selected Writings of Dorothy Day,* ed. Robert Ellsberg (New York: Knopf, 1983), 286.

Scripture Index

Scripture Index